The Press on Trial

Recent Titles in
Contributions to the Study of Mass Media and Communications

The Press on Trial

Crimes and Trials as Media Events

Edited by
LLOYD CHIASSON JR.

Contributions to the Study of Mass Media and Communications,
Number 51

GREENWOOD PRESS
Westport, Connecticut • London

Library of Congress Cataloging-in-Publication Data

The press on trial : crimes and trials as media events / edited by
Lloyd Chiasson Jr.
    p.   cm.—(Contributions to the study of mass media and
communications, ISSN 0732–4456 ; no. 51)
   Includes bibliographical references and index.
   ISBN 0–313–30022–4 (alk. paper)
   1. Trials—United States.   2. Mass media and criminal justice—
United States. I. Chiasson, Lloyd, 1947– . II. Series.
KF220.P74   1997
345.73′02—DC21   96–53030

British Library Cataloguing in Publication Data is available.

Library of Congress Catalog Card Number: 96–53030
ISBN: 0–313–30022–4
     0–275–95936–8 (pbk.)
ISSN: 0732–4456

First published in 1997

Greenwood Press, 88 Post Road West, Westport, CT 06881
An imprint of Greenwood Publishing Group, Inc.

Printed in the United States of America

The paper used in this book complies with the
Permanent Paper Standard issued by the National
Information Standards Organization (Z39.48–1984).

10 9 8 7 6 5 4 3 2 1

Every reasonable effort has been made to trace the owners of copyright
materials in this book, but in some instances this has proven impossible. The editor and publisher will be glad to receive information leading to more complete acknowledgments in subsequent printings of the
book and in the meantime extend their apologies for any omissions.

This book is for the good Lord—Father, Son, and Holy Spirit—who gave me whatever ability I possess. It is also for my wife, Shannon, my daughters, Marnie and Cassidy, and my parents, Helen and Lloyd. All give me the substantial and continuing love that sustains me.

Contents

Preface

The Opening Statement

Unlike life with all its shades of grey, a trial is black or white, someone is guilty or innocent; there is crime, there is justice, there is punishment. Perhaps it is that simplicity most of us find so compelling, and perhaps that is the reason trials so often grip our attention. We gravitate to the natural drama of a trial, and some have significance that far exceeds our understanding. The trial of a carpenter's son, for example, still holds the world's attention after 2,000 years.

Perhaps the intoxicating mystery of a trial is that elusive concept called *justice*. Laws differ by country and by tradition, but justice is the common goal. From the Salem witch trials to the spectacular trials of the century that come along every five years or so, America has defined itself through its search for justice. It is what we blindly stumble after in life and what we hope to attain in court. It may be wishful thinking, of course, to believe that we can bottle and dispense in a courtroom what we can hardly identify in life, but God bless us, we try.

This book is about that search. It is also about how we in America judge what is fair and equitable and true. It is about people: judges, attorneys, juries, and more important, the accused, the media, and the public. It is about beliefs and customs and values. Finally, it is about sixteen trials, each of which has significance in the history of America.

It is a trial with no significance, one that never happened, that is partly responsible for the birth of this text. It is the by-product of a Jack Lemmon movie titled *How to Murder Your Wife*. Although the film costarred one of the most beautiful women ever to grace the screen, Virna Lisi, the real star of the movie and the moving force behind this academic tome is the "Globbida Globbida machine" most of us know simply as a cement mixer. It is allegedly the Globbida Globbida machine that eats Lemmon's wife, the voluptuous Ms. Lisi, after Lemmon allegedly throws her into the bowels of that evil machine.

Lemmon is brought to trial, and the evidence piles up against him. Just as his bleak plight appears hopeless, Lemmon affects a new defense strategy. In a shocking twist, he admits to the murder, but claims that murdering one's wife is justifiable homicide. Upon hearing this moving defense, the all-male jury unanimously shouts "not guilty" before showing unrestrained exuberance with its opinion by carrying the victorious Lemmon out of the courtroom on its collective shoulders.

So how do we go from Jack Lemmon and the Globbida Globbida machine to a book about sixteen of the most significant trials in American history? Actually, rather easily. After seeing *How to Murder Your Wife*, I was reminded of a trial that generated every bit the drama as did Mr. Lemmon's. In fact, the resemblance between the two trials is remarkable, although they are separated by two centuries. The year is 1735, a similar verdict is returned, and a similar reaction from the jury results. Newspaper editor John Peter Zenger is charged with seditious libel. The trial, and a verdict of guilty, are but a formality since all the jury has to do is establish the fact that Mr. Zenger has published an article critical of a local public official. It doesn't matter whether what was written was true or not. The law is simple: the greater the truth, the greater the libel. In short, John Peter Zenger is walking in quicksand with lead shoes. Then something remarkable happens: The greatest trial lawyer of the day dramatically enters the courtroom. Stately, confident, renowned for his knowledge of the law, Andrew Hamilton is in every way a colonial Perry Mason. In that moment John Peter Zenger must have been the most relieved man in the Americas. But only for a moment. For as soon as he addresses the court, Hamilton does the most remarkable thing: He admits that his client is guilty! Just like Jack Lemmon, he asks for acquittal even though guilt is unquestionable. And just like in *How to Murder Your Wife*, the all-male jury unanimously finds the defendant not guilty in spite of the evidence. And, of course, the jurors carry Zenger out on their shoulders.

After seeing *How to Murder Your Wife*, I asked myself, if Jack Lemmon's trial made for an interesting tale, wouldn't other trials—real trials with real people and real drama—be even better? The answer, of course, is this text. You be the judge.

Although no drama catches the interest of the American public more than a spectacular trial, rarely does the crime embody the natural suspense of the trial that follows. The crime is reported; it is big news, but then it quickly diminishes in news value. But the trial, particularly in recent years, lingers, and drama builds. It is a play whose actors are real, whose stage is a courtroom, whose audience is a jury.

The true American theater is the courtroom. How the public views that stage is often left to the media. The jury renders a judgment, but public opinion often determines the final verdict in terms of the lasting historical significance of the crime, the trial, and the accused. This was true when John Peter Zenger defended his right to free speech in 1735, and it has proven true for every "trial of the century" since. The reason is relatively simple: Trials are media events and media coverage impacts their importance.

This is not to say that trials have no lasting significance beyond how the public perceives them. A trial can have long-reaching significance beyond what the media write and beyond what the public thinks. It can rewrite the Constitution; it can lead to war; it can revamp institutions; it can mold public opinion; it can change society. Some trials, primarily because of the accompanying media coverage, have brought about these results.

What follows is the story of sixteen trials in American history. Each chapter relates the history of events leading up to the trial; each describes the persons involved; and each shows how the crime and subsequent trial were reported. This collection is not an esoteric study of the effects of media coverage, nor a series of essays on the role of the judiciary regarding First and Sixth Amendment issues. It is the story of sixteen crimes, the subsequent trials, and the media coverage of each. Most important, it relates the historical significance of those happenings.

In chronological order, the trials include colonial printer John Peter Zenger in 1735; the murder trials associated with what became known as the Boston Massacre in 1770; the murder trial of abolitionist John Brown in 1859; the trial of those charged with the Haymarket riot in 1886; the trial of Lizzie Borden for the murder of her father and stepmother in 1892; the trial of Harry K. Thaw for the murder of well-known architect Stanford White; the bizarre trial of several of the Chicago Black Sox baseball players in 1921; the 1925 "monkey" trial of John Thomas Scopes for teaching evolution in a Tennessee school; the numerous trials of the Scottsboro boys for rape; the 1935 trial of Bruno Hauptmann for kidnapping and murdering the child of famed aviator Charles Lindbergh; the espionage and perjury trial of Alger Hiss in 1949–50 and the trial of the Rosenbergs for wartime espionage soon after; the trial in 1969 for conspiracy to incite violence by the anti-establishment "radicals" known as the Chicago Seven; the 1970 murder trial of Charles Manson; the military trial that same year of Lieutenant William Calley for premeditated murder of villagers in My Lai, Vietnam; and the most publicized trial in American history, the O. J. Simpson murder trial in 1995.

Few of these trials ended as happily as did Jack Lemmon's or John Peter Zenger's. But their stories are rich; they are colored by life, and, for various reasons, they are historically important. So for that I say thanks to John Peter, to Virna, to Jack, and, most important of all, thanks to the Globbida Globbida machine.

Lloyd Chiasson Jr.

Acknowledgments

I would like to thank the contributors to this volume, a remarkably gifted group of people who have been a pleasure to work with. Thanks also to the editors at Greenwood, true professionals in every way. I know because twice they have succeeded in making me look good. Thanks to Connie Sirois for the wonderful layout job. Thanks to Mike Maher, both for his insightful ideas and for his willingness to help a friend in need. And, finally, special thanks to former student and good friend, Tel Bailliet, the editor's editor.

The Press on Trial

1

The Case of John Peter Zenger
(1735)

"A Monkey . . . about 4 foot high"

Gene Wiggins

As the story goes, the old Texas trial lawyer received a telegram in his Dallas office from a wealthy family way out in west Texas. The family was seeking the veteran lawyer's help in defending a son who was charged with murder, following a shoot-out on the streets of the little town. The lawyer's calendar was full so he sent back a telegram politely refusing the request. Soon after, a second telegram arrived from west Texas, promising the lawyer $250,000 to defend the young man. The patriarch of the west Texas family got an immediate answer from the Dallas lawyer, that read: "Arriving on noon train (STOP) Bringing three eyewitnesses."

Guaranteed results in an American court of law are, of course, not quite as certain as the above story would indicate. However, the American press and legal journals are full of accounts where the outcome of a trial was determined by some unusual action by a member of the court. Judges have issued decisions that defied legal logic, attorneys have used tactics or antics that fiction writers couldn't have dreamed up, and trial participants haven't always been the quiet, respectful persons they were expected to be. Juries, of course, have gone so far afield from the evidence and issued such outrageous judgments that the results actually have wound up in Hollywood.

Such courtroom behavior has resulted in mixed receptions from the general public. At times, decisions contrary to law or accepted legal authority have been condemned by large segments of society—witness the O. J. Simpson trial of 1995.

At other times, such decisions have been received with popular acclaim, with the defendant or some other court participant hailed as a hero—witness the John Peter Zenger trial of 1735.

Witness a cast of characters right out of a Neil Simon play. Witness the poor, abused printer, ably portrayed by Mr. Zenger; witness the young, inexperienced, and politically keen judge, stoically played by Stephen Delancey; witness the wicked, but admirably greedy governor, impeccably portrayed by William Cosby; witness the distinguished and famous trial lawyer, brilliantly acted by Andrew Hamilton.

Witness a trial that could not have been scripted better by Edward Albee, that was the result of a family feud, that should never have seen the light of a courtroom, that couldn't be won, but was, and that laid out, in straightforward, almost clinical language, the ground rules for an amendment to a document that has served as the political, social, and religious backbone to the United States for more than 200 years. Witness the conception of the First Amendment to the Constitution. Witness, also, one of the strangest, and most dramatic, trials in American history.

And, of course, it all happened in New York.

The trial of John Peter Zenger received as much attention, on a relative scale, as did any trial in the history of the United States. Accounts of the trial and subsequent events were printed all over the colonies, in England, and on the European continent. Zenger's trial has been studied from many aspects, including political, religious, and legal angles. While the trial supposedly arose from political differences, it also resulted from problems of greed, egotism, and personal bitterness between various individuals and factions in the city of New York. Such problems have been the root cause of trials in America ever since, but this trial laid the foundation for future challenges to unyielding authority and political chicanery.

The city of New York in 1735 was nothing like the modern metropolis of today. It was small, barely 10,000 people, a fifth of those were slaves. Like most small towns today, everyone knew everyone, which made for strong friendships and even stronger animosities. Many citizens were descendants of the original Dutch colonists; people with influence and financial stability. However, after the English occupied the colony in 1664, most of the Dutch and English citizens found themselves victims of generally oppressive governments and administrators. Governors had vast power granted by the Crown and governed as they wished, answering only to authorities in London.[1]

Politically, New Yorkers generally split into two major factions which most historians refer to as the Popular and Government parties. Most of the general population—blue-collar workers and merchants—supported the leaders of the Popular Party. In addition to the development of political factions, personal feuds and rivalries further divided the people. Foremost among these feuds was one between two of the most prominent families in the colony—the Morrises and the Delanceys. Lewis Morris was a widely respected aristocrat who served as counselor, assemblyman, and chief justice of the Supreme Court. Stephen Delancey was a member of the wealthy merchant class who also served in the Assembly. Two major clashes between the men—one over a trade policy issue and the other over Delancey's right to serve in the Assembly—left no room for warm relations.[2] This family feud also exacerbated existing political problems that resulted in the most reported trial of the time, and in retrospect, the most important of the entire colonial period.

Into this arena of conflict high-stepped a new figure in 1732—Governor William Cosby. Appointed by the Crown following the death of Governor John Montgomerie in July 1731, Cosby was of Anglo-Irish aristocracy, a man obsessed with greed and one who possessed a haughty nature and little sympathy for the common man. He was also a man who had just been removed from his post as governor of the island of Minorca for political chicanery that even the London authorities couldn't overlook. Cosby, however, had the good fortune—some spelled it foresight—to have married the sister of the Earl of Halifax. He was also good friends with the Duke of Newcastle, who no doubt managed the new appointment in New York.[3]

During the thirteen-month interim, Rip Van Dam, a popular Dutch merchant born in New York, served as governor. When Cosby arrived, he received a cordial welcome by New Yorkers, but upon learning of Cosby's actions in Minorca, another soon-to-be opponent of the new governor, Cadwallader Colden, expressed the general feelings of the majority of the colonists: "How such a man, after such a flagrant instance of tyranny and robbery, came to be intrusted with the government of an English Colony and to be made Chancellor and keeper of the King's conscience in that Colony, is not easy for a common understanding to conceive."[4]

Time needed for Crosby to create trouble: none.

With little delay, Cosby set about proving Colden right by showcasing such prodigious greed that only his astounding pettiness dwarfed it. Cosby criticized the Assembly for voting him what he considered a small stipend in payment for services supposedly rendered while he was in London. The Assembly raised the payment, but Cosby still showed no appreciation. No doubt members of the Assembly, as well as average New Yorkers, must have wondered what kind of new governor they had inherited. Van Dam soon found out. While disputing with the Assembly, Cosby demanded of Van Dam half the payments he received as acting governor, using a document from London that Cosby said authorized such payment. The shrewd old Dutchman wasn't about to turn over half the money he had received to this pompous aristocrat without a fight. So Van Dam graciously agreed to split his salary—but only if Cosby would split what he had received since the day he was appointed, which amounted to over 6,000 pounds.

Cosby now faced the first of many dilemmas. Propelled by pathological avarice, he decided to sue Van Dam for the money. The problem was, he just couldn't figure out how to do it. The Supreme Court had no equity jurisdiction, and Cosby couldn't sue in Chancery Court since he was the chancellor. He didn't dare sue in common law because a jury verdict against him (not at all unlikely) would be disastrous.[5] The scheming Cosby then decided to create a new jurisdiction. Supreme Court judges would now be Barons of the Exchequer. This court, essentially the Supreme Court with additional powers akin to the defunct but once almighty Star Chamber, would hear the case. Cosby then instructed the attorney general to bring an action there.

If nothing else, Cosby proved greed could be complicated.

Lewis Morris Sr. was chief justice of the Supreme Court while James Delancey, a member of the family disliked by the Morrises, had only recently returned from studying at the bar in London and was the newly appointed second judge on the court. The third judge was Frederick Philipse, a man who followed the lead of Delancey and the Government Party. Morris quickly ruled that the court, no matter what its name, lacked jurisdiction and chastised the new governor for creating such a court of equity without the consent of the legislature.[6] Cosby's reaction was simplicity itself. He removed Morris from the bench and elevated Delancey to the position of chief justice. Not bad for a kid fresh out of law school.

Needless to say, Morris was incensed at such high-handed actions by Cosby. So, too, were Van Dam's attorneys, William Smith and James Alexander. Smith was one of the most prominent lawyers in the city, later serving as attorney general and justice of the Supreme Court. Alexander, a brilliant and fiery idealist who helped found both Princeton University and the American Philosophical Society, had "escaped" England after the failed rebellion of the Jacobists. Above all, Alexander was a man who loved a fight, legal or political.

By now, the general population of the New York colony was getting downright fidgety about Cosby, whose backdoor shenanigans painted a splendid portrait of a colonial carpetbagger. People were hearing stories of such allegedly underhanded dealings as Cosby's attempt to disenfranchise the Quakers and to extort land from those receiving land grants. Little wonder that local folks were moving quickly to the side of the Popular Party since its leaders—Morris, Alexander, and others—were opposing the governor and his Government Party at every turn.

It is at this point in our drama that the press became involved. Only one newspaper existed in New York at this time. William Bradford, who had left Philadelphia after encountering difficulties there, moved to New York and established the *New York Gazette* in 1725.[7] Although Bradford was not a strong supporter of the Government Party, he had learned his lesson in Philadelphia and stayed out of trouble with the administration. As a reward, he was named the official printer and received a lucrative payment each year. Upon discovering the financial windfall of being a puppet, Bradford could hardly afford to offend the existing powers. He never objected publicly when Cosby placed one of his own henchmen, Francis Harison, in charge of editorial policy.[8] Harison was a scoundrel who, like many of his ilk, seemed to warrant a label that certainly didn't make him a successful crook. He was "dumb and devious," a dangerous and often laughable combination for a fellow who attempted so many shady deals that he eventually had to return to England to escape punishment.

As is often the case with the dumb and devious, Harison took his assignment seriously and immediately began to trumpet the successes, however mythical, of his political boss. The *Gazette* carried numerous accounts of the noteworthy deeds of the governor while, at the same time, lambasted those who opposed Cosby's efforts. Needless to say, Morris, Alexander, Van Dam, and other supporters of the Popular Party were the targets of Harison's poorly written, but stinging, comments.

One more major character was missing from the play, a person whose involvement in the events to this point was nonexistent. He was a man who really had little to do with the subsequent attacks upon Cosby and his forces, and many scholars feel he was not much more than a scapegoat for some members of the Popular Party. However, because Cosby chose to prosecute him, his name—John Peter Zenger—is synonymous with freedom of the press in America.

Time needed for the leaders of the Popular Party to decide if they needed an opposing voice to the *Gazette*: not much.

Morris, Alexander, and their friends knew they needed something more than pamphlets and open letters to combat the *Gazette's* attacks, so they chose a local printer, Zenger, and encouraged him to begin a second newspaper. So began the *New York Weekly Journal* on November 5, 1733. Zenger fit the description of many newspaper publishers of the period. He was a printer more than a journalist. He had learned his trade through years of apprenticeship for a printing business. He printed many of the open letters, pamphlets, and other materials for the Popular Party members before beginning the newspaper at their behest.

Historians generally agree that Zenger's printing was good, but his journalistic abilities were limited. John Tebbel wrote that Zenger wasn't qualified by intelligence or ability to lead the fight against Cosby and labeled him as an "indifferent printer and an untalented writer."[9] James Melvin Lee commented that Zenger's contributions to his newspaper were "easily discovered by their poor spelling and by their grammatical errors."[10] However, early journalism historian Frederic Hudson claimed Zenger was a "good printer . . . and something of a scholar."[11]

No records exist to verify who among the Popular Party crowd approached Zenger with the idea of a second newspaper to answer the scathing comments Harison was writing for the *Gazette*. Alexander, a prolific writer for the *Journal,* was surely one of them, along with Morris. A second newspaper in New York would be risky business financially, so some backing would be needed initially. As one writer observed: "Not many of the 10,000 people in the town . . . were readers of anything. More preferred to shoot quail in the brush along Broadway."[12]

A milestone in American journalism could be observed if the creation of the *Journal* is viewed as the establishment of an independent paper to oppose a powerful political group. Perhaps the best view of the event is to see it as the creation of one politically partisan publication to oppose another.

For the most part, Zenger was the printer of the *Journal* and Alexander the chief editorial writer, or as Frank Luther Mott described Alexander, "the *de facto* editor."[13] Other backers and contributors to the publication included Lewis Morris Sr., Lewis Morris Jr., Cadwallader Colden, and William Smith. Zenger's biographer, Livingston Rutherfurd, claimed Zenger entered the "newspaper scheme from a commercial point of view only, and without any adequate idea of the results which were to be accomplished."[14] Whatever Zenger's feelings were at this time, his supporters had far more ambitious ideas for the *Journal*. Over the next year and a half, however, Zenger warmed to the task and became an ardent opponent of Cosby and a strong supporter of the Popular Party.

The field was set, the troops ready. Cosby's opponents had found the man to carry the battle, and the vehicle—the *Journal*—was created. Now for the engagement. One of the first editions of the new newspaper carried a long essay on liberty of the press, much of which was extracted from Cato's Letters. This series of writings, then available in four volumes, had been written and published in London a decade earlier by Thomas Gordon and John Trenchard. Alexander, who had read *Cato* many times, used these arguments for freedom of the press as effectively west of the Atlantic as did Gordon and Trenchard in England.[15]

So began the first newspaper war in the colonies. But the battle was more than one between two newspapers; it was a battle between forces of unbridled authority and greed and those who felt liberty itself was at stake.

Frontal assaults on the furious governor never abated. Nor did the biting comments about his henchman, Harison, cease. So intense were the words of Alexander and Morris that at one point Harison wrote that another word for liar was "Zenger." Since the articles did not identify the authors in the *Journal,* the only visible target was Zenger. What was driving Cosby mad was that he couldn't prove it. Only the printer, Zenger, was publicly identified, and Cosby knew this poor German was only the tool. He wanted the culprits behind Zenger.

Cosby desperately sought some means of punishing his tormentors. It soon became obvious that he cared less whether the means of punishment were legal or not. And more and more, Cosby's attention began to turn to the one visible character on the battlefield—John Peter Zenger. Why not try another tactic? Cosby sought help from the Assembly and the magistrates to seize the newspaper and destroy all copies. Although the Assembly turned a deaf ear to his requests, the offending copies of the *Journal* were seized anyway by old reliable Francis Harison, ever ready to do the governor's dirty work. But he couldn't get anyone to burn the newspapers. Eventually, Harison had a slave burn the papers as he stood by and watched.[16]

The sharp-witted writers for the Journal were quick to seize upon any situation to embarrass the governor and his friends. When Morris opposed one of Cosby's hand-picked candidates for the assemblyman seat from Westchester, the sheriff managed to exclude some of Morris's Quaker supporters. Morris won anyway. The mental picture of the chubby little sheriff prancing around in his red uniform and cocked hat was too much to pass up. Loaded with more than a little satire, the following ad, which everyone knew was aimed at the sheriff, appeared in the Journal.

A Monkey of the larger Sort, about 4 foot high, has lately broke his chain and run into the country. . . .
Having got a Warr Saddle, Pistols and Sword, this whimsical Creature fancied himself a general; and taking a Paper in his Paw he muttered over it, what the far greatest Part of the Company understood not. . . .[17]

Copies of Zenger's newspaper were selling as fast as they were printed. In fact, several editions had to be reprinted to meet the demand. Zenger even considered publishing a second edition on Thursday to accompany the usual Monday edition.[18]

For months the attacks continued as Cosby frantically sought some means of punishing his tormentors. At last, the governor and his cohorts hit upon the proper combination that they felt would halt the onslaught. Cosby would charge Zenger with seditious libel, thereby halting publication. The attorney general bypassed the grand jury and charged Zenger.

Time needed for Zenger to be arrested for publishing "seditious libels": one year.

The *Journal* publisher was arrested on November 17, 1734, imprisoned by the authorities, and was kept there month after month awaiting trial.

Cosby and his legal cronies should have felt comfortable with events at this point. After all, new Supreme Court Justice Delancey, mouthing Cosby's charges, said Zenger's published comments contained scandalous, malicious, libelous material. That point cleared up, the die was cast. Existing libel law clearly guaranteed a conviction.

True to their natures, however, certain members of the Government Party couldn't resist attempting so many illegal and underhanded tactics before the trial that even the most unbiased observer would have condemned their efforts. They used a court that the Assembly and other upstanding members of the colony refused to recognize as legitimate, a court that also had been stacked with the governor's own hand-picked men, Delancey and Philipse. Bail was set so high that poor Zenger had no hope of being released to print his newspaper.

To make matters worse, the Cosby supporters disbarred Zenger's attorneys, thus denying him proper legal representation. The court appointed a spineless defense attorney, John Chambers, who was afraid to challenge any of the illegal proceedings. As a final blow, a court official attempted to stack the jury, and the court itself tried to disallow any proper arguments against the libels. What could Zenger and his friends do to fight such underhanded legal tactics? A look at each of the maneuvers attempted by the court party gives the answer.

Recall that Cosby had appointed the Supreme Court members as Barons of the Exchequer, giving them powers that had not been used in over a century in England. The Assembly had been ignored and, for the most part, opposed such an action. Cosby had booted Lewis Morris off the court, elevated Delancey to the chief justice seat, and made Philipse the second judge. A third judge was not appointed.

To combat such efforts, Zenger's attorneys, James Alexander and William Smith, officially challenged the legality of the justices' appointments and their right to hear such a trial. This so incensed Delancey that he disbarred the pair and forbade them to practice their profession henceforth. The newly appointed attorney, Chambers, refused to make such challenges on behalf of his client and seemed more than willing to go along with whatever the court declared. He did, however, plead his client not guilty and asked for a trial during the next term.

Time Zenger spent in jail awaiting trial: nine months.

The trial date was set for August 4, 1735, a long time for Zenger to wait in a jail cell to have his day in court. But that day was somewhat darkened when his friends arrived at the court clerk's office on the evening of July 25, 1735, to help select forty-eight names from the freeholder's book as a panel for the jury. To their amazement they found that the names had already been selected and the list of the "struck jury" prepared.

Zenger's friends argued that many of the names were of persons who were not freeholders (voting citizens) and that the balance were the governor's "baker, tailor, shoemaker, candle-maker, joiner, etc."[19] Strenuous objections got them nowhere and the court clerk steadfastly refused to allow them to help select another forty-eight names. Chambers argued at court the next day that the names were chosen improperly, and the court allowed forty-eight names to be chosen from the freeholder's book in the presence of all parties. A jury was eventually seated that was satisfactory to both sides.

Time needed for the *Journal* to begin printing again: one week.

The following week after Zenger's arrest no *Journal* was published, but two weeks after his arrest, on November 25, 1734, Zenger resumed publication. The issue contained an apology from Zenger for missing a week's publication and contained an explanation about his arrest. He dictated through the "hole" in his cell door to his wife and servants, who then published the newspaper.[20] He took the opportunity to lambaste Cosby and Harison for his troubles. But what he did not do was reveal who had written the articles that the government claimed were libelous. It is well to note that Zenger was the first American newspaperman to establish the tradition that journalists would protect their sources, even to the point of imprisonment. Those who wrote the articles remained silent, and Zenger protected their identities.[21]

The day of the trial arrived at last. The court party must have entered the courtroom with a smug attitude on August 4, 1735. After all, English law provided that a person could be punished for libel even if the damaging words were true. And it was acknowledged by the court that a person who disseminated the libel—someone like the printer—also could be punished. The court would decide if the words were indeed seditious libel and all that would be left for the jury to decide was if the hapless Zenger was the printer of the words, something he could not deny since he was the owner and publisher of the newspaper.

In addition to having the law on their side, members of the Government Party were confident that Zenger's court-appointed defense attorney, John Chambers, was inept. So, it must have been quite a shock for the two justices to enter the packed courtroom on that warm summer day and see the distinguished white-haired gentleman sitting at the defense table with Zenger. The man: Andrew Hamilton, a venerable Philadelphia lawyer said to be near eighty years in age. Whether in awe of the famed lawyer or frightened of a strong public reaction to a negative decision, Delancey never questioned the right of Hamilton to serve as counsel for Zenger.

Time needed before Hamilton admitted his client was guilty: two minutes.

Hamilton, retained by Alexander and Morris to defend Zenger, never relinquished control of the courtroom even at the outset when it seemed as if the old warrior had given away any chance of acquittal by acknowledging that Zenger was indeed guilty, that he had in fact published the words the court alleged as libelous! The prosecutor, surprised by such an admission, arose and announced that there was little to do except for the jury to return a verdict for the king. "Not so neither," spoke out Hamilton. "Before you make my client a libeler . . . the words themselves must be libelous, that is 'false, scandalous and seditious,' or else we are not guilty."[22]

Hamilton was a few decades ahead of his time with this legal interpretation, and the court quickly pointed out that the law did not allow truth to be considered in a libel decision. But Hamilton had not earned his fame without developing a bulldog mentality. With the jury hanging on his every word, the old lawyer retorted that he would question whether just complaints of men who suffered under a bad administration are actually libels. Hamilton challenged the prosecutor to prove the facts false, and the defense would then admit to the libels.

Delancey interrupted to instruct Hamilton that the court would not permit truth to be used in evidence since "a libel is not to be justified; for it is nevertheless a libel that it is true."[23] Hamilton then launched into a long speech, explaining that all the legal precedents came from the Star Chamber a century earlier and that the jury had the right to determine the facts and the law. At this point, young Delancey again interrupted to lecture Hamilton on the law. The jury did not have that right, explained Delancey. At this point, the following exchange took place between Delancey and Hamilton:

Delancey: Mr. Hamilton, the court have delivered their opinion, and we expect you will use us with good manners; you are not to be permitted to argue against the opinion of the court.

Hamilton: With submission, I have seen the practice in very great courts, and never heard it deemed unmannerly to . . ."

Delancey [interrupting]: After the court have declared their opinion, it is not good manners to insist upon a point, in which you are over-ruled.

Hamilton: I will say no more at this time; the court I see is against us in this point; and that I hope I may be allowed to say.

Delancey: Use the court with good manners, and you shall be allowed all the liberty you can reasonably desire.[24]

The chief justice had fallen for the bait. The distinguished old lawyer replied, "I thank your honour." Then he turned from the judge, looked directly at the jury and said:

Then, gentlemen of the jury, it is to you we must now appeal; for witnesses to the truth of the facts we have offered, and are denied the liberty to prove; and let it not seem strange, that I apply myself to you in this manner; I am warranted so to do both by law and reason.[25]

Hamilton explained to the jury that while he admitted to his client being the printer of the allegedly false words, the facts were not committed "in a corner," but were known by everyone to be true.

Hamilton challenged the prosecutor to define libel and then afterwards asked him, for the jury to hear, by what rule could we know whether the words are malicious, defamatory, or tend to breach the peace. Was the writing done ironically or in all seriousness? How are the words to be understood, and who decides what they mean? Delancey broke in to say that "those" who judge the words must decide whether the words are scandalous or ironical, tend to breach the peace, or are seditious.

Hamilton had him. The tide of battle in the courtroom visibly turned when Hamilton again thanked Delancey for his remarks and retorted: "Then it follows that those 12 men must understand the words . . . to be scandalous . . . and when they understand the words to be so, they will say we are guilty of publishing a false libel. . . . "[26] Hamilton then informed the court, for the jury's benefit, that the jury had the right to determine both law and fact, and where the jury had no doubt of the law, it should do exactly that.

What followed was a long, in-depth discussion by Hamilton, directed at the jury, of liberty, the meaning of freedom, and the abuse of that freedom by many in power. He essentially urged the jury to ignore the law and use its own power to reject the court's insistence on limiting the jury's ability to determine what is right and just. "If you should be of opinion that there is no falsehood in Mr. Zenger's papers, you will, nay you ought to say so; because you do not know whether others (the court) may be of that opinion."[27]

Part of Hamilton's summation is worthy of note here, as these words have rung down through the years as a call for men to defend liberty wherever the challenge arises. He concluded:

The question before the court and you, gentlemen of the jury, is not of small or private concern; it is not the cause of a poor printer, nor of New-York alone, which you are now trying: no! It may, in its consequence, affect every free man that lives under a British government on the main of America. It is the best cause: it is the cause of liberty! and I make no doubt but your upright conduct, this day, will not only entitle you to the love and esteem of your fellow citizens; but every man who prefers freedom to a life of slavery, will bless and honour you, as men who have baffled the attempt of tyranny, and who, by an impartial and uncorrupt verdict, have laid a noble foundation for securing to ourselves, our posterity, and our neighbours, that, to which nature and the laws of our country have give us a right—the liberty—both of exposing and opposing arbitrary power . . . by speaking and writing truth.[28]

A noble challenge to the twelve jurymen. Did they listen to the words? A rather officious instruction to the jury followed by a deflated Delancey, in which he told them not to worry about deciding the law, that the court would handle that little chore. And then the jury retired.

Time needed to reach a decision: ten minutes.

As the jury returned, the packed courtroom quieted before jury foreman Thomas Hunt uttered those wonderfully improbable words: "Not guilty."

Pandemonium broke out in the room. So much noise, in fact, that Delancey threatened to punish those in attendance. To his credit, Delancey did not set aside the judgment, which he had the power to do, nor did he hold Hamilton in contempt for arguing to the jury something Delancey had earlier forbidden. Perhaps the chief justice understood that the jury decision came not so much from Hamilton's eloquent plea, but from a popular feeling among the people.

The crowd, along with the delirious attorneys and friends of Zenger, retired to the Black Horse Tavern and celebrated long and hard. Zenger, however, missed the celebration party. He had to return to jail and was not freed until the following day after an order from the court was received. Zenger did have the opportunity to take part in the hero's farewell to Hamilton, who sailed out of New York harbor the following day to the thunder of cannon salutes.

What did this victory mean to Zenger and his friends? What impact did it have on freedom of expression then and later? No law was changed, and no law would be changed in America until the beginning of the nineteenth century. The decision ran counter to every aspect of English libel law. Obviously, colonial authorities moved cautiously following this decision, and few problems of censorship or charges of seditious libel arose during the remainder of English rule.

Time needed before the trial had an impact on the colonies: none.

A seed for a still distant revolution was planted in the New York courtroom. Stories of the great legal victory were told and retold right up to the Revolution. For decades reprints of Hamilton's version of the trial were published in both America and England. The verdict certainly impacted colonial leaders as well as the general population, and the notion that a free press and the right to express dissatisfaction with arbitrary power gained important ground with Americans.

Time needed for the results of the trial to be enacted into law: fifty-six years.

The residue of the Zenger trial could also be found in documents such as the Bill of Rights and the Constitution, which provide for freedom of expression and for the jury's right to determine law as well as fact.

In 1738, the *Pennsylvania Gazette* printed a letter from a Londoner quoting a learned man of law who said if Hamilton's principle "is not law, it is better than law, it ought to be law, and will always be law wherever justice prevails."[29]

Ultimately, justice somehow did prevail. In a case rich with scoundrels, paybacks, and simmering animosities, great truths emerged and thrived. In the winding river of American history, the legal principles and precedents John Peter Zenger established for future generations remained long after the German immigrant's battle was over.

NOTES

1. Livingston Rutherfurd, *John Peter Zenger* (New York: Arno Press, 1970), 3.

2. Vincent Buranelli, ed., *The Trial of John Peter Zenger* (New York: New York University Press, 1957), 5–7, 10–11.

3. Ibid., 8–9. See also William L. Chenery, *Freedom of the Press* (Westport, Conn.: Greenwood Press, 1977), 110–111.

4. Buranelli, *The Trial of John Peter Zenger*, 9.

5. Maud Wilder Goodwin, *Dutch and English on the Hudson* (New Haven, Conn.: Yale University Press, 1919), 196. See Also Michael R. Belknap, *American Political Trials* (Westport, Conn.: Greenwood Press, 1981), 25.

6. Rutherfurd, *John Peter Zenger*, 25.

7. Goodwin, *Dutch and English on the Hudson*, 197.

8. Buranelli, *The Trial of John Peter Zenger*, 20.

9. John Tebbel, *The Compact History of the American Newspaper* (New York: Hawthorn Books, 1969), 22.

10. James Melvin Lee, *History of American Journalism* (Garden City, N.Y.: The Garden City Publishing Co., 1923), 40.

11. Frederic Hudson, *Journalism in the United States* (New York: Harper and Brothers, Publishers, 1873), 81.

12. Jonathan Daniels, *They Will Be Heard* (New York: McGraw-Hill Book Company, 1965), 12–13.

13. Frank Luther Mott, *American Journalism* (New York: The Macmillan Company, 1942), 32.

14. Rutherfurd, *John Peter Zenger*, 29.

15. Buranelli, *The Trial of John Peter Zenger*, 31.

16. Ibid., 35–37.

17. Mott, *American Journalism*, 32.

18. Robert W. Jones, *Journalism in the United States* (New York: E. P. Dutton and Company, 1947), 90.

19. Stephen Parks, ed., *Three Trials: John Peter Zenger, H. S. Woodfall and John Lambert.* (New York: Garland Publishing Co., 1974), 9. This is the official account of the trial as written by Andrew Hamilton that was reprinted for decades after the trial. This account was printed for London publisher J. Almon in 1765.

20. Hudson, *Journalism in the United States*, 83.

21. Jones, *Journalism in the United States*, 94.

22. Chenery, *Freedom of the Press*, 116.

23. Ibid., 118.

24. Parks, *Three Trials*, 25.

25. Ibid., 25.

26. Ibid., 28.

27. Ibid., 44.

28. Ibid., 45–46.

29. Mott, *American Journalism*, 37.

2

The Case of the Boston Massacre
(1770)

"A . . . melancholy Demonstration"

Carol Sue Humphrey

Monday, May 4, 1970. A warm spring day at Kent State University in northeastern Ohio. Twenty-year-old Sandy Scheuer has spent part of the morning walking her neighbor's dog, Heavy. Now she hurries across campus to make her speech-therapy class. As she walks past the crowd of antiwar demonstrators and National Guardsmen near Taylor Hall, gunshots ring out. When the shooting stops, Sandy Scheuer lays in her own blood, dead. Three others, also students, are killed in what will become one of the most agonizing chapters of the anti-Vietnam movement in the United States.[1]

The horror at Kent State University (now known as Kent University) developed out of the growing opposition to American involvement in the war, and protests began on campus as early as 1968. The demonstrations focused on the presence of a Reserve Officers' Training Corps (ROTC) at Kent State. By 1970, more students had joined the protests, but the numbers involved represented only a minority of the student population.

On April 30, 1970, President Richard Nixon announced the U.S. invasion of Cambodia. During the next several days, students at Kent State rallied in opposition to this action. On the evening of May 2, the demonstrators firebombed the ROTC building, burning it to the ground. Local police, fearing further trouble, placed a curfew on the town and asked for assistance from the state. Governor James Rhodes sent in the National Guard.

For several days, the two groups faced off. Students hurled insults and curses at the troops, while guardsmen were determined to prevent any further student violence. On the morning of May 4, the final confrontation occurred. Students threw rocks and chunks of concrete at the guardsmen, who responded with tear gas in an attempt to disperse the crowd. Just after the supply of tear gas ran out, the National Guardsmen believed they heard a single shot. The response was a three-second volley that left four students dead and ten people wounded.

America recoiled in horror, unable to accept that Americans had killed Americans, that a college campus in Ohio had turned into a battlefield, that the killing fields were not thousands of miles away but at home. Americans everywhere asked the same question: How could it happen? What few realized, however, is that this was not the first time in America that the military and citizenry had confronted one another with deadly results. Two hundred years before, the cold, snow-covered streets of Boston turned blood red. And the aftermath was much the same: Public outrage followed by claims of innocence. The final result: an ever-widening chasm between public opinion and government policy. Just like Kent State, the question of guilt never was put to rest. The Boston Massacre still remains a mystery.

March 5, 1770. A quiet night in downtown Boston. A light snow fell earlier in the day, and Private Hugh White of the Twenty-ninth Regiment walks his sentry post in front of the Custom House at the corner of King Street and Royal Exchange Lane. White, nor anyone else for that matter, does not seem worried about walking a sentry post alone. But on this cold night a group of young apprentices confront the sentry, taunting him, and calling him names. The name-calling eventually develops into a one-sided snowball fight. Fearing for his life because the crowd is growing and starting to threaten him verbally, White calls for the Main Guard to come to his aid. Under the command of Captain Thomas Preston, a squad responds. By the time they reach the Custom House, the church bells of Boston are ringing (indicating a fire or some other kind of trouble), and a large mob gathers in front of White's sentry post.[2]

It is not clear what happened next. Preston attempted to march his men back to the barracks, but couldn't because of the size of the mob facing him. Cries of "Fire" seem to come from everywhere. Later, many in the crowd said Preston ordered his men to fire into the crowd, but his presence in front of the troops when the first shots rang out undermines this idea. Whether ordered to do so or not, the soldiers fire. Suddenly, several people lay bleeding in the snow. Five were either dead or mortally injured and six others were wounded. Captain Preston quickly marched his men to Murray's Barracks and waited to see what local authorities would do. Both he and his men were arrested early the next morning.[3]

Although the exact details of the event are still impossible to determine, it is clear that a growing animosity between the citizens of Boston and the British troops stationed there would erupt into a violent confrontation. Three years earlier the Townshend Acts levied taxes on important products like tea, glass, and paper. When word spread that the taxes would be used to pay the British appointees who administered the colonies, simmering animosities quickly came to a boil. The radical Sons of Liberty protested, and troops arrived in Boston in October 1768 to enforce the customs regulations that many rebellious Massachusetts merchants either failed to obey or chose to ignore. During the next seventeen months, tensions mounted. Town leaders wanted the troops removed because they represented an attempt by British authorities to control local government. Residents wanted the troops gone because they believed that the troops, who were working at various jobs around town, lowered wages for everyone by accepting lower pay. The potential for conflict steadily grew. Minor verbal confrontations between troops and the citizens of Boston became a regular occurrence—the locals called the soldiers *Bloodybacks* and *Lobsters* because of their red coats—and the long New England winter probably heightened tensions as young Bostonians often threw snowballs, some encasing stones, at the British troops. It may have been such a snowball that started the Boston Massacre and eventually led to the withdrawal of the British troops from Boston.

In the week following the massacre, the local newspapers published accounts of the event. Although edited in different ways, the accounts almost certainly had the same original source: Samuel Adams, the leader of the fiery Sons of Liberty in Boston. Not surprisingly, the report of the massacre in the Boston press blamed the tragedy on the troops and their superiors. The scope of the guilt reached all the way to Governor Francis Bernard, who made the ultimate mistake by asking for troops to be sent to Boston, the colonial hotbed of radicalism. The *Boston Gazette's* account opened with the following editorial comments:

The Town of Boston affords a recent and
melancholy Demonstration of the destructive
Consequences of quartering Troops among Citizens
in a Time of Peace, under a Pretence of supporting
the Laws and aiding Civil Authority; every
considerate and unprejudic'd Person among us was
deeply imprest with the Apprehension of these
Consequences when it was known that a Number of
Regiments were ordered to this Town under such a
Pretext, but in Reality to inforce oppressive
Measures; to awe & controul the legislative as well
as executive Power of the Province, and to quell a
Spirit of Liberty, which however it may have been
basely oppos'd and even ridicul'd by some, would
do Honor to any Age or Country.[4]

Such hyperbole reflected the role of the press in North America throughout the eighteenth century. Newspapers provided news of events outside the town, but knowledge of local events came through other sources, primarily word-of-mouth. Boston's papers in 1770 were all weeklies, and their readers probably already knew the details of community happenings before the newspaper became available. The Boston Massacre illustrates this well. The event occurred on the evening of March 5, and three of the five Boston papers had appeared that very day. It was a week before an edition of these news sheets appeared again. By that time, in all of Boston and its surrounding areas, people were talking about the massacre. Consequently, the newspaper accounts of the tragedy did not really serve to inform people of the details of the event. Rather, they functioned as a means to unify public opinion by placing the blame on the "enemy"—British authorities—and served to heighten the stress and conflict between government officials and those leaders in the colonies who sought more freedom of action in local affairs.

Those who opposed Great Britain quickly seized on the Boston Massacre as a wonderful propaganda opportunity in their fight for colonial autonomy. Samuel Adams led in the quick production of a variety of materials that depicted the incident as an example of British tyranny. Besides the detailed description of the massacre, Adams and the Sons of Liberty organized elaborate funerals for the victims of the massacre that portrayed each as a martyr to the cause of liberty. Probably the most famous piece of propaganda came out of the shop of Paul Revere, who obtained a copy of a drawing of the massacre, done by Henry Pelham. Without permission, Revere engraved the drawing and had it printed. A grossly inaccurate rendering of the massacre that showed the troops standing in a tight formation and firing into the bloodied crowd, the print circulated widely and most people at that time, and for years afterwards, believed it to be a true depiction of what happened that March evening. The goal of Adams and the Sons of Liberty was not so much truth and accuracy in reporting, but propagation of hatred for British rule.

Throughout the months between the massacre and the trials, the newspapers carried little specific information. Firebrands like Adams missed a wonderful opportunity for weekly propaganda. However, the lack of comment in the local press does not mean that the media played no role in the aftermath of the Boston Massacre. The Boston Massacre quickly became part of the conflict between the colonies and the mother country. As such, part of the battle took place in Great Britain as local leaders and British officials in Massachusetts tried to convince the government in London that the other group was causing all the problems. In attempts to influence the king and his advisers—the final arbiters—both sides turned to a media form even older than the newspaper—the pamphlet.

Journalism historians have always recognized the role of the press in the coming of the Revolution, and the weekly news sheets of the colonies played the primary role in disseminating ideas throughout the countryside. But Bernard Bailyn disagrees, writing that it was in pamphlets "that much of the most important and characteristic writing of the American Revolution appeared."[5] As is often the case, the truth lies somewhere in the middle. Colonial printers, and the men who wrote for them, did not immediately turn to their weekly news sheets alone as a means to express political ideas. Pamphlets continued to be printed in large numbers.[6] It was only in the 1780s, with the appearance of larger papers and ones that published more than once a week, that newspapers finally became the major forum for the expression of political opinions.

The Boston Massacre, and the printed response to it, reflected the continued usefulness of pamphlets. Government officials in Massachusetts, in an attempt to get their view of the conflict before the British government, rushed John Robinson to England following the massacre. Once he arrived, he supervised the publication of a pamphlet entitled "A Fair Account of the Late Disturbances at Boston." Contained in this publication were a group of military depositions concerning the event and an affidavit from Andrew Oliver, the secretary of the colony, that described raucous council meetings following the massacre. In more than one deposition, government officials were threatened if they did not get the army out of Boston.[7]

Town leaders spent several days after the confrontation gathering the testimony of people in the crowd at the time of the shootings. These materials, along with an account of the massacre by James Bowdoin, were published as "A Short Narrative of the Horrid Massacre in Boston . . . To which is added, An Appendix." The bulk of the pamphlet consisted of ninety-six depositions. Ninety-four placed the blame on the soldiers or other government officials. Copies of this pamphlet were hurriedly sent to Great Britain in hopes that officials there would believe the troops caused all the trouble.[8]

Although principally aimed at British officials, town leaders also hoped "A Short Narrative" would help convince any wavering citizens that the military was completely to blame in the case of the Boston Massacre. Officially, town leaders ordered that all extra copies of the pamphlet be impounded in order not to prejudice potential jurors. However, the pamphlet did circulate in Boston prior to the trials and possibly influenced public opinion concerning the massacre.[9]

When the soldiers involved in the Boston Massacre were finally arraigned on September 7, 1770, they faced their accusers with three capable lawyers to defend them: Robert Auchmuty, Josiah Quincy, and John Adams, the cousin of Sam Adams and a known sympathizer of the Sons of Liberty. The defense team quickly asked for, and was granted, separate trials for Captain Preston and his men. The reasoning for this was simple: Try them together and Preston tells the jury he didn't order the soldiers to shoot. The soldiers are then left with but one defense: Preston gave the order. Result: a confused jury hangs them all. So with much relief, the defense began to prepare for the trials to come.

Preston's trial began on October 24. The impaneling of the jury took quite some time since the defense, in seeking as impartial a jury as possible, challenged many potential jurors. When the jury was finally seated, there was little doubt as to the trial's outcome. Most of the jurors either lived outside of Boston or were locally known as supporters of the government. Still, the trial lasted much longer than normal—six days, when the norm for a murder trial was less than a day. Throughout the trial, the jury was sequestered in Boston. The prosecution spent two days calling witnesses who testified that Captain Preston had ordered his men to fire. In cross-examination the defense showed that the witnesses disagreed about whether Preston had been standing in front of or behind the troops when the order was given. The defense witnesses emphasized the unruliness of the crowd and denied that Preston had given the order to fire. When both sides gave their closing arguments, it quickly became clear that the prosecution had not been able to prove beyond "reasonable doubt" that Preston had ordered his men to fire into the crowd. The case went to the jury at 5 p.m., October 29. It apparently reached a verdict in three hours, but the outcome was not reported to the court until 8 the next morning. The verdict: not guilty.[10]

The trial of the eight soldiers did not begin until November 20 because the court had to ride the circuit and handle cases in several communities surrounding Boston. Once more, when that jury process was completed, no juror came from Boston. The defense, however, had a much higher hurdle to jump in this trial: the deaths of five people due to gunshot wounds inflicted by the defendants. The question before the jurors: Did the soldiers have sufficient justification to shoot into the crowd? The prosecution emphasized the animosity the troops had for townspeople before the massacre. The defense concentrated on the events of the evening of March 5, showing that the crowd had been unruly and had threatened the soldiers with clubs and sticks.

But great trials are hardly great without at least one surprise witness, and John Adams provided one when he called Richard Palmes, a prominent Liberty man. Palmes had been prevented from leaving town when Adams had gotten a court order forcing him to stay. Palmes was, at best, a reluctant witness but he would prove to be Adams's best. Palmes, you see, had spoken with Preston just as the shooting started.

Palmes told the jury of his abbreviated conversation with the captain: "Sir," said Palmes, "I hope you don't intend the soldiers shall fire on the inhabitants. He said, 'by no means.' The instant he spoke I saw something resembling snow or ice strike the grenadier on the Captain's right hand. . . ."

Palmes reluctantly continued, saying that the grenadier had "fired the first gun." Although others also testified that Preston gave no orders to shoot and that the soldiers' response was made in self-defense, Palmes's testimony was crushing to the prosecution since, as Adams emphasized to the jury, he was "an inhabitant of [the] town [and] therefore not prejudiced in favor of [the] soldiers."[11]

In a masterful closing argument, John Adams called on the jury to put their political opinions aside:

Facts are stubborn things, and whatever may be our wishes, our inclinations, or the dictates of our passions, they cannot alter the state of facts and evidence. Nor is the law less stable than the fact. If an assault was made to endanger their lives, the law is clear; they had a right to kill in their own defence. If it was not so severe as to endanger their lives, yet if they were assaulted at all, struck and abused by blows of any sort, by snowballs, oyster-shells, cinders, clubs, or sticks of any kind, this was a provocation, for which the law reduces the offence of killing down to manslaughter, in consideration of those passions in our nature which cannot be eradicated.

To your candor and justice I submit the prisoners and their cause. The law, in all vicissitudes of government, fluctuations of the passions, or flights of enthusiasm, will preserve a steady, undeviating course. It will not bend to the uncertain wishes, imaginations, and wanton tempers of men. . . . "Tis deaf, inexorable, inflexible. On the one hand, it is inexorable to the cries and lamentations of the prisoner; on the other, it is deaf, deaf as an adder, to the clamors of the populace."[12]

Adams believed that a favorable verdict was certain. He was right. The case went to the jury at 1:30 p.m., December 5, 1770; by 4 p.m. the jurors had returned. Of the eight defendants, two were convicted of manslaughter and six were acquitted of any wrongdoing. According to the *Boston Gazette*, "the soldiers were discharged from Court in high Day-Light; and went their Way thro' the Streets, with little, if any Notice."[13] With little fanfare, the trials of the soldiers accused of murder in the Boston Massacre came to a quiet end.

Throughout the trials, which began in October and ended in December, the Boston newspapers provided little coverage, apparently reflecting a lack of attention to the trials. Brief reports about the trials taking place appeared, as did brief statements about the verdicts. The newspapers, however, failed to give any details of the testimony at the trials or the arguments of the lawyers. John Adams's brilliant closing argument was not published in the local press.

If one used the newspapers of the fall of 1770 to judge the significance of the Boston Massacre trials, one would be tempted to belittle their importance. Such a conclusion, however, would be a mistake. The Boston Massacre, and the trials following it, constituted pivotal events in the growing conflict between Great Britain and the colonies.

The newspapers did not play a major role in informing or influencing the public *during* the trials, but this was not the case *after* the trials. No one appreciated the potential impact of the press in such a situation more than Samuel Adams. Writing under numerous aliases, Adams used the weekly news sheets during the Stamp Act crisis in 1765 and later in protesting the Townshend duties. The *Boston Gazette* provided the main outlet for Adams's ideas. It is unclear, however, why Adams did not turn to the newspapers more in the months prior to and during the Boston Massacre trials. Perhaps he simply assumed that Captain Preston and the soldiers would be convicted. When that did not happen, Adams turned to the press as an outlet for his frustration and as a means to galvanize public opinion against the British.

Beginning on December 10, 1770—the same day that the final official report of the trials appeared—and continuing through January 28, 1771, a series of essays appeared in the *Boston Gazette*. Writing as "Vindex," Adams used the pages of the *Gazette* to retry the cases. In the end he could not change the verdicts, but he did convince many a Bostonian that the trials had not resulted in a fair judgment for everyone involved.[14]

Over the course of two months, Adams deftly used the press to shape public opinion about the massacre and to turn it into a major crime by the British royal government. Through Adams's skillful writing, Captain Preston, the eight soldiers, and the entire British government were portrayed as the murderers of five patriots killed in front of the Boston Customs House that bitter March evening.

At first, Adams praised all of the participants in the trials for their conscientious efforts in carrying out their respective assignments. However, he quickly moved to the issue of whether the soldiers were justified in firing into the crowd. Adams questioned why the soldiers did not just retreat to the barracks.[15] Adams also wrote that there existed ample proof the soldiers had stirred up the crowd and caused the trouble in front of the Customs House. "The behavior of the party as they went from the main guard discover'd an haughty air—they push'd their bayonets and damn'd the people as they went along."[16] According to Adams's Monday morning analysis, the troops brought the trouble on themselves by stirring up the crowd with their own belligerent attitudes.

Throughout the series of essays, "Vindex" continually returned to the issue of who was at fault on the night of March 5, 1770. In a piece published on December 31, he concluded that during the trials, "not a single instance was prov'd, of abuse offer'd to Soldiers that Evening, previous to the insolent behavior of those who rush'd out of Murray's Barracks, with Cutlasses, Clubs and other Weapons, and fell upon all whom they met." Rather, there had been many instances of the troops "insulting and even assaulting the Inhabitants in every part of the Town. . . ."[17]

Adams left the final judgment up to the people of Boston, but his language leaves no room for doubt as to who he believed was responsible for the Boston Massacre.[18] He concluded that the soldiers pushed the crowd too far and that the people responded to the threats in self-defense. "Vindex" wrote that after the initial shots into the crowd the soldiers continued to fire because their commanding officer did not control them: "Capt. Preston, at so alarming a juncture, took no method to prevent the rest from firing, if what was testified in court is to be credited; or, if his own account must be rely'd upon, he exerted no authority over his men, but used expostulations only."[19]

Adams also emphasized the barbarity of the event. In doing this, he presented to the public questionable evidence never aired at the trial. Of particular importance was the issue of Private Kilroy's bayonet, which "was prov'd to be the next morning bloody five inches from the point." Adams stated that many believed the bayonet had fallen into human blood "which ran plentifully in the street," which accounted for its condition the next morning. But, it was "much more likely that this very bayonet was stab'd into the head of poor Gray [one of the dead] after he was shot." Adams reported that "such an instance of Savage barbarity there undoubtedly was.—It was sworn before the Magistrate who first examined into this cruel tragedy." However, when the case came to trial, the witness who made this statement was out of the province and could not attend to testify. Adams believed that government collusion lay behind this.[20]

Beside asking why certain witnesses did not appear for the prosecution, Adams questioned the validity of witnesses who testified for the defense. In particular, he challenged the evidence given by Andrew, a slave, which supported the story that the crowd threw coal at the sentry. The great propagandist declared that Andrew was "remarkable for telling romantick stories in the circles of his acquaintance." People believed Andrew's testimony, Adams wrote, primarily because "his master, who is in truth an honest man, came into court and swore to his character." Adams hinted that the master may be mistaken because "no man knows so little of the real character of his servant, as the master himself does: It is well known, that the Negroes of this town have been familiar with the soldiers; and that some of them have been tamper'd with to cut their master's throats: I hope Andrew is not one of these."[21] Such comments weakened the strength of defense testimony, at least in the minds of many who already believed the soldiers were guilty.

Adams also attempted to put events in historical perspective: "[T]he trial of the soldiers concern'd in the carnage on the memorable 5th of March, was the most solemn trial that ever was had in this country, was pronounc'd from the bench. To see eight prisoners bro't to the bar together, charg'd with the murder of five persons at one time, was certainly, as was then observ'd, affecting."[22]

Finally, Adams slyly reversed himself on the issue of how good a job those involved in the trial had done. He declared that "I am not about to arraign the late jurors before the bar of the publick." But, he concluded, "they are accountable to God and their own consciences, and in *their* day of trial, may God send them good deliverance."[23]

For Adams, justice had not been served through the trials of those involved in the Boston Massacre. Perhaps colonists felt a measure of justice was meted out ten years later with Cornwallis's surrender at Yorktown in 1781. In any case, Adams's opinion remained the dominant one for decades. Until well into the nineteenth century, most Americans believed that murder had been committed in front of the Customs House on that cold, snowy evening in March 1770.

NOTES

1. James A. Michener, *Kent State: What Happened and Why* (New York: Fawcett Crest, 1971), 355–357.

2. Hiller B. Zobel, *The Boston Massacre* (New York: W. W. Norton, 1970), 184–195.

3. Ibid., 195–205.

4. *Boston Gazette*, 12 March 1770.

5. Bernard Bailyn, *The Ideological Origins of the American Revolution* (Cambridge, Mass.: Belknap Press of Harvard University Press, 1967), 2.

6. The fact that Thomas Paine is remembered both for writing *Common Sense*, a pamphlet, and *The Crisis*, a series of newspaper essays, reflects the continued usefulness of both mediums.

7. Zobel, *Boston Massacre,* 212–213. This pamphlet never appeared in its entirety in Massachusetts, but copies of it did reach Boston and parts of it appeared in newspapers in other colonies.

8. Of the remaining two depositions, one was basically neutral as to blame, while the other blamed the townspeople, but a footnote declared that "no credit ought to be given to his deposition." Quoted in Zobel, *Boston Massacre*, 213.

9. Ibid., 213–214.

10. Ibid., 241–265.

11. *Boston Gazette*, 3 March 1771; Zobel, *Boston Massacre*, 263.

12. John Adams, *The Works of John Adams*, ed. Charles Francis Adams (Boston: Little, Brown, 1856), 1:113–114.

13. *Boston Gazette*, 17 December 1770.

14. It was not until the nineteenth century that many people came to believe that the verdicts in the Boston Massacre trials had been fair. Prior to that time, many Americans believed that justice had not been served and that the soldiers had been able to "get away with murder." John Adams disagreed. Years later, he described his service as defense attorney as "one of the most gallant, generous, manly and disinterested Actions of my whole life, and one of the best Pieces of Service I ever rendered my Country." John Adams, *Diary and Autobiography of John Adams*, ed. Lyman H. Butterfield et al., 4 vols. (Cambridge, Mass.: Harvard University Press, 1963), 2: 79.

15. "Vindex," *Boston Gazette*, 10 December 1770.

16. Ibid.

17. Ibid., 31 December 1770.

18. Ibid., 28 January 1771.

19. Ibid.

20. Ibid., 17 December 1770.

21. Ibid., 7 January 1770.

22. Ibid., 17 December 1770.

23. Ibid., 21 January 1771.

3

The Case of John Brown
(1859)

"John Brown still lives."

Bernell Tripp

A gaping mob watched in silence as the prisoners straggled from the jail and proceeded diagonally across the street to the courthouse, filing between rows of troops holding bayoneted rifles. Rumors circulated that eighty soldiers had been dispatched to guard the five men, three whites and two Negroes, who had been in custody since October 17, 1859. Hordes of spectators filled every space in the courtroom—pressing around the bar area surrounding the prisoners and along the walls, before spilling out into the hallways and onto the porch. Charlestown, West Virginia, teemed with newspapermen, militia, and citizens anxious to catch a glimpse of the man and his followers who had staged the vicious attack against peaceful citizens in Virginia. Despite the short trip, one prisoner, Aaron Stevens, had to be supported by two bailiffs—his body smeared with blood and grime as he suffered from three bullets in his head, two in his breast, and one in his arm. His forehead also bore the mark of a rifle bullet that had failed to penetrate his skull.

However, it was the leader who strode at the head of the bedraggled band at which most of the spectators gawked. Old John Brown marched into the midst of his foes, head erect, and eyes glaring defiantly around him at the crowd and the eight magistrates presiding over the court of examination. Reporters would later point out that capture and confinement by his enemies appeared not to have softened—and certainly had not broken—Brown's spirit. Like Stevens, the 6-foot-tall Brown also bore signs of the pitched battle at Harpers Ferry a week earlier. His peculiarly shaped head was covered with long gray hair matted with grime and caked blood from a sabre cut. In sharp contrast to the dirt, blood, and gunpowder residue, pale blue eyes, almost a clear gray, challenged the hostile faces that surrounded him. His only allies seemed to be the four men standing next to him: Stevens, Edwin Coppic, John Copeland, and Shields Green.

As the prisoners stood before the eight Justices of the Peace, the sheriff read the commitment charges, each carrying the death penalty—treason, murder, and inciting slaves to insurrection. Two lawyers, C. J. Faulkner and Lawson Botts, both Virginians and slavery advocates, were called forward from their places in the crowd, and the prosecution, Charles B. Harding, attorney for Jefferson County, and Andrew Hunter, counsel for the state, asked the prisoners if they would accept the two men as counsel. Twice Brown refused, while the other four assented to the arrangement. After the first request, Brown remarked:

Virginians: I did not ask for any quarter at the time I was taken. I did not ask to have my life spared. The Governor of the State of Virginia tendered me his assurance that I should have a fair trial; but under no circumstances whatever, will I be able to attend to my trial. If you seek my blood, you can have it at any moment without this mockery of a trial.[1]

And so began the most partisan, political trial of the nineteenth century. So began the end for Old Osawatomie Brown. So began one of the final steps of the long path leading the country toward civil war.

Previously thought killed in the fight against the Virginia militia, but later discovered to be wounded only slightly despite several sabre cuts, Old Osawatomie Brown was very much alive and eager to plead his own case before the press and the world. Consequently, the press, as well as the people, would be forced to decide for themselves if Brown was indeed a madman or a martyr. The question still lives.

Thus began the preliminary hearing of a man whose life and actions were at one moment atrocious to many Americans, yet understandable to others, applauded by the North, yet feared by the South. John Brown was at the heart of the matter, and the matter was human bondage. His crimes and trial perhaps marked the cusp of public opinion in a struggle older than the country.

Let there be no drama. Brown was guilty under the law. He was found guilty; he was condemned; he was hanged. But there is much more to the trial and death of John Brown than benign statements of fact. Newspapers for and against Brown attempted to use the raid, the trial, the sentencing, and the execution to propagate their beliefs across a country rapidly heading for the unthinkable: war within.

John Brown's trial, then, would become a crucible in deciding the question of slavery. It was important to newspapers simply because it was the news, and at the same time, it was propaganda. It was *the* event, and readers throughout the country would look to journalists to provide them with information and guidance.

This is not to suggest that the country wasn't already charged with the excitement and controversy surrounding slavery. Newspapers, as well as citizens, were choosing sides, and each new event was judged for its media impact and persuasive value in garnering support for either proslavery advocates or abolitionists. The Nat Turner and Denmark Vesey uprisings were "proof" in the South that slaves needed to be controlled. The 1837 murder of St. Louis editor Elijah Lovejoy had already provided the abolitionists with a martyr and concrete evidence of the brutality of those who promoted the continuance of slavery. As time passed, there was no reconciliation between the regions and the only significant change was the strength of feelings. The last thing slavery sympathizers needed was another martyr, something feared when rumors abounded that Brown had been lynched by the soldiers who had captured him.

Journalists first viewed Brown's capture as a victory for slavery supporters. One of the more violent and radical abolitionists—a madman who served as an example of just how unstable antislavery advocates were—would no longer plague southern slaveholders.[2] However, this sense of triumph gradually disintegrated into fear. By his very nature, and by his treatment of the blacks around him, Brown easily inspired blacks to rally in support of his efforts. Since the Nat Turner rebellion of 1831, Southerners had begun to fear their own creation: the enemy within; the one working in the kitchen, or in the barn, or in the fields.

To free blacks and slaves, the leader at Harpers Ferry was more than a man—he was a symbol who conferred dignity and worth upon his black followers. This devotion to Brown, with his condemnation of slavery as the sin of all sins, motivated many blacks to follow him without question.[3] Fear that Brown's failed raid at Harpers Ferry might ignite a great slave uprising was real. Andrew Hunter, appointed as special prosecutor by the governor, seemed to agree that the "raid was not the insignificant thing which it appeared to be before the public, but that it . . . was the incipient movement of the great conflict between North and South."[4]

This was perhaps the greatest fear of Southerners: not the threat of war so much as the potential for slave insurrections and the crumbling of a way of life. Activities of all blacks in the South, even seemingly innocent actions, were viewed with suspicion. Initial reports of the raid stated that as many as 600 to 900 Negroes were expected to revolt.[5] Even during Brown's incarceration, rumors circulated that an army of slaves and abolitionists were plotting to march across Virginia's borders and free Brown. This scenario had the antislavery army massacring all white men, women, and children, while burning everything in their path.[6]

Newspapers capitalized on this hypothetical, citing numerous incidents of Southern paranoia. According to a *Richmond Enquirer* article, reprinted in the *New York Times*, the raid was proof that abolitionists were madmen determined to undermine the rights of slaveholders in the South.[7] During the siege at Harpers Ferry, Baltimore newspapers printed detailed stories of a dangerous ringleader who commanded 300 "strapping negroes" (later 500 to 700) who were slaughtering whites and causing a great deal of trouble.[8] And on October 27 the *New Orleans Daily Picayune* asked the question no one in either region wanted answered: "Are the thinking men of the North ready for civil war—a war of vengeance, embittered by the hottest fanaticism? Will they recognize the desperado, Osawatomie Brown, as a martyr in a good cause . . . ?"

By comparison, some Northerners viewed Southern fear of Brown's actions as advantageous to the antislavery cause. Abolitionist Thomas Wentworth Higginson, one of six well-known men thought to have been part of the conspiracy, wanted Brown to disprove the theory that all slaves were as submissive as Harriet Beecher Stowe's ultimate propaganda figure, Uncle Tom. By doing so, the slaves would prove that they possessed the core of American political, social, and economic ideals—the willingness to fight for their freedom—and force whites to understand the reasoning behind their need for enfranchisement.[9]

At the heart of this slave uprising was a New Yorker raised to abhor slavery and discrimination in all forms. John Brown was born May 9, 1800, in Torrington, Litchfield County, Connecticut, the second son of Owen and Ruth Mills Brown. His father, a tanner and shoemaker, had also been an abolitionist, a legacy that son John would pass on to his own children.[10]

By 1856, Brown was a contributor to the *Ram's Horn*, a black weekly owned and operated by Willis A. Hodges in New York City, and he often sent money and supplies to be used in aiding the runaways' assimilation into a new life in Canada.[11] However, after Brown and his sons waged war on the proslavery settlers in the Kansas territory, and after he butchered five proslavery settlers near Osawatomie, Kansas, in 1856, many people in both regions saw Brown's "executions" as either the work of a madman or a religious zealot. The following year, President James Buchanan labeled the man now widely known as Old Osawatomie an outlaw and offered a reward for his capture.[12]

Brown escaped to Canada, however, and remained free until October 1859. Then on Sunday, October 16, Brown and twenty-one men took control of the town of Harpers Ferry. By the next day, Brown's forces were embroiled in an unrelenting battle with the state militia, having killed or taken several residents hostage and controlling the United States armory and both bridges leading into town. At dawn on October 18, Brown and his followers were overrun by a company of U. S. Marines, under the direction of then-Colonel Robert E. Lee, who had moved into the town during the night.[13]

Only twelve of the twenty-two men survived. John E. Cook, a former schoolteacher in Harpers Ferry, and other members of the raiders' rearguard stationed at the schoolhouse, fled into the mountains. Brown's two sons, Watson and Oliver, were casualties of the raid. Oliver died at the armory, and his body was wrapped in the arms of free black Dangerfield Newby as a joke, before both were tossed into an unmarked hole on the bank of the Shenandoah River.[14] Watson, bleeding internally, died twenty hours later in the guardhouse after the group was captured. After his death, Watson's body was supposedly shoved into a box and taken away to Winchester Medical

College for medical dissection.[15]

The conditions and the treatment of the prisoners provided ample opportunity for both sides to analyze Brown and the U. S. slavery policy. Separated from his son after their capture, Old Brown lay more than thirty hours on the floor of the superintendent's office of the armory, listening to the drunken carousing and the gunfire from his own Sharps rifles and revolvers taken by looters who were threatening to lynch him. For Brown, a lynching might have been preferable to a public trial and execution. It could have provided the abolitionists with yet another martyr—this time, one who had a stronger connection to blacks, who were becoming an increasingly integral part of the movement.[16] A lynching, however, could never have had the impact of a capture, an indictment, a trial and, finally, an execution. So began partisan and regional media campaigns that shoved the slavery issue to the top of the news agenda.

Despite Brown's hopes, the prisoners were transported to Charlestown, the Jefferson County seat, before a lynching could occur. After the five men were safely ensconced in the jail, Hunter was determined to indict, try, and execute Old Brown and his men within ten days. According to Virginia law, anyone involved in a slave insurrection could be tried under this accelerated process.[17]

The men remained in jail for five days before they were brought into the court for their arraignment.[18] During the incarceration, newspapers were limited to providing analysis of Brown's life and philosophies, as well as background material on the prisoners. Many editors used this opportunity to contemplate the outcome of the trial and its effect on the slavery issue.[19] However, because of rumors that Hunter was attempting to limit access to the prisoners, Brown soon became fearful that the people would never hear the truth about his actions and beliefs. In a hastily arranged press conference in his cell, the old renegade bluntly, guiltlessly, righteously, preached his innocence of wrong-doing. Said Brown: No acts of violence except those necessary to implement his plans were ever committed. Yet Brown's beliefs were of little interest to the reporters salivating for the spectacle the upcoming trial was certain to create. The journalists had been handpicked by Hunter, including the Associated Press reporter and the *New York Herald* correspondent, Gallagher, who soon became Old Brown's ally.[20]

Having already made up their minds about the past events, the reporters often were more interested in Brown's frequent speeches during the trial than the evidence or other witnesses' testimony. When asked on the day of the preliminary examination if he would accept the aid of Faulkner and Botts, Brown appealed to Gallagher and the other reporters in the courtroom. He reiterated his request for counsel who would defend his rights to a fair trial.[21] Down came the gavel as the presiding magistrate issued preemptory orders that "the press should not publish detailed testimony, as it would render the getting of a jury before the Circuit Court impossible."[22] Faulkner also expressed a desire not to serve as counsel because he had been among those

men who had subdued Brown's party at Harpers Ferry. He was requested to
remain at least until the closure of the preliminary examination.[23]

The preliminary examination moved quickly. Eight witnesses, seven of
whom had been hostages at Harpers Ferry, were called to testify about the
capture of the residents, the occupation of the armory, the battle, the
casualties of the fight, the rebels' professed philosophies and purpose, and
the treatment of the hostages. By 5 p.m., the prisoners had been remanded for
trial and brought before the grand jury.[24] Court reassembled at 10 a.m.,
October 26. According to one press account:

The prisoners were brought in, accompanied by a body of armed men. Cannon were
stationed in front of the Court House and an armed guard were patrolling around the
jail. Brown looked something better and his eyes were not so much swollen. Stevens
had to be supported, and reclined on a mattress on the floor of the court
room—evidently unable to sit. He has the appearance of a dying man, breathing with
great difficulty. The prisoners were compelled to stand during the indictment, but it
was with difficulty, Stevens being held upright by two bailiffs.[25]

At noon the Grand Jury reported a "true bill" against each of the
prisoners, whom they declared "evil-minded and traitorous persons . . . not
having the fear of God before their eyes, but being moved by the false and
malignant counsel of other evil and traitorous persons, and the instigations of
the devil."[26] Faulkner had already departed, and the court appointed Thomas
C. Green, mayor of Charlestown, to hear the indictments, along with Botts,
who decided to remain on the case. The five prisoners were charged with
confederating to make rebellion against Virginia, conspiring to induce slave
insurrections, and committing murder upon four men.[27]

The prisoners' pleas of not guilty surprised no one, and Hunter readily
agreed to requests for separate trials. This way, he could try Brown first. At
this point, Botts reiterated Brown's earlier plea for a two- or three-day delay
to heal from his wounds.[28] Hunter objected vehemently, fearful of another
uprising as well as an attempt to rescue the prisoners. Following testimony
from the prison physician that Brown was physically able to stand trial (in
fact, Brown could not stand at all, and throughout the trial was not seated
with the defense counsels but laid on a cot instead), Judge Parker ruled that
Brown's trial should begin immediately.[29]

For slavery supporters, this was probably the worse tactical decision the
state could have made. The excitement and sentiments about the case were
already extremely passionate. A wiser alternative would have been to delay
the trial until attitudes calmed. The spectacle of wounded prisoners on trial
for their lives when they seemed too weak to defend themselves elicited
sympathy and support from journalists and citizens throughout the North.
Even those who had been outraged by Brown's actions at Harpers Ferry were
equally affected by the description of a haggard Brown, weak from unhealed
wounds, having to attend his trial while lying on a cot.[30] Northern editors

hastened to point out how swiftly slavery supporters were willing to move, trampling moral rights and human dignity to maintain their way of life.

Immediately after the raid, reactions among the press had been decidedly mixed on the events at Harpers Ferry. Most editors could not determine if Brown was a madman driven insane by his cause or a martyr motivated by his beliefs. Abolitionist editor William Lloyd Garrison was repulsed by Brown's violent actions and professed his opposition to the raid.[31] Similarly, *New York Tribune* editor Horace Greeley, who was among those mentioned by Democratic proslavery newspapers in the North as being culpable for Brown's deeds, fully expected the prisoners to pay for their crimes: "The prisoners in fact have no defence, and their case will probably be speedily disposed of."[32]

Later, Greeley and the *Tribune's* tone changed considerably as Brown was repeatedly denied delay requests because of his health or to prepare a complete defense against such serious charges. During the trial, for example, the *Tribune* wrote that authorities wanted "a full five-act tragedy. . . . It is a pretty scheme—a scheme worthy of Virginia . . . "[33]

Feelings quickly shifted in Brown's favor. Each day of the trial brought more instances in which newspapers depicted the entire process as unfair. It was difficult not to notice how the trial was beginning to take a toll on Brown. During the afternoon session on October 26, Brown, who had declared himself unable to rise from his bed, was carried into the courtroom on a cot. Most of the time he lay quietly with his eyes closed and the covers pulled up close to his chin.[34]

Daily dispatches from Hunter's "authorized" group of journalists revealed numerous surprises for the readers. Brown's dissatisfaction with his counsel, the prosecuting attorney's personal bias in the case, and the concern over the consequences of the outcome provided constant conflicts to be reported. Most carried full transcripts of each day's testimony. On October 27, the first full day of testimony and opening arguments, Brown's attorney attempted to enter an insanity plea despite Brown's protestations. Such a move would have defeated Old Osawatomie's plan to put slavery on trial. Consequently, before the judge or the prosecution could respond, Brown raised himself up in bed and remarked, "I will add, if the Court will allow me, that I look upon it [insanity plea] as a miserable artifice and pretext of those who ought to take a different course in regard to me, if they took any at all, and I view it with contempt more than otherwise."[35]

It was obvious Brown felt that he'd get a fairer trial—or at least a trial that martyred him and furthered his cause—if he had counsel who could be trusted to understand his motivation. It was not surprising when, after several disparaging comments in court against his attorneys, both Botts and Green demanded to be dismissed from the case. Brown, who certainly had vast experience in explaining, and defending, himself, now had what he wanted—himself as a client. Yet this was just the beginning of the most significant day of the trial. According to Associated Press reports, it was a damaging day for Brown, but one wonders how his predicament could have been worse.

The same day Botts and Green resigned, John Cook was captured. Thought to be Brown's first recruit for the raid at Harpers Ferry, Cook was brought to the jail, loudly blaming his involvement in the incident on Brown. Cook told anyone within hailing distance that Brown was a Pied Piper in complete control of his minions. The defense was dealt yet another significant blow when the prosecution entered as evidence the Constitution and Ordinance of the Provisional Government for the area Brown had intended to free through his ill-advised resurrection. This damning evidence had been written by the old man himself. In addition, a large bundle of letters and papers from other abolitionists thought to be involved in the planning of the raid was admitted into evidence. But there was more. Testimony from some of the hostages—particularly Henry Hunter, the prosecutor's son—about the murder of one of the hostages increased spectators' hostile sentiments.[36]

And still the day was not done. A young Boston attorney arrived at the trial, not to participate but to report details back to Northern abolitionist leaders. Beyond spying for Brown supporters such as Wendell Phillips and John Andrew, George H. Hoyt was to arrange for Brown's escape. Except Brown didn't want to escape. He wanted to stay; he wanted the story to grow; and he wanted to die. Said Brown: "I am worth now infinitely more to die than to live."[37]

Although Hoyt stayed, observed, and visited Brown in his jail cell, the old man was as tough-minded with friend as foe. He would not be deterred.

The following day the arrival of Brown's Northern counsel, Samuel Chilton of Washington and Henry Griswold of Cleveland, did not provide the relief Brown expected. Since the attorneys based their case on the legalities of the indictment, the case in Brown's defense was inordinately swift. Following a break for Sunday, both sides concluded arguments on Monday, October 31, at 1:30 p.m., and the jury retired.

After deliberating for forty-five minutes, the jury returned. Spectators filled the courtroom, pressing against the railings, out through the hall and beyond the doors. Like an early morning fog in a West Virginia hollow, a stillness blanketed the room. Brown sat up in bed to hear the verdict: guilty, guilty on all counts. Guilty of treason, guilty of conspiring and advising with slaves and others to rebel, guilty of murder in the first degree. Then he lay down quietly and said nothing.

Two days later, Judge Parker sentenced Brown while the jury retired for deliberation in Coppic's trial. It had been assumed that all the prisoners would be condemned and executed on the same day. Brown, then, was surprised when asked if he wished to say why sentence should not be passed. The old man rose from his seat near his counsel, rested his hands lightly on the table, and issued his last words to the public. He said, in part:

I deny every thing but what I have all along admitted—the design on my part to free the slaves. . . . I believe to have interfered as I have done, as I have always freely admitted I have done, in behalf of His despised poor, was not wrong, but right. Now, if it is deemed necessary that I should forfeit my life for the furtherance of the ends of justice, and mingle my blood further with the blood of my children, and with the blood of millions in this slave country whose rights are disregarded by wicked, cruel, and unjust enactments—I submit: so let it be done. . . .[38]

Despite an overflow crowd in the courtroom, there was complete silence during Brown's speech. And then the judge sentenced Brown to be hanged on Friday, December 2. One man applauded but was quickly suppressed. Brown, who had remained silent throughout, was taken back to his cell. Meanwhile, after an hour of deliberation the jury found Coppic guilty on all counts.[39]

The remaining days of Brown's life were spent writing letters to family and friends.[40] Newspapers were rife with speculation over whether Brown would remain in custody long enough to hang. Again, fear ran rampant in the South while the reason for that apprehension quietly wrote his will.[41] By the time his execution day arrived, the old man had been imprisoned in the Charlestown jail for forty days. He had entertained numerous journalists in his cell during that period, particularly during his last days. Correspondents filled Northern and Southern newspapers with accounts of these visits and those of others who came to console Brown. And the media event continued to grow.

On the day of his execution, however, Brown was alone. No dispatches were to be sent out without prior approval from authorities. Charlestown officials had limited access into the city, and many northern editors, feared to be abolitionists planning to rescue Brown, were barred from the event.[42] From 8 a.m. until 10 a.m., military troops arrived and positioned themselves at the site. Lines of pickets and patrols numbering nearly 3,000 soldiers encircled the place of execution for fifteen miles, with more than 500 troops posted around the scaffold. Only about 400 citizens were present, along with what few reporters had been allowed to attend the event.[43]

When Brown disembarked at the field, without benefit of clergy, the scaffold and the rope, shipped in from Kentucky, had been made ready. With little delay, Brown was led up the scaffold; the noose was set; the trap door opened; the old man hanged. After swinging for thirty-eight minutes, the body was cut down and delivered to his widow at Harpers Ferry.[44] It was then taken to North Elba, where abolitionist orator Wendell Phillips gave the eulogy. John Brown's body was laid to rest on December 8.[45]

Newspaper accounts included specific details of the execution, along with coverage of meetings and mourning sessions held to honor him. Mourners gathered throughout the United States and Canada—including Montreal; Rochester; New York; Plymouth; Concord; New Hampshire; New Bedford; Albany; and Fitchburg—to remember this most controversial of men.[46] Many editors lauded his death sentence.[47] The *Weekly Portage* (Ohio) *Sentinel*, published in Brown's old hometown, viewed the execution as proper penalty for the crimes of one who had always been a "lawbreaker."[48] Others, such as the *Baltimore American*, hoped Virginia might "settle down" after the execution, comparing Brown's death to that "of a Thug, dying by the cord with which he had strangled so many victims."[49]

However, other newspapers like Greeley's *Tribune* provided Brown with the martyr status the antislavery movement would need to give impetus to the cause. A particularly large meeting in Boston was detailed in abolitionist newspapers throughout the country. The desk for the speakers was adorned with a likeness of Brown, a cross, a laurel wreath, placards with quotes from Brown, and an "insurrectionary emblem" of a warrior with his foot on a tyrant. The message on the emblem read: SIC SEMPER TYRANNIS ("So be it ever to tyrants"). The December 9 issue of the *Liberator* declared: "It is no use. Old Brown will have his day. He is the hero of the hour, and fills every ear with the story of his daring, of his fall, and of his fate." The day following his execution, the *Springfield Republican* wrote: "John Brown still lives." Later, Ralph Waldo Emerson wrote that Brown had "made the gallows glorious like the cross."[50]

Other papers simply exploited the entire affair. *Frank Leslie's Illustrated Newspaper*, which pictured elaborate wood carvings of the execution, was, according to the owner, "the most important paper we have yet issued."[51]

The following year, on July 4, 1860, blacks and abolitionists would make a pilgrimage to North Elba to remember Old Brown. He was saluted by such notable journalists as Frederick Douglass, James Redpath, and William Lloyd Garrison as a patriot worthy of the respect of the country's Founding Fathers.[52] The passage of time and impending civil unrest had softened the impressions of many Americans toward Brown and his actions. Despite literally being tried, convicted, and sentenced in the press, Brown had achieved his ultimate goal of promoting the atrocities of slavery. And even those who had not approved of his actions grudgingly acknowledged his ability to foresee the violent thunderclouds filling the horizon.

NOTES

1. *New York Herald*, 26 October 1859; quoted in Thomas Drew, *The John Brown Invasion: An Authentic History of the Harper's Ferry Tragedy* (Boston: James Campbell, 1859), 25.

2. See, for example, *New York Herald*, 20 October 1859; *Cleveland Weekly Leader*, 26 October 1859; *Hartford Evening Press*, 20 October 1859; *Freedom's Champion* (Atchison City, Kansas), 22 October 1859; *New Orleans Daily Picayune*, 22 October 1859.

3. Benjamin Quarles, ed., *Blacks on John Brown* (Urbana: University of Illinois Press, 1972), xiii.

4. Quoted in Truman Nelson, *The Old Man: John Brown at Harper's Ferry* (New York: Holt, Rinehart & Winston, 1973), 200.

5. *New York Tribune*, 18 October 1859.

6. Oswald Garrison Villard, *John Brown, 1800–1859: A Biography Fifty Years After* (Boston: Houghton Mifflin Co., 1910), 478–479.

7. *New York Times*, 29 October 1859.

8. *Baltimore Patriot*, 18 October 1859; *Baltimore American*, 17 October 1859; *Baltimore Exchange*, 18 October 1859.

9. See Stephen B. Oates, *To Purge This Land with Blood: A Biography of John Brown* (New York: Harper & Row, 1970), 238; Tilden G. Edelstein, *Strange Enthusiasm: A Life of Thomas Wentworth Higginson* (New Haven, Conn.: Yale University Press, 1968), 224–225.

10. F. B. Sanborn, *The Life and Letters of John Brown, Liberator of Kansas, and Martyr of Virginia* (Boston: Roberts Brothers, 1891), 12.

11. Bernell Tripp, *Origins of the Black Press in New York, 1829–1849* (Northport, Ala.: Vision Press, 1992), 52–53.

12. Lloyd Chiasson Jr., ed., "Old Osawatomie Brown: Martyr or Madman?" *The Press in Times of Crisis* (Westport, Conn.: Greenwood Press, 1995), 69.

13. *Baltimore Patriot*, 17 October 1859; *Baltimore American*, 18 October 1859; *Baltimore Exchange*, 18, 19 October 1859.

14. Nelson, *The Old Man: John Brown at Harper's Ferry*, 198.

15. *New York Herald*, 6 December 1859; James Redpath, *The Public Life of Capt. John Brown, with an Auto-Biography of his Childhood and Youth* (Boston: Thayer and Eldridge, 1860), 288.

16. Nelson, *The Old Man: John Brown at Harper's Ferry*, 203.

17. Villard, *John Brown, 1800–1859: A Biography Fifty Years After*, 644.

18. Nelson, *The Old Man: John Brown at Harper's Ferry*, 206, 229.

19. See, for example, *New York Times*, 21 October 1859; *New York Herald*, 20 October 1859; *Hartford Evening Press*, 20 October 1859.

20. Nelson, *The Old Man: John Brown at Harper's Ferry*, 207.

21. Drew, *The John Brown Invasion: An Authentic History of the Harper's Ferry Tragedy*, 26.

22. Associated Press telegraph report. Reprinted in Redpath, *The Public Life of Capt. John Brown, with an Auto-Biography of his Childhood and Youth*, 294.

23. Ibid.

24. Redpath, *The Public Life of Capt. John Brown, with an Auto-Biography of his Childhood and Youth*, 298.

25. Ibid., 301.

26. Drew, *The John Brown Invasion: An Authentic History of the Harper's Ferry Tragedy*, 26.

27. Ibid.

28. Redpath, *The Public Life of Capt. John Brown, with an Auto-Biography of his Childhood and Youth*, 300; Drew, *The John Brown Invasion: An Authentic History of the Harper's Ferry Tragedy*, 27; *New York Herald*, 27 October 1859.

29. Ibid.

30. *New York Herald*, 28 October 1859; *New York Times*, 27 October 1859.

31. *Liberator*, 21 October, 1859.

32. *New York Tribune*, 25, 28 October 1859.

33. Ibid., 16 November 1859.

34. *New York Times*, 27 October 1859; Redpath, *The Public Life of Capt. John Brown, with an Auto-Biography of his Childhood and Youth*, 308.

35. Ibid.

36. As cited in Richard O. Boyer, *The Legend of John Brown* (New York: Alfred A. Knopf, 1973), 18.

37. *New York Herald*, 29 October 1859; *New York Times*, 29 October 1859.

38. Redpath, *The Public Life of Capt. John Brown, with an Auto-Biography of his Childhood and Youth*, 340–342.

39. Ibid., 342–343.

40. Ibid., 344–372.

41. *Liberator*, 4, 25 November 1859; *Tallapoosa (Alabama) Times* and *Philadelphia Christian Observer*, reprinted in *New York Times*, 25 November 1859; *New York Herald*, reprinted in *Liberator*, 18 November 1859.

42. *Baltimore American*, 1 December 1859; *New York Times*, 2 December 1859.

43. *Liberator*, 2, 9 December 1859; *New York Times*, 3 December 1859.

44. *New York Times*, 3 December 1859; Associated Press report, reprinted in the *New York Times*, 3 December 1859.

45. Villard, *John Brown, 1800–1859: A Biography Fifty Years After*, 561.

46. *Liberator*, 9 December 1859; *New York Tribune*, 3 December 1859.

47. *New York Herald*, reprinted in *Liberator*, 18 November 1859; *Richmond Enquirer*, reprinted in *New York Times*, 2 December 1859; *New York Observer* and *Central Presbyterian* (Richmond, Virginia), reprinted in *Liberator*, 25 November 1859.

48. *Weekly Portage (Ohio) Sentinel*, 7 December 1859.

49. *Baltimore American*, 7 December 1859.

50. Louis L. Snyder and Richard B. Morris, eds., *A Treasury of Great Reporting* (New York: Simon and Schuster, 1962), 124.

51. Ibid., 125.

52. *Liberator*, 27 July 1860.

4

The Case of the Haymarket Riot
(1886)

"This is the happiest moment in my life!"

Kittrell Rushing

Just a few minutes before noon, November 11, 1887, four condemned men were paraded up the stairs of a Chicago jail gallows. The men were dressed in muslin shrouds, arms tied to their chests, their hands cuffed.

The murmuring of 200 spectators dropped to absolute silence.

Jailers shuffled the bound men over four trap doors. Nooses were positioned around the necks of the convicted anarchists. One of the men, August Spies, indicated the noose was uncomfortably tight. He smiled a quiet "thank you" when the hangman adjusted the rope.

The heads of the men were covered with black hoods.

Suddenly, Spies called out from inside his hood: "There will come a time when our silence will be more powerful than the voices you strangle today!"

Spies's outburst brought reactions from the three other hooded men. Fifty-year-old Adolph Fischer loudly proclaimed, "Hurrah for anarchy. . ."

Before Fischer's shout ended, his companion George Engel cried, "This is the happiest moment in my life!"

Confederate veteran and activist newspaperman Albert Parsons pleaded, "Will I be allowed to speak, O men of America? Let me speak, Sheriff Matson! Let the voice of the people be heard. . . ."

Parsons's cry ended in midsentence.

The trap doors fell open. The ropes snapped taunt. The four men struggled for a moment and went limp, swaying before the spectators.[1]

The four deaths marked the end of the beginning of the first nationwide "Red Scare." Other supposed leftist threats—organized labor, socialism, communism—would give birth to fear, misunderstanding, and violence throughout the twentieth century, but it was the Haymarket bombing in Chicago the night of May 4, 1886, that signaled the beginning of an ideological bogeyman that would dominate the political psyche of the United States for the next 100 years. The Haymarket riot and subsequent trial and executions also marked a major setback for the labor movement in the late nineteenth century, and the 1887 executions effectively ended the anarchist movement in the United States.[2]

By today's standards, the 1886 trial of the Haymarket "anarchists" was a charade. Few trials in U.S. history reflect a greater miscarriage of justice. The verdict was flawed, the adjudication of the trial was tainted, and the behavior of the press was unconscionable. In short, the accused were probably innocent of the charges, the judge was prejudiced, and the reportage was both subjective and sensational. The morning of May 5 the *Chicago Tribune* called for the lynching of the "dynamite orators," the "cowards," and the "foreign Socialists" responsible for the riot,[3] and from that day until the men hanged nineteen months later, the press led the cry for their deaths.

As was the journalistic style of the era, little distinction existed between the "news" and "editorials" of the newspapers. Within days of the arrests of the eight suspects, newspapers pronounced those arrested guilty and called for swift justice.[4] Under the headline, "Anarchist Murders," the *Chicago Tribune* reported that "seven [sic] of the anarchist conspirators" had been indicted for murder; and there seemed to be "no doubt that the anarchists planned wholesale murder, arson, and pillage."[5] The *Tribune* told its readers that the accused "should be made to suffer the penalty of their crime without unnecessary delay. Swift justice in this case is needed as a warning and an example."[6]

It is clear the concept, rather than the crime, ignited editorial fervor. Moreover, semantics may have been more important than concepts. Historian Bruce Nelson writes that throughout the 1870s the workingmen's parties in Chicago had been labeled "Communist" by the press, although the terms *Socialist* and *Communist* were often used interchangeably. Beginning in 1881, the press began to use the term *anarchists*, and, according to anarchist Albert Parsons, "to denounce us as enemies to all law and government." In response "we began to allude to ourselves as anarchists, and that name which was at first imputed to us as a dishonor, we came to cherish and to defend with pride."[7]

If anarchists puffed with pride from the old metaphor, "A rose by any name," the Chicago press in the 1880s seemed intent to rewrite a children's adage instead: "Sticks and stones may break your bones, but names will get you arrested."

And so it was that the social tensions came to a head on May 4, 1886. That spring evening, August Spies arrived late at Haymarket Square and was surprised that the evening rally had not begun. The rally was to protest the previous day's shootings by police of McCormick factory strikers. Spies found a number of men standing about the square in small groups, apparently waiting for someone to take charge.

Spies called to the men, instructing them to join him in front of Crane Brothers' factory. He climbed onto a flatbed wagon parked at the curb and began to speak. The crowd grew. Spies's intention was to hold the group together until the arrival of his friends and fellow anarchists Albert Parsons and Samuel Fielden.

Spies was angry. The men were angry and frustrated. The attack on the striking workers by police the day before had increased their sense of powerlessness. Police had killed several of the protesters, wounded others, and the men felt that they were no closer to achieving their goals of improved working conditions and better wages.

Spies told the growing Haymarket crowd of his experiences the day before. "I was addressing a meeting of 10,000 wage slaves," he said. "They did not want me to speak. The most of them were good church-going people. . . . I spoke to them and told them they must stick together. . . . Then the police came and blood was shed!"[8]

According to court testimony, Spies talked to the Haymarket crowd for about twenty minutes from the wagon platform. During the speech, Parsons arrived. Spies recognized his friend and turned over the platform. One biographer described Parsons, a self-proclaimed anarchist, as a "successful spell-binder of the old school."[9] Parsons reviewed for his audience the frustrations of their "eight-hour movement," which called for cutting the then standard ten–hour workday to eight hours and increasing hourly wages.

Parsons told the men they were slaves to the capitalist lords of labor, and that the attack by the police the day before was the result of their masters' attempt to deny workingmen their rightful voice and just rewards. Parsons spoke for almost an hour, then turned to Samuel Fielden, who challenged the men to stand firm in their resolve.

A slight rain began to fall, and the crowd began to break up. Someone suggested the meeting move to a nearby saloon. Fielden asked the crowd to wait, he needed only a moment to finish his speech.

As Fielden made his closing remarks, a contingent of Chicago police from the neighborhood station arrived. The officer in charge moved toward the platform.

Fielden spoke directly to the officer, saying loudly, "We are peaceful . . ." He did not finish.

Someone, a person never identified, tossed an explosive device, into the area between the police and the crowd. The bomb exploded with devastating effect, immediately killing at least one policeman and maiming several others. People ran, screamed, pushed one another to escape. Police fired into the crowd, wounding a number of the fleeing workers. Some witnesses later said the police were firing wildly, some shots hitting brother officers.

Within minutes the square was empty except for the police, the wounded, and the dying. Newspaper headlines the next morning across the nation screamed that the anarchists' revolution had begun.[10]

Framed by inequity and fueled by ideology, a new era in American history had arrived.

It was a revolution long feared by the country's leading capitalists. That fear was a consequence of the increasingly huge chasm separating the burgeoning immigrant working classes from the upper class of the Gilded Age. The 1880s labor upheaval in the United States was one result of the country's dramatic shift to an industrial economy. The shift reflected the great post–Civil War social changes that occurred in the United States, especially in the North.

Accompanying and exacerbating the wrenching of the social order was a huge influx of cheap European labor. These immigrants formed an underclass positioned beneath craftsmen and skilled workers. By the mid-1880s the class difference between employer and factory worker was striking and continuing to grow.[11] By the mid-1880s the "haves" more often than not viewed the "have nots" as commodities, machines rather than men. Jay Gould perhaps best captured the philosophy of the tycoon in the Gilded Age with straightforward pragmatism: "labor is a commodity that will in the long run be governed absolutely by the law of supply and demand."[12]

Nationwide, big business either ignored or refused to admit that poverty and inequity flourished in the boom that characterized the industrial growth in the second half of the nineteenth century. But poverty did exist. Unfortunately for many, it conquered. City slums, government apathy, disease, incredibly harsh working environments, and intense poverty were later well documented by the muckrakers[13] and lessened with the growth of the Progressive movement.

Capital, represented by men like Jay Gould, John McCormick, and Andrew Carnegie, denied that labor shared inadequately in the wealth of the nation. McCormick adamantly refused to listen to the complaints of his laborers, and in June 1886, he ordered protesting workers locked out of his Chicago factory. McCormick explained he would not give up his right to hire and fire as he pleased, that he would not be "dictated to" by employees.[14]

On May 3, police attacked and fired on striking McCormick workers. Twenty-four hours later the Haymarket bomb exploded.

Eight men were arrested in connection with the bombing. Each had been active in the Chicago eight-hour movement; each was an avowed anarchist; each was known to authorities as a labor activist; each was known to police and to the city's business community as a labor agitator. All but one was foreign-born, yet none were charged with the throwing of the Haymarket bomb. The men were tried, as the prosecutor told the jury in his opening statement, "for endeavoring to make anarchy the rule."[15]

In reality, the men were tried because they supported a cause frightening to the upper classes. Several of the accused men had advocated in speeches and in print the rights of labor (loudly advertised by capitalists as socialism), and they were in the forefront of the "radical" eight-hour movement.

The first speaker the night of the Haymarket bombing had been August Spies, the German-born editor of the *Arbeiter-Zeitung*. The day before, Spies had been at the McCormick plant. He had just finished speaking to the more than 5,000 McCormick strikers when club-wielding police waded into the crowd, opening fire on the demonstrators, killing two, and wounding five or six. Spies hurried from the scene to his newspaper office where he wrote and ordered printed what came to be called the "revenge circular."[16]

The circular later played a prominent part in the Haymarket trial. It exhorted, "REVENGE! WORKINGMEN! TO ARMS!" The text of the handbill briefly reviewed the McCormick affair and then proclaimed:

If you are men, if you are the sons of your grandsires, who have shed their blood to free you, then you will rise in your might Hercules, and destroy the hideous monster that seeks to destroy you.
To arms, we call you to arms![17]

The circular was signed, "Your Brothers."

The headline of the original bill carried the word "Revenge" in large type. The headline was changed and the word "Revenge" removed after only 200 to 300 circulars of a 20,000-run were printed. Nevertheless, prosecutors later pointed to the circular as evidence of the accused men's intention to foment revolution and murder.

Spies was born in central Germany in 1855, the son of a government official. He was seventeen when his father died; he moved to America and settled in Chicago. Sometime after 1875 Spies became active in the Socialist movement. After his conviction two years later, Spies spoke to the court at length, vehemently condemning his conviction and death sentence.

I have been indicted on a charge of murder. . . . There is no evidence produced by the State to show or even indicate that I had any knowledge of the man who threw the bomb, or that I, myself had anything to do with the throwing of the missile. . . . If there was no evidence to show that I was legally responsible for the deed, then my conviction and the execution of the sentence is nothing less than willful, malicious and deliberate murder.[18]

Michael Schwab, a Bavarian immigrant, struck some court observers as looking like the "ideal German professor."[19] He was ardent in his devotion to socialism and had worked as a reporter for Spies's *Arbeiter-Zeitung* for about two years before the Haymarket bombing. Schwab told the court that its sentence meant he was "condemned to die for writing newspapers articles and making speeches." He said his only crime was in speaking out against injustice. "It is idle and hypocritical to think about justice," Schwab told the court. He said the defendants had not been tried for murder. They were tried, he said, for their beliefs.[20]

Thirty-six-year-old Oscar Neebe was not an intellectual. Although active in the labor movement for about ten years when the Haymarket bomb was thrown, Neebe at best had only a surface knowledge of socialism and anarchism. However, police found a red flag and a revolver in his home the week after the bombing, and for these discoveries, claimed Neebe, he had been arrested, tried, and sentenced to die.[21]

Adolph Fischer, a twenty-eight-year-old German immigrant, worked as a compositor for at least two Socialist newspapers. He had been with the *Arbeiter-Zeitung* for about three years. Fischer also had worked with George Engle in founding the *Anarchist,* a Socialist newspaper that survived only a few issues. Fischer was described by one biographer as a "zealot who would not hesitate to sacrifice his life for the 'cause.'"[22]

Louis Lingg was only twenty-two in 1886, the youngest of the eight on trial. Also a German, he had moved to Switzerland in his teens, became active in the Socialist movement, and immigrated to the United States in 1885.

George Engel, another German immigrant, had been in the United States about twelve years when the Haymarket riot occurred. According to one historian, Engel's social views probably could have been traced to an unhappy childhood, an eye disease that made him almost blind, and years of poverty. From jail Engel wrote, and later proclaimed to the court, that his only crime was being a member of the International (the world Communist movement). Engel told the court: "On the night on which the first bomb in this country was thrown, I was in my apartment at home. I knew nothing of the conspiracy which the State's Attorney pretends to have discovered."[23]

Samuel Fielden, one of two non-Germans in the group, was a teamster, and had come to the United States eighteen years before from Lancashire, England. Fielden was about forty, had worked all his life, and had been active in the radical labor movement for a number of years. He was not noted for a deep intellect nor for an ability to articulate the cause for which he would hang. However, in his statement to the court, Fielden spoke at length about his life, his labor activities, the evils of capitalism, and his innocence of any crime.[24]

Fielden's participation in the Socialist movement was probably motivated more by religious and humanitarian beliefs than any deep commitment to anarchist principles. Fielden had the reputation of being "easy-going" and "mild-mannered." One contemporary said of Fielden's supposed part in the Haymarket affair that "to conceive of him as in any way a dangerous person seemed a suggestion of humor."[25]

A leader, an orator, and the only American-born of the group, Albert Parsons was the old man among the anarchists. He could trace his ancestry to the Revolutionary War, and he was a Confederate army veteran. When the Civil War broke out, Parsons, then a thirteen-year-old printer's apprentice, immediately enlisted in the Confederate army. At war's end he founded a Texas newspaper, the *Waco Spectator.* Parsons's politics changed, he became a Republican, a "scalawag," and he was forced to give up the newspaper. He became part of Texas's reconstruction government, advancing to a high position in the Internal Revenue Service in Austin. Parsons married a woman of mixed race (probably a black Creole), and the relationship, coupled with his Republican convictions, may have contributed to his move from Texas to Chicago in 1873.[26]

Parsons found work in Chicago as a compositor. He joined a typographical union, and within a few months became a leader in the labor movement. According to one biographer, Parsons shifted steadily to the Left after he arrived in Chicago, and by 1884 he had broken with the Socialists and increasingly identified with more radical anarchists. He began editing the labor newspaper *Alarm,* and he was the recognized spokesman of the movement.

Only one lawyer of any standing in the community would agree to defend the anarchists. Captain William Black was recruited by a small legal defense committee. Black then recruited two young lawyers to aid in the task.[27]

Black and his team knew there was trouble ahead, and they asked Judge John G. Rogers, the man who had overseen the indictment phase of the proceedings, for a change of venue and a change of judges. Black believed the chances of a fair trial in Chicago were, in his words, as likely as an anarchist being elected mayor. In addition, Rogers had shown what Black interpreted as flagrant prejudice in his instructions to the grand jury that ordered the indictments.

Captain Black requested the case be transferred from Rogers's court. The requests were refused by the state's attorney, Julius Grinnell. The accused men were convinced that Rogers's behavior during the pretrial phase proved his prejudice against them, and the defense wanted the trial transferred to the court of Judge Murray Tuley. Tuley was known in Chicago as an "able and fair jurist." Grinnell objected, and after some negotiation, the two sides finally agreed on Judge Joseph Gary who, until the Haymarket trial, had the reputation of running an impartial court.[28] The defense might have been better off with Rogers. Gary let it be known throughout the trial, both in his commentary and his rulings, that he believed the men were guilty. Gary refused defense motions for separate trials for the defendants, and his rulings during jury selection ensured a biased jury.[29]

The jury was not selected in the usual manner. One historian, citing Governor J. P. Altgeld's contemporary description of the voir dire, observed:

[I]nstead of having a number of names drawn out of a box that contained many hundred names, as the law contemplates shall be done in order to insure a fair jury and give neither side the advantage, the trial judge appointed one, Henry L. Ryce, as a special bailiff to go out and summon such men as he, Ryce, might select to act as jurors. . . . He boasted while selecting jurors that he was managing this case; that these fellows would hang as certain as death; that he was calling such men as the defendants would have to challenge preemptorily and waste their challenges on, and that when their challenges were exhausted they would have to take such men as the prosecution wanted.[30]

Judge Gary and State's Attorney Grinnell apparently knew what Ryce was saying and doing. Ryce admitted he confined his selection to "certain classes that were clerks, merchants, and manufacturers." The defense team protested to the court that the behavior of Ryce and his public statements prejudiced their clients' rights, but the judge refused to act.[31]

Throughout the jury selection and trial, the *Chicago Tribune* gave the story immense play, condemning the accused, and calling for "swift justice." The jury was not sequestered and had easy access to the paper. Only a few days before the trial began the *Tribune* reported the death of a seventh policeman. The newspaper announced that sixteen of the injured police were still confined to bed. According to the paper, the slow healing of their wounds was due to the use by the anarchists of poison in the bomb.[32] The use of poison was never confirmed, however, and no mention of it was made at the trial.

The prosecution made no attempt to link any of the accused men to the Haymarket bombing. State's Attorney Grinnell argued that the speeches and writings of the men on trial were evidence enough to make them responsible. The actual identity of the bomber was not important, claimed the prosecution, who never made any attempt to present evidence of who actually threw the bomb. The *Tribune* supported the prosecution's conspiracy argument: "no maudlinsentimentality should interfere with the course of the law. The men who conspired to destroy the city which opened its hospitable arms to them should be treated as any other murderous conspirators."[33]

A review of the prosecution's case indicates that none of the men on trial could have thrown the bomb. Engel was not at the Haymarket the night of the explosion. Lingg, an admitted bombmaker, was no where near the square. Fischer was at Zepf's Hall, a nearby saloon off the square. Albert Parsons and his wife left the Haymarket as Fielden began to speak. Spies was on the platform while Fielden was speaking. Schwab was making a speech on Chicago's North Side. Neebe was not in the vicinity of the Haymarket, and no testimony during the trial connected Neebe in any way with the bombing.

Not one of the indicted men was linked to the actual bombthrowing, and only one of the men on trial, Lingg, could be tied to bombmaking. The only man who possibly could be connected to the throwing of the bomb, Rudolph Schnaubelt, disappeared. Police never found him.

The verdict was, as expected, guilty as charged. Spies, Schwab, Fielden, Parsons, Fischer, Engel, and Lingg were sentenced to be hanged. Oscar Neebe was sentenced to fifteen years in prison. Neebe's verdict crushed him, according to one observer. No real case existed against the young worker. Even Grinnell said the Neebe case was weak. Early in the trial, prosecutors discussed setting him free. However, the state decided to proceed because, Grinnell said, dropping the charges would have a negative effect on the cases against the other prisoners.[34]

Parsons, Spies, Engel, and Fischer were hanged November 11, 1887. Just hours before he was scheduled to die, Louis Lingg committed suicide by blowing off his jaw with a small bomb smuggled into his jail cell by someone never identified. The day before the executions, the sentences of Schwab and Fielden were reduced to life imprisonment. Six years later Schwab and Fielden were pardoned by Governor John Altgeld and released from prison. In his written justification for the pardon, Altgeld said the Haymarket jury selection had been unfair, the trial judge had been prejudiced, and because the actual bomb thrower was never identified, no one could have known beyond a reasonable doubt if the bomber had read or heard the views of the convicted men, much less whether the bomber had been influenced by their views.[35]

Altgeld's justification of his pardons did not mention the press' influence on the trial. It could have. It should have. The news coverage given to the Haymarket affair was rabid, distorted, and emotional. The violent nature of the event, as well as animosity toward leftist philosophies, certainly molded reportage. The Haymarket bombing and trial were unquestionably "news," but the coverage given to the Haymarket affair reflected a philosophy of journalism more old than new. It was basically a reflection of the opinionated reporting that characterized nineteenth-century journalism.

The last quarter of the nineteenth century, however, was a period of journalistic transition. The large metropolitan newspapers were changing. The mid-1880s marked a period in which newspapers were beginning to adopt modern journalistic values of independence, impartiality, unbiased story selection and reporting. Many papers were also moving from a traditional emphasis on editorial content to an emphasis on news.[36] This was not the case with Haymarket coverage. From beginning to end, from metro daily to country weekly, news about the bombing and the trial was inaccurate, sensational, and apparently designed to appeal to reader prejudice, and the coverage apparently had an impact on prospective jurors. Ernest Zeisler, writing seventy years after the trial, quoted one of the jurors, George Porter, responding to questions during jury selection. Said Porter: "I believe what I read in the papers; I believe that the parties are guilty. I would try to go by the evidence, but in this case it would be awful hard for me to do it."[37]

The judge overruled the defense's challenge, and Porter was impaneled.

The record demonstrates that the judge was prejudiced, the jury biased; and the weak protesting cries from the few outraged by the trial were ignored. Those cries of protest, although muted with the passage of years, echo even today. Each May, a small group of sympathizers gathers at the Martyr's Monument in Chicago's Forest Home Cemetery to remember the convicted men.

Two monuments exist to those involved in the Haymarket affair. One, the Martyrs' Monument, stands over the graves of the convicted anarchists. The monument was dedicated on June 25, 1893, and today it and the graves over which it stands are seen by some as a shrine to free speech and the minority's right to disagree with the majority.[38]

The second monument, the Haymarket Riot Statue, is a 9-foot bronze of an 1880s Chicago policeman. A tribute to the police officers killed in the bombing, the memorial was erected in 1889 near the site of the riot on Randolph Street. The bronze statue has been blown up by unknown persons several times since 1889, most recently in 1970. It now stands in the protected courtyard of the Chicago Police Academy.[39]

NOTES

1. Henry David, *The History of the Haymarket Affair: A Study in the American Social-Revolutionary and Labor Movements* (New York: Russell and Russell, 1958), 463.

2. Bruce C. Nelson, *Beyond the Martyrs: A Social History of Chicago's Anarchists, 1870–1900* (New Brunswick, N.J.: Rutgers University Press, 1988), 216.

3. *Chicago Tribune*, 5 May 1886.

4. See, for example, *Chicago Tribune*, 8 May 1886; *New York Times*, 22 July 1886.

5. *Chicago Tribune*, 28 May 1886; see also Ernest Bloomfield Zeisler, *The Haymarket Riot* (Chicago: Alexander J. Isaacs, 1956), 27–28..

6. *Chicago Tribune*, 28 May 1886.

7. Quoted from Nelson, *Beyond the Martyrs: A Social History of Chicago's Anarchists, 1870–1900* (New Brunswick, N.J.: Rutgers University Press, 1988), 154–155.

8. David, *The History of the Haymarket Affair: A Study in the American Social-Revolutionary and Labor Movements*, 200.

9. Ibid., 201

10. See, for example, "Anarchy's Red Hand," *New York Times*, 5 May 1886; and "Bullets and Bombs," *Chattanooga Daily Times*, 5 May 1886.

11. David, *The History of the Haymarket Affair: A Study in the American Social-Revolutionary and Labor Movements*, 5–9.

12. Ibid., 7.

13. William David Sloan and James D. Startt, eds., *The Media in America: A History* (Northport, Ala.: Vision Press, 1996), 366–376.

14. David, *The History of the Haymarket Affair: A Study in the American Social-Revolutionary and Labor Movements*, 187.

15. Ibid., 253.

16. Nelson, *Beyond the Martyrs: A Social History of Chicago's Anarchists, 1870–1900*, 188.

17. David, *The History of the Haymarket Affair: A Study in the American Social-Revolutionary and Labor Movements*, 191–192.

18. Lucy Parsons, "Famous Speeches of the Eight Chicago Anarchists," in *Mass Violence in America*, ed. Robert M. Fogelson and Richard E. Rubenstein (New York: Arno Press and the *New York Times*, 1969), 11.

19. David, *The History of the Haymarket Affair: A Study in the American Social-Revolutionary and Labor Movements*, 334.

20. Ibid., 334.

21. Ibid., 335.

22. Ibid., 336.

23. Ibid., 340.

24. Parsons, "Famous Speeches of the Eight Chicago Anarchists," 40–64.

25. David, *The History of the Haymarket Affair: A Study in the American Social-Revolutionary and Labor Movements*, 341.

26. K. K. Campbell, ed., *The Autobiography of Albert R. Parsons*. Labor Day 1995 [Toronto: eye WEEKLY, 1995] (http://www.interlog.com/eye/Misc/Labor/ Haymarket). The race of Parson's wife was an issue of note in many newspapers. For example, Mrs. Parsons was described in the *New York Times* and the *Atlanta Constitution* as a negro *(sic)* or "Parsons' Dusky Wife." See "Anarchy's Red Hand," *New York Times*, 5 May 1886; and "Battle of the Bums," *Atlanta Constitution*, 6 May 1886. The *Chattanooga Daily Times* indicated Mrs. Parsons was "mulatto" in "The Anarchist's Defense," *Chattanooga Daily Times*, 15 May 1886.

27. David, *The History of the Haymarket Affair: A Study in the American Social-Revolutionary and Labor Movements*, 230–231.

28. Ibid., 231–232.

29. Ibid., 239–250.

30. Zeisler, *The Haymarket Riot*, 34.

31. Ibid.

32. Ibid., 36.

33. Ibid., 28; *Chicago Tribune*, 28 May 1886.

34. David, *The History of the Haymarket Affair: A Study in the American Social-Revolutionary and Labor Movements*, 316–318.

35. Zeisler, *The Haymarket Riot*, 83–84.

36. Sloan and Startt, *The Media in America: A History*, 245–254.

37. Zeisler, *The Haymarket Riot*, 38.

38. "The Haymarket Martyrs," Chicago-Kent College of Law, Illinois Institute of Technology (http://www.kentlaw.edu/ilhs/haymkmon.htm).

39. "1886 The Haymarket Riot," *Chicago Historical Information* (http://cpl.lib.uic. edu/004chicago/timeline/haymarket.html).

5

The Case of Lizzie Borden
(1893)

"Elizabeth Borden took an ax"

Donald R. Avery

It was too hot in Fall River, Massachusetts, late that August morning in 1892 to do much more than hang around. John Cunningham, the local newsdealer, was doing just that at Hall's Livery Stable watching the proprietor, Mark Chase, work on the carriage brought in by Mrs. Adelaide Churchill's hired man, Tom Bowles. It was simply too hot and muggy to pay much attention to anything but finding a cool breeze. Cunningham hadn't paid much attention when the carriage came in, but when Mrs. Churchill ran into the livery stable shortly before noon, out of breath, yet calling loudly for Tom, he took notice.[1]

Mrs. Churchill told Tom to find the nearest physician; there was great urgency in her voice. Cunningham couldn't hear everything that Mrs. Churchill breathlessly told Tom, but one thing was clear: Something dreadful had happened at the house of Andrew and Abby Borden across Second Street from the livery stable.

Cunningham hurried from the stable and crossed Second Street to the nearest store to use the telephone. Anyone who knew newsdealers across America would not have been surprised to hear him ask the operator to connect him with the *Fall River Daily Globe*.[2] The newspaper claimed its reporter was the first on the scene but the evidence from Cunningham's testimony was that he made four telephone calls, to the *Daily Globe*, the *Fall River Daily Herald*, and the *Fall River Evening News*. Cunningham told the newspapers that someone had brutally murdered Andrew and Abby Borden. The telephone call gave the newspapers their greatest scoop, and from that moment Fall River would never be the same.

After he had taken care of business, Cunningham made his fourth telephone call: He called the police.

Relations had been strained in the Borden household for years but had taken a particularly nasty turn in the two years before the blood-letting.[3]

Most of the theories about the motive for the Borden murders argue that the nastiness of those years could not help but lead to murder. The theories range from greed to illegitimate children to incest to homosexuality.[4] No matter the motive, the Borden's was a decidedly unhappy household.

Abby Borden was probably not thinking about happiness shortly before 9:30 that August 4 morning as she hauled her 200-plus pounds upstairs to tidy up the guest room. She was still feeling the effects of yesterday's nausea and vomiting that had afflicted everyone in the house except Lizzie: food poisoning or maybe something intentional. She would never know. Long ago she had reached an accommodation with her place in life: a loveless marriage, two stepdaughters who clearly despised her, and a social life that had abandoned her even before she married. Although, she would admit to herself she had been lighter in those days. Still, her weight had been a problem for years, so much so that she rarely went outside the house anymore unless it was to have dinner with her sister and that only about once a month.

She was standing almost upright rearranging items on the bureau with her back to the door. Nothing in her attitude indicated that she heard the small steps crossing the room behind her. Abby's first awareness was also her last. The first blow from the hatchet to the back of her skull was so deep that she was dead before her heavy body hit the floor with a sound that should have been audible throughout the small house. Only the murderer knew whether she uttered a sound in surprise. More than likely the only sound after Abby's body hit the floor was the chop, chop of the hatchet as it struck her head, neck, and shoulders repeatedly, a total of twenty blows. After Abby was surely dead, the murderer remained someplace on the premises for the next hour and a half. Both Lizzie and the maid, Bridget continued to do their chores in the house until Andrew Borden came home about 11 a.m.

Andrew Borden had been downtown tending to his various business interests, but because he still did not feel well, had decided to return home early for lunch. He found Lizzie and the maid, Bridget, at home. Abby was not there to greet him. This was so unusual that he asked Lizzie where her stepmother was, and Lizzie said she didn't know, but that Abby had received a note about a sick friend and had gone out earlier. This was a surprise, but Andrew simply felt too under the weather to question her further. He thought he'd just lie back on the sitting room sofa and rest his eyes a few minutes. Bridget was in her third floor room resting from the previous day's vomiting, and Lizzie said later that she had gone to the barn to look for lead for a fishing trip she planned. She left the screen door at the side of the house unlocked.

It is possible that Andrew heard something, a step, an intake of breath, something to arouse him from his stupor for one of the hatchet chops struck his head a glancing blow, slicing an ear and imbedding the weapon in his shoulder. In the end it made no difference. When the murderer was finished, Andrew's head had received ten chops, and his body remained in the position both Lizzie and Bridget recalled. Having finished his or her work the murderer made a miraculous escape.[5] Lizzie claimed she had been outside no more than twenty minutes, although the time frame varied, depending upon whom she was talking to later.

Almost from the moment the newspapers stories were released in the afternoon, the press and crowds of the curious began to gather. No one would have recognized that they were facing a defining moment in American press history, and by the end of the decade the new aggressive journalism of those building publishing empires would have a new name: "yellow journalism."[6] The Borden case was one of the pieces. Few doubted from the beginning that the Borden murders were a city room and circulation department's dream. They needed no further evidence than the fact that by sundown of the first day more than 2,000 people had gathered outside the Borden house. Most of the crowd didn't go home that night, and the numbers swelled the following day. Indeed, all of the public events associated with the case, the discovery of the bodies, the arrest, the inquest, the preliminary hearing, and the trial, drew huge crowds.

While smaller newspapers were contracting with local reporters and anyone else they could find to serve as correspondents, some twenty-five of the largest dailies sent reporters and in some cases papers were willing to absorb the extra expense of assigning more than one writer.[7] Stories appeared in newspapers all over the world.[8] In their drive to find material, no fact or rumor, however minute, was beyond inclusion in the latest report. As the case wore on, planted stories and even planted rumors and evidence[9] from all sides became the order of the day.

Five people occupied 92 Second Street on August 4, 1892: Andrew Borden, seventy; his second wife, Abby, sixty-three; his daughters from his first marriage, Emma, a spinster at forty-one; Lizzie, thirty-two, also unmarried; and Bridget Sullivan, the Irish maid.[10] Despite enormous wealth, Andrew Borden, gave new meaning to the word "miser." Worth the modern equivalent of $12 million, he would not install indoor plumbing or gas or electric lights. The *Daily Globe* reported in a headline that Borden was honest but "Devoted to Money Getting." The body of the story was more specific in describing what it saw as a traditional New Englander:

Andrew J. Borden was a peculiar man in many respects. While his tall, neatly clothed figure was familiar to all the older citizens, he had few intimates and was reticent to a marked degree. When he started in life his means were extremely limited and he made money by saving it. The habits of economy and thrift which he formed then, clung to him to the last and although his income of last years was very large, he lived modestly and continued to count the pennies.[11]

The story concluded by pointing out that Borden "at times appeared to lack sympathy" and really had no friends and no interests beyond making money.[12] One writer went even further, saying that "he had no socially redeeming qualities."[13]

Abby was a spinster at thirty-eight when she married Andrew and took on the role of mother in the household. While Emma insisted on calling her "Mrs. Borden," Lizzie called her "mother" until the years just before the murder. By August 4, 1892, both sisters referred to Abby as Mrs. Borden if they acknowledged her at all.[14] Abby was viewed by Lizzie and Emma as the classic stereotype of the stepmother, an interloper with designs on the children's birthright. In her trial testimony, Emma said of Abby, "We never felt that she was much interested in us."[15] The daughters' hate for Abby seemed obvious to everyone. Lizzie and Emma had not spoken to their stepmother in perhaps two years except to maintain a smooth order in the small house, and relations with their father also had been strained in recent years.[16]

Emma was an enigma. Apparently reconciled to spinsterhood, she was withdrawn from life outside the Borden house, hated her stepmother with a passion that was remarked on both before and after the murders, was estranged from her father, but was devoted to her younger sister, Lizzie.[17] No photograph of the adult Emma exists, only a courtroom drawing showing her covering her face with her hands as she sits next to Lizzie.[18] She was described by the newspapers in a number of unflattering ways with the reporter for the *New York Times* being not altogether unkind: "She is over forty years of age, and looks it—a little old fashioned New England maiden, dressed with exceeding neatness in plain black, with the impress of a Borden in every feature."[19]

Lizzie on the other hand, was in many ways the opposite of her sister. She was more outgoing, not at all timid, was still able to talk with her father, but was unmarried at thirty-two, shared Emma's hate for her stepmother, and could be arrogant and outspoken. Most newspaper descriptions of Lizzie Borden were less evenhanded than the following:

By the way, the strangers who are here begin to notice that Lizzie Borden's face is of a type quite common in New Bedford [where the trial was held]. . . . Some are fairer, some are younger, some are coarser, but all have the same general cast of features—heavy in the lower face, high in the cheekbones, wide at the eyes and with heavy lips, and a deep line on each side of the mouth.[20]

Bridget, who had worked for the Bordens for two of the six years she had been in America, apparently told just about everyone she talked to outside the house about what a queer bunch the Borden family was.[21]

Over the years, virtually everyone associated with the case has been put forward as the murderer. Included in the list of suspects were Lizzie, where most evidence points, Emma, Bridget, Uncle John Morse, Andrew's illegitimate son William, and several other unnamed perpetrators cited at the time by newspapers. In the days following the murders newspapers speculated widely—and somewhat colorfully—about itinerant mule skinners, mad Portuguese, skulkers about the Borden property, and others.[22] One local newspaper placed its suspicions immediately on "a missing Swede, said to be a farm hand, or on some tenant with who [sic] Mr. Borden is supposed to have quarreled."[23]

At first, suspicion fell on a visiting uncle, John Morse, the brother of Borden's first wife, but under pressure from the media, community leaders, and the clergy,[24] an inquest was quickly held and Lizzie was arrested and charged with the murder. Nine months later she was acquitted of all charges in a trial tainted by probable perjury, judicial mismanagement, outright fraud, and ultimately by the culture of Fall River.[25]

First-day stories tended to use words such as "fiend," "most terrible tragedy," and other fevered terms,[26] and the typical story was consistent with nineteenth-century reporting: heavy in style, short on accuracy, and almost certain to inflame passions.

Perhaps the greatest consistency in reporting over the next nine months was the wild disregard of facts and the media's failure to correct inaccuracies. In fact, one recent writer has argued that much of the reporting was fiction.[27] Due to the practice of rarely giving attribution, it is difficult to determine how much reportage was based on interviews, hearsay, and how much was created in the fertile minds of the reporters. Virtually every story contained the writer's assessment of the latest theory or bit of gossip. Many newspapers printed wrap-up stories, usually on the weekends.[28] The wrap-ups were often an opportunity for the newspaper to put its particular spin on recent events concerned with the case.

As has often been the case with criminal trials in America, the press coverage was instrumental in the conduct of the investigation, trial preparation, trial conduct, and the verdict. From the moment of the initial reports, authorities felt constant pressure from the public and officials to find the killer or killers, bring them to justice, and let the community get on with its life. Despite the fact that the *New York Times* reported that authorities were suspicious of Lizzie's uncle in its initial story, by the second-day story Lizzie had become a suspect.

Some newspapers covered everything they could get their hands on, including transcripts of hearings and the trial. Others were as likely to report rumor as anything else. A final group of newspapers—one with the most influence on public perceptions and the conduct of the proceedings and trial itself—would report only what their reporters could generate. This group depended more than others upon information supplied by those close to the case—police, lawyers, friends, and enemies of the Bordens. They were absolutely ripe to be had by those with an agenda to promote. Two stories from the case make the point. Both stories were published early in the case and had opposite effects.

The first story was an interview with Hiram Harrington, the husband of Andrew Borden's only sister, reported in the *Fall River Daily Globe*. Harrington, whom Lizzie called a suspect at her inquest, pointed at Lizzie clearly as the murderer:

> If Mr. Borden died, he would have left something over $500,000, and all I will say is that, in my opinion, that furnishes the only motive, and a sufficient one, for the double murder. I have heard so much now that I would not be surprised at the arrest any time of the person to whom in my opinion suspicion strongly points. . . . Lizzie is haughty and domineering with the stubborn will of her father and bound to contest her rights. There were many animated interviews between father and daughter. Lizzie is of a repellent disposition and after an unsuccessful passage with her father would become sulky and refuse to speak to him for days at a time.[29]

Harrington told the newspapers that he knew a great deal about Andrew Borden's finances and relations within the Borden household. He may have gotten some information from Emma, who remained friendly with Harrington's wife, but it is certain that neither Andrew nor Lizzie had confided much in him in recent years. While his interview seemed important at the time and he testified at the inquest, he disappears from the story before the trial. No newspaper ever challenged his story even after they knew much of what he said was not true.[30] As the crowds around the Second Street address grew, there was renewed pressure to find the killer, and the public sentiment began to turn sharply toward Lizzie as the murderer.[31]

A bungled job of reporting also greased that precipitous slide in public opinion against Lizzie. The newspaper with the largest circulation in New England—the *Boston Daily Globe*—was tricked by a detective hired by the Fall River police into running a story it had not independently verified. On page 1 of the August 10 edition, a thirteen-column story offered up a motive and proclaimed twenty-five new witnesses had been found that pointed to Lizzie's guilt.[32]

Among the claims were that Lizzie was pregnant by Uncle John Morse, that she had admitted it to her father the night before the murders, that a witness had seen Lizzie in the upstairs bedroom where Abby Borden died looking out the window at the time of her murder, that Bridget said Lizzie had promised her money if she would not talk to the police, that Lizzie had committed the murders during an epileptic seizure, and that Lizzie murdered her parents because her father had killed her pet pigeons some months before. Among the stack of headlines associated with the "scoop," the newspaper pointed out that its circulation was increasing and that "Globes Were Bought by Thousands." It was a wonderful coup for the newspaper. If only it had been verified. Therein was a journalistic error as large as the headlines: The material was created out of the fertile imagination of the detective paid by the *Boston Daily Globe* for an exclusive story.[33]

The *Boston Daily Globe* began backtracking almost immediately under pressure from the police, defense attorneys, and other newspapers. The following day, the newspaper got an admission from the detective that he had made up most of the story. It ran a retraction:

The *Globe* feels it is its duty as an honest newspaper to state that is has been grievously misled in the Lizzie Borden case. It published on Monday a communication that it believed to be true evidence. Some of this remarkably ingenious and cunningly contrived story undoubtedly was based on true facts. The *Globe* believes however that much of it is false and should never have been published. The *Globe* being thus misled has innocently added to the terrible burdens of Miss Lizzie Borden. We hereby tender our heartfelt apology for the inhuman reflection on her honor as a woman and for any injustice the publication reflected on her.[34]

From this point public sentiment and support shifted to Lizzie, and the state never regained its momentum. As one writer has put it, "The outcome was that newspapers everywhere began to rally behind Lizzie's cause. A wave of sympathy was building."[35] Long before the end of the trial newspapers were pointing out that the state's case seemed too weak to convict.

The public began to admire the hard edge that Lizzie showed to the world. One writer has argued that the public became very positive in its view of Lizzie calling her "America's Wasp Princess. . . . People couldn't say enough nice things about her icy calm."[36] She took that advantage into her trial.

June 6, 1893. It was somewhat cooler than the previous August along the south coast of Massachusetts and just as they had begun to do so on the day of the murders, crowds began to gather for a glimpse of the historic spectacle. But it was not the weather or the crowds of the curious that was of greatest concern to those charged with the conduct of the Lizzie Borden case. It was the judicial climate. Because the media's coverage during the previous ten months had so poisoned the minds of those in Fall River, it was decided to move the trial to New Bedford, a town ten miles away. In the era before broadcasting, ten miles was another world.

The high-priced defense team and equally powerful prosecution and judicial teams represented the best available in the state. There was a former governor of Massachusetts, a future attorney general, and even a future justice of the Supreme Court of the United States. The audience was made up of reporters and a few regular citizens, predominantly female observers. One newspaper ran a picture of women at the trial under the headline, "Group of Valentines and Daisies."[37] The "Daisy" everyone was there to see, of course, was Lizzie.

In addition to the local press, there were forty-two out-of-town reporters representing forty newspapers.[38] The reporting of the trial was generally more accurate than other reportage surrounding the case. However, it was no less sensational. A number of newspapers, notably the *Fall River Daily Globe*, often carried verbatim reports of the trial testimony. Reporting of jury selection and opening statements were in depth, often with embellishments, which helped place the reader in the courtroom.

During the course of the trial judicial maneuvering made it apparent that the jury would not hear several pieces of important testimony, most notably Lizzie's contradictory inquest testimony and testimony concerning her attempts to buy poison.

Newspapers reported every tiny detail inside and outside the courtroom. For some newspapers, it was enough to publish a nearly verbatim report of the day's activities.[39] Other newspapers reported only dispatches from other publications.[40] The majority of newspapers with reporters on the scene reported the courtroom story, but also looked elsewhere for "color."[41] It was not uncommon for a newspaper's coverage of a day at the trial to run several columns reporting virtually every word spoken by attorneys and witnesses.

The prosecution took seven days to present evidence that included testimony mostly from those associated with the murder scene. The *New York Times* stated the view held by most of the press: "On every legal point the prosecution has been defeated, and this has greatly lessened the strength of their case."[42] The defense took a day and a half to present character witnesses, none of whom were strongly challenged by the prosecution.

Following the attorney's closing arguments, Judge Justin Dewey stepped down from the bench to deliver the charge to the jury. It was unprecedented; it was bizarre; it was devastating in its effectiveness. *He simply instructed the jury to find Lizzie Borden innocent.*[43] Telling the jury that he was so sure that Lizzie was innocent he felt it necessary to explain why; he then began to take apart the prosecution's case. Concerning Dewey's actions, the *Fall River Daily Globe* wrote: "The charge was more an argument in favor of the defendant than it was an instruction in the law and offering evidence."[44] Almost immediately Dewey came under attack for violating the laws of Massachusetts.[45]

It took the jury one vote and one hour to find Lizzie innocent of the murders.

Lizzie was free but not forgotten. Inside and outside the courtroom the crowds cheered when Lizzie was found innocent. She did not leave the courthouse immediately, but sat in her carriage while hundreds filed passed. She touched a hand here, spoke a word there, even kissed babies as they were held up to her. Her triumph lasted until Sunday when Lizzie made her first attempt to reenter Fall River society by going to church. When she sat on the pew purchased by her father years before, those churchgoers nearby moved away. She remained isolated for the rest of her life.[46]

In a few months Lizzie and Emma had sold the Second Street property and bought a thirteen-room Victorian on The Hill. Her attempt to thrust herself into the high society of Fall River failed. One writer has argued that her major faux pas was in naming the house, a totally unacceptable practice in the sober Yankee country of Fall River.[47] She not only named her house, Maplecroft, but also changed her own name. Lizzie was not a name to associate with high society. She became Lisbeth of Maplecroft. It was too much for Yankee society, and she was functionally ostracized.[48]

Over the years, newspapers continued to report her various activities, including an arrest for shoplifting, a rumored marriage, a supposed lesbian relationship with an actress, her move into Fall River society, her rejection by that society, and her lonely, outcast final years. Even her death in 1927 has not silenced the voices that have found her fascinating at best and an obsession at worst. One newspaper got to the heart of the matter the day following the acquittal: "That was the end of one of the greatest modern criminal trials, and it left the people where they began, asking one another who killed Mr. and Mrs. Borden."[49]

Lizzie Borden's greatest adversary proved not to have been the prosecutor, the power of the bench, not even her own confused testimony. From the day of the murders, the *Fall River Daily Globe* haunted her.[50] Its stories constantly exhorted the police, challenged the court of public opinion, and maintained an accusatory tone, all apparently designed to see Lizzie convicted of the crime. The acquittal had no effect on the newspaper. On the first anniversary of the murders the newspaper published a recap of the murder, in excruciating detail, with the finger of implication pointed directly at Lizzie.

Much as the killer of Andrew and Abby Borden had chopped away long after the victims were dead in 1892, the newspaper continued to hack away at Lizzie over the years, never missing an opportunity to remind its readers, and Lizzie, that no murderer had ever been brought to justice. It continued to publish anniversary stories every year for thirteen years. Its twelfth anniversary story was typical:

Who knows, even now, that the vile-minded murderer may not be at large in the community walking, stalking. . . . He—or she—is enjoying at least the waking hours of daily life very much as the neighbors, well fed, well dressed, well waited on, however the still hours of the night may be passed, whether in solace of refreshing slumber, or in the viewing of phantom pictures of the hideous scenes of twelve years ago this morning. Who can tell.[51]

The anniversary stories were all page 1, several columns, continued inside the newspaper. Virtually every paragraph referred to the killer as "he" followed by "or she." No one would likely be fooled into believing that the newspaper was talking about anyone other than Lizzie.

Unaccountably, the last of the anniversary stories was published by the *Fall River Daily Globe* the following year. As if recognizing the futility of its vendetta, the newspaper shifted its tack in its final assault. Page 1 of the newspaper contained the following headline decks:

GREAT WRONG
IS RIGHTED AFTER 13 YEARS OF MISREPRESENTATION.
NO MURDERS WERE COMMITTED ON AUGUST 4, 1892,

DESPITE THE BELIEF THAT ANDREW AND ABBY
BORDEN DIED IN THAT MANNER.

With tongue firmly in journalistic cheek, the newspaper called the murders a false rumor and then asked rhetorically why the public spread such stories. The newspaper finished its final attack with the following bit of gallows humor:

The Globe [sic] suggests that its readers forget the past and its cruel errors of judgment, and its suspicions of pure and lofty souls and remember just one thing for all time: THERE WERE NO BORDEN MURDERS! BOTH THE VICTIMS OF 13 YEARS AGO DIED AS THE RESULT OF EXCESSIVE HEAT![52]

While the *Fall River Daily Globe* no doubt thought it had had the final word, history has proved it wrong.

In 1994 a play whimsically titled *A Musical Tragedy in Two Axe* was produced; in 1996 Jack Beeson's opera, *Lizzie Borden*, was revisited after a twenty-year hiatus; no less than one movie and several television shows have retold Lizzie's story; and rarely a month goes by that some new newspaper story, book, academic journal article, magazine piece, or a student paper does not appear to keep alive arguably the most popularly celebrated murder and criminal trial in American history.[53]

Lizzie Borden has gained the rarest sort of celebrity: morbidity. A newsletter based upon the 1892 murders called *The Weekly Hatchet* is published to this day, and in 1996 the Borden House opened as a "bed and breakfast" largely catering to visitors with a yen to get "up close and personal" with the bloody story. To suggest that Lizzie's story is timeless is no overstatement. For years after the murders, children everywhere jumped rope to various versions of the "Fall River Hoedown." Lizzie lives forever in verse.

Elizabeth Borden took an ax
And gave her mother forty whacks
And when the job was nicely done
She gave her father forty one![54]

NOTES

1. Frank Spiering, *Lizzie* (New York: Random House, 1984), 40.
2. *Fall River Daily Globe*, 5 August 1892.
3. Lizzie's inquest testimony, *New Bedford Evening Standard*, 12 June 1893.
4. See Ann Scholfield, "Lizzie Borden Took an Axe: History, Feminism, and American Culture," *American Studies*, April 1993, 91–103.
5. The facts of the case, found in the trial transcript but rarely in the newspapers,

was that about 9:30 a.m. someone took an axe to Abby Borden and hacked her to death in the upstairs guest room. During the next hour or so Lizzie and Bridget were engaged in mundane chores about the house, the former ironing handkerchiefs in the dining room and the latter cleaning windows on the first floor. Shortly before 11 a.m. Andrew Borden returned home from a trip to his properties downtown. Both Lizzie and Bridget spoke to him when he lay back on the parlor sofa to rest a bit before the midday meal. Bridget went to her room on the third floor to rest before lunch, and Lizzie claimed she went to the barn to look for lead sinkers to use in fishing. Sometime during the following twenty minutes someone hacked Andrew to death. His body was discovered by Lizzie returning from the barn. Abby's body was found somewhat later by a neighbor. Lizzie biographers almost without exception agree "she done it." Not all recent writers agree that Lizzie was the culprit. See generally, Spiering, *Lizzie*, who argues that Emma did the deed; Arnold Brown's *Lizzie Borden: The Legend, The Truth, The Final Chapter* (Nashville, Tenn.: Rutledge Hill Press, 1991), 159, who finds the murderer Andrew's illegitimate son, William; and Edward Radin, *Lizzie Borden: The Untold Story* (New York: Simon and Schuster, 1961), who argues simply that Lizzie did not commit the crime.

6. George Everett, "The Age of New Journalism, 1883–1900," in *The Media in America.: A History*, ed., William David Sloan and James D. Startt (Northport, Ala.: Vision Press, 1996), 275.

7. Spiering, *Lizzie*, 57.

8. Reuters produced the early coverage for its international clients. However, for the trial many foreign newspapers sent their own reporters or hired correspondents on the staffs of U.S. newspapers and magazines.

9. See Brown, *Lizzie Borden: The Legend, The Truth, The Final Chapter*, 226–229.

10. Ibid., 35.

11. *Fall River Daily Globe*, 5 August 1892.

12. Florence King, "A Wasp Looks At Lizzie Borden," *National Review*, 17 August 1992, 24–28.

13. Brown, *Lizzie Borden: The Legend, The Truth, The Final Chapter*, 58. For a similar description, see also Arthur S. Phillips, *The Phillips History of Fall River* (Fall River, Mass.: Dover Press, 1944, 1946), 3–6.

14. *New York Times*, 17 June 1893.

15. Ibid.

16. Victoria Lincoln, *A Private Disgrace: Lizzie Borden By Daylight* (New York: G. P. Putnam's Sons, 1967), 94–97.

17. Brown, *Lizzie Borden: The Legend, The Truth, The Final Chapter*, 41–43.

18. From the *Illustrated American*, cited in Spiering, *Lizzie*, 142.

19. *New York Times*, 17 June 1893. See also reports from the *New York Herald*, 17 June 1893; *Fall River Daily Globe*, 16 June 1893; and the *New York Sun*, 17 June 1893 for other even less flattering descriptions of Emma Borden.

20. *New York Sun*, 7 June 1893. Descriptions of court officers, defendants, and witnesses were common during this period. See also *Boston Globe, Providence Journal, New York Times, New York Sun, New York Herald, Fall River Daily Globe,*

New Bedford Times, 6 June 1893.

21. *Fall River Daily Globe*, 7 June 1893.

22. *Fall River Daily Globe*, 4 August 1892. Imbedded within the newspaper's story of the murders was a report that two young men had been arrested for speeding on a horse and were being held as suspects in the murders. Nothing was ever mentioned of the two again.

23. *Fall River Daily Globe*, 4 August 1892.

24. Spiering, *Lizzie*, 57.

25. See generally Lincoln, *A Private Disgrace: Lizzie Borden By Daylight.*

26. See generally the *Fall River Evening News, Fall River Daily Globe*, and the *Fall River Daily Herald*, 4 June 1892 for local commentary on the murders.

27. See generally Spiering, *Lizzie.*

28. See particularly the *Fall River Daily Globe*. Indeed, its coverage was arguably the most extensive.

29. *Fall River Daily Globe*, 6 August 1892. See also the *Fall River Daily Herald*, 5 August 1892.

30. Much like the contemporary press, the newspapers reporting the Borden case were constantly looking for the new angle and paid almost no attention to old news, good or bad.

31. See particularly the *Fall River Daily Globe*, 6 August 1892 for the newspaper's listing of clues that point toward Lizzie.

32. *Boston Daily Globe*, 10 August 1892.

33. Spiering, *Lizzie*, 98–99.

34. *Boston Daily Globe*, 11 August 1892.

35. Spiering, *Lizzie*, 101.

36. King, "A Wasp Looks At Lizzie Borden," 24–28.

37. *Fall River Daily Globe*, 12 June 1893.

38. Lincoln, *A Private Disgrace: Lizzie Borden By Daylight*, 215.

39. See the New York *Times.*

40. This was particularly true of the small newspapers or more distant publications around the country such as the *Chicago Journal, St. Louis Post Dispatch, Springfield (Massachusetts) Republican*, and the foreign press, most notably the *London Evening Echo, London Sphere, London Morning Post.*

41. Most of the newspapers in the northeast fit this category. See particularly the *Boston Globe, Boston Daily Advertiser, Boston Sunday Post*, the three Fall River newspapers mentioned elsewhere, *New York Times, New York Sun, New York Herald, New York World, Providence Journal.*

42. *New York Times*, 16 June 1893.

43. Spiering, *Lizzie*, 275–280.

44. *Fall River Daily Globe*, 21 June 1893.

45. Spiering, *Lizzie*, 184

46. Ibid., 183.

47. Lincoln, *A Private Disgrace: Lizzie Borden By Daylight*, 302.

48. Ibid.

49. *New York Sun*, 21 June 1893.

50. Spiering, *Lizzie*, 201.

51. *Fall River Daily Globe*, 4 August 1904.

52. *Fall River Daily Globe*, 4 August 1905.

53. Among the hundreds of major works about the Borden case the most important is probably the earliest: Edwin H. Porter, *The Fall River Tragedy* (Fall River, Mass.: J. D. Monroe, 1893). Porter was a reporter for the *Fall River Daily Globe* and covered every aspect of the case from the murders to acquittal. Lizzie was so unhappy with the work that she bought up all but four copies of the book shortly after it was released.

54. Lizzie Borden: (http://web2.xerox.com/digitrad/song=FALLRIVR)

6

The Case of Harry K. Thaw
(1907)

"You have ruined my wife!"

Janet S. Boyle

> I was born into a world of much more sunlight and less smoke than now, a
> world of ringling horse cars, ragtime music, cakewalks and Floradora
> Sextets, and a sense that the coming new century would be the biggest and
> the best.
>
> —Mae West, *Goodness Had Nothing to Do with It*

Alabaster arms twine softly around the velvet garnet ropes. The girl's
champagne laughter tinkles like Christmas bells off the crystal chandelier as
she swings naked into its circle of luminescence, her hair a fiery auburn
pennant in her wake. Her pointed toes pierce the paper parasol at the top of
the arc,[1] then, enticing the light onto her slim calves and thighs, beckon it
again into the shadows as the swing begins its backward course. The hands of
the pusher caress briefly before propelling the swinger upward again.

Such images surely titilated readers of New York City's some fifteen
newspapers[2] (many of them sensational "yellow press" dailies),[3] as they
devoured the details of events leading to the June 25, 1906, murder of
architect Stanford White and the subsequent trials of Pittsburgh millionaire
Harry K. Thaw for the crime.

The motive? The Gibson Girl, the ethereally beautiful artist's model and
showgirl, Evelyn Nesbit. *The Girl in the Red Velvet Swing*. Described as the
first "supermodel,"[4] Evelyn Nesbit was already well known by her
photographs to readers of the daily press when the murder occurred, and her
pivotal role in a steamy love triangle with the perpetrator and his victim
inflamed the public's desire to know everything about both her and the
murder.[5] Within a week of the crime, the *New York World* was selling an
extra 100,000 copies a day.[6] The *New York Evening Journal* melo-
dramatically proclaimed: "The flash of that pistol lighted up an abyss of
moral turpitude, revealing powerful, reckless, openly-flaunted wealth."[7] The

comparatively staid *New York Times* gave the story almost daily front-page coverage through the end of August 1906 and again when the trial began in January 1907. Irvin S. Cobb, who covered the trial for the *New York Evening World,* later wrote that the Thaw case had

wealth, degeneracy, rich old wasters; delectable chorus girls and adolescent artists' models; the behind-the-scenes of Theaterdom and the Underworld, and the Great White Way; the abysmal pastimes and weird orgies of overly aesthetic artists and jaded debauchees.[8]

It was a fitting spectacle for turn-of-the-century New York City.

In 1900 New York burgeoned with nearly 4 million souls, the result of industrialization, urbanization, and immigration. Both sea and land trade thrived, thanks to pioneers such as Commodore Cornelius Vanderbilt and John Jacob Astor. Factories produced goods and products that were hustled to and fro by a million miles of railroad tracks whose construction bankrupted hundreds of companies and ruined farmers. Telegraph lines across the continent and cables on the floor of the Atlantic enabled communication between New York and its far-flung dominions. And the investment banks of New York managed the money. By 1900, half of all revenues of the U.S. government were levied as custom-house duties at the Port of New York, and these duties were piled into the banks of Manhattan for later use in the development of the country. This was in addition to the banks' holdings of revenues generated by producers of everything from iron to glass, from clothing to nails. New York was overwhelmed by its money; skyscrapers proclaimed the city's wealth like stone and steel exclamation points, millionaires' mansions erupted along Fifth Avenue, and newly installed electric light illuminated all.[9]

Stanford White, forty-eight years old in 1901, was one of the city's premier citizens and perfectly suited to the position. Native New Yorker, genius architect of Madison Square Garden, he was not content merely to design a building's external structure. The whole of a project consumed him, so that his ideas and influence extended to its interior design and ambiance; the occupation of "interior decorator" emerged in response to White's example.[10] When designing Madison Square Garden, he was concerned with "how it would look, how it would feel, when the cigarette smoke curled up into the yellow spotlights—how the color would *sound* when the band struck up, how the arena would *smell* when the scents of powder and perfume and the acrid odors of excitement were mixed."[11] To one client seeking White's advice on her bedroom decor, he replied: "Any color as long as it is red."[12] White's style, energy, and passion produced seemingly endless displays for the city's wealth—he created homes, churches, sculptures, public buildings; he filled his structures with the finest furniture, rugs, and tapestries he could find in Europe; and he organized balls and banquets whose menus and floral arrangements he created.[13] The flamboyant architect gave to the city and its society the benefits of his 200-year-old lineage of New York gentility, his architectural skills honed under the likes of Henry Hobson Richardson, and his broader artistic concepts learned at L'École des Beaux Arts in Paris. Stanford White, the arbiter of New York style, was in constant demand.

He swam on a wave of prestige that lifted him like a Titan. . . . Not a day passed without hearing something new about him. His flaming red hair could be seen a mile; and every night at the opera he would come in late, not purposely advertising himself, but intuitively knowing that every millionaire in town would see him, and that the galleries would whisper, and even the supers on the stage would mutter: *There's Stanford White.*[14]

And he loved beautiful young women.

Considerably less sought after than White was Harry Kendall Thaw of Pittsburgh. The Thaw family, including ten children, was among the elite of Pittsburgh, intimates and peers of the Mellons, the Carnegies, and the Fricks. William Thaw, Harry's father and a shrewd businessman, had accumulated a fortune from coal mine leases, franchises in railroad feeder lines, and successful manipulations of stocks and bonds, so that when he died in 1889, Harry became heir to a $40 million legacy. The elder Thaw considered his son an idler, and the perspicacity that had served him so well in his business dealings evidenced itself in his will, in which he stated that "with great regret and reluctance and solely from a sense of duty, I hereby cancel and revoke any and all provisions of my said will directing payment of money or property to my said son, Harry Kendall Thaw." Harry's inheritance was to be managed by a trust fund which would dole out no more than $2,400 a year after he reached the age of twenty-one. Harry's mother later raised her son's yearly allowance to $80,000 a year, a sum on which he could live comfortably.[15]

Harry had difficulty in school, never seeming to be able to stick to any one thing except finding trouble. His stated intention to study law at the University of Pittsburgh was not fulfilled, and from that university he went to Harvard, where he gambled and drank heavily. He was expelled from Harvard following an incident in which he chased a cab driver down the street with a shotgun.

Harry then decided he would enjoy his inheritance in Europe where he entered society through endless dinners, teas, tours, and parties. At one such extravagant party Harry hosted, he was the only male in attendance with 100 beauties of the stage. He reportedly had an expensive piece of jewelry set beside each woman's plate.

Harry continued his rowdy living and maintained his reputation as an eccentric playboy upon returning to New York. After being refused membership in an exclusive club, he rode a horse into its elegant lobby. He drove an automobile through the front window of a shop whose employees had insulted him. He liked to associate with actresses, and gossip along

Broadway had it that a prominent madam provided girls for Harry to whip. It was rumored that one woman sued him for luring her back to his apartment and beating her severely with a dog whip.[16] In 1901, Harry Thaw was thirty years old, and *Floradora* was a phenomenally successful musical on Broadway.

Evelyn Nesbit's father, a Pittsburgh lawyer, died when she was eight years old. Her widowed mother attempted to support herself, Evelyn, and Evelyn's younger brother by letting rooms, but she was unsuccessful. Forced to sell most of the family's belongings, Mrs. Nesbit moved to Philadelphia, where she hoped to become a dress designer. Though she was a capable seamstress, she had no experience, and Evelyn, at age fourteen, abandoned the thought of school and began working in a department store to help support the family.[17]

Through the artist John Storm, whose sister lived in the same boardinghouse as the Nesbits and who was stunned by Evelyn's beauty, Evelyn was introduced to Violet Oakley, a designer of stained glass windows, and from this beginning the fourteen-year-old began posing for Philadelphia artists and illustrators. Her face appeared in books, magazines, and newspaper supplements, and soon both mother and daughter realized that Evelyn's work as a model could earn more money than their department store jobs. Taking a chance and carrying a letter of introduction, the family relocated to New York in 1900, where Evelyn soon enjoyed success as a model for some of the outstanding artists of the city. George Grey Bernard sculpted her as *Innocence*, later on view in the Metropolitan Museum of Art, and the famed Charles Dana Gibson portrayed Evelyn as *The Eternal Question* in a pen-and-ink profile which became enormously popular. But New York newspapers such as the *Sunday World* and the *Sunday American* were now using live models for hats, shoes, stockings, and gowns in their newly conceived fashion pages, and Evelyn Nesbit, seeing that being a photographer's model in the public eye was more lucrative than posing for artists, became the photographers' darling, the "Beautiful Model of New York Studios,"[18] a phenomenon.

It was only a brief matter of time until a theatrical agent approached Evelyn and her mother, and, in 1901, the nymphet made her debut on the New York stage in the musical *Floradora*. She was sixteen.

The affairs of beautiful chorus girls with prominent men were so commonplace that the most successful joke at the turn of the century was this brief dialogue:

First Chorus Girl: I found a pearl in an oyster at Rector's last night.
Second Chorus Girl: That's nothing. I got a diamond necklace out of an old lobster at Delmonico's.[19]

The other chorus girls called Evelyn "the kid" and edited their conversations when she was present, but in spite of her youth, neither she nor her mother could possibly have been confused about the environment in which Evelyn was now entrenched. One biographer postulated that her mother placed Evelyn out there hoping to attract the man with the most money.[20] This the girl did.

Shortly after joining the company, Evelyn was introduced to Stanford White, who descended upon her with the same fervor he brought to his architectural projects. Their first meeting took place at one of his opulent apartments, where he invited Evelyn and another girl for luncheon, and where Evelyn first saw the red velvet swing. White whisked mother and daughter out of their boardinghouse, ensconcing them snugly in a hotel directly opposite the theater in which *Floradora* was playing. Flowers arrived daily, and one of his first gifts to Evelyn was a red cloak that he and Mrs. Nesbit agreed made Evelyn look like Little Red Riding Hood. He sent her to the dentist to have an imperfect front tooth fixed. He gave her fine clothing, jewelry, and books. And in the fall of 1901, with her mother away visiting her son at school after having left her daughter in White's care, he made Evelyn his mistress. Shortly thereafter, he moved the Nesbits again, this time to a lavish hotel, where, characteristically, he had decorated the rooms himself, choosing for Evelyn's bedroom red carpet and white satin walls.

But though he presented Evelyn to Manhattan society at his splendid Madison Square Garden Tower parties and ornamented her with diamonds and furs, he always spent his weekends on Long Island with his family, and it was his wife who accompanied him on his trips to Europe. White's reputation for fidelity to his mistresses was less than stellar, and with his interest in her waning after about a year, it behooved Evelyn to consider some of the many other offers she received.

Harry Thaw's first timid approaches, occurring when Evelyn was already involved with White, were rebuffed. After a while he began sending Evelyn flowers with $50 bills wrapped around them and taking her to dinner at New York's finest restaurants when White was occupied elsewhere. His persistence eventually paid off. For vague health reasons, Stanford White had enrolled Evelyn in a private boarding school for young women, and six months later she underwent surgery for an attack of "acute appendicitis." Thaw suggested that Mrs. Nesbit and Evelyn accompany him on a trip to Europe, where Evelyn could recuperate from her ordeal. Mrs. Nesbit agreed. It was on this trip that Evelyn first witnessed Thaw's jealousy, temper tantrums, and erratic behavior, and it was on this trip that Thaw first proposed marriage. She declined, and after repeated importations from Thaw, she revealed that Stanford White had plied her with drugged champagne and taken her virginity, and that both Harry and his family would be humiliated by his marriage to one of White's girls. Mrs. Nesbit soon tired of the tour and returned to America. Harry and Evelyn then traveled as man and wife, his obsession with her ruination by White growing and his marriage proposals continuing. During this time he subjected Evelyn to bondage and beatings and introduced her to cocaine use.[21]

Notwithstanding the pain and degradation Evelyn had suffered, and over the objections of Harry's proper Pittsburgh family, the showgirl and the millionaire married in 1905.

On June 25, 1906, Evelyn and Harry dined at the famous Martin's prior to attending the premiere of the musical *Mamzelle Champagne* at the Madison Square Garden Tower Theater. During dinner, Evelyn passed Harry a note informing him that Stanford White was in the restaurant. Their dinner concluded in a subdued manner but without incident, and the Thaws walked the few blocks from the restaurant to the theater. Harry left their table shortly after they had been seated. Well into the show, Stanford White made his entrance and proceeded to his reserved table near the stage. Harry Thaw approached White's table, pulled a revolver from under the overcoat he wore anomalously in the summer heat, and shot White three times.

"Thaw Murders Stanford White" and "'He Ruined my Wife,' Witness Says He Said" proclaimed the *New York Times* the following day.[22] "You deserve this. You have ruined my wife!" Thaw said at the fatal moment, according to the *New York Sun*.[23] No matter what he did or did not actually say, Harry Thaw's action ignited an explosion of factual and sensational reportage such as the nation had never seen. It gave birth to innovations in jury treatment and media coverage, and it facilitated the emergence of women as a force in the molding of public opinion.

On the days following the murder, the *Times* ran articles on Stanford White's career, Harry Thaw's family, Thaw's history of instability, and Evelyn Nesbit's connection with White. Opinions about Thaw's sanity were printed, opinions coming from Pittsburgh associates to White's architectural firm partner to Thaw's jailers to the alienists of the day. "Crazy," said some. "Sane," declared others.[24] The head of the Society for the Suppression of Vice told a *Times* reporter that Thaw had approached him before his marriage to Evelyn concerning "revolting orgies" held in White's Madison Square Garden Tower studio and the "atrocities perpetrated upon girls" in that studio.[25] The Cleveland pastor of John D. Rockefeller stated that the murder "reveals an absolutely rotten situation socially in New York" and that "men should be more careful about their relations with other men's wives,"[26] implying justification for the crime while demonstrating a rather unique theological approach to adultery.

From his prison cell, Harry Thaw explained to reporters that he had shot White because the architect "ruined" young girls. Newspaper reporters were frustrated in their attempts to obtain confirmations or denials from White's friends, for those friends either could not be found or would say nothing about White's revelries in general or his relationship with Evelyn Nesbit in particular. In July, the *Evening Journal* began to serialize the story of Susie Johnson, who had been "The Girl in the Pie" at a famous stag party given by White. At this party White and twenty-eight of his friends partook of a lavish dinner, served by an equal number of young girls, none of them more than twenty years old, and all of them naked, or nearly so, for the festivities. At the culmination of the party, a huge pie was wheeled into the room, and at the appropriate moment in "Sing a Song of Sixpence," little postpubescent Susie emerged nude from the pie amid a flurry of birds. White lifted Susie out of the pie and disappeared with her to his private apartment, leaving his guests to their own pleasures.[27] According to Susie Johnson, Stanford White abandoned her after making promises of support. She committed suicide a few years later.

Reporters revealed that Thaw had hired detectives to follow White who in turn had hired detectives to find out who was shadowing him. Girls were found who stated that the parties given by White and his coterie were indeed depraved; others were found who stated that all the girls who attended those parties were fully aware of the implications in the $20 gold piece each was given, and that they were free either to stay and participate or to leave.

Harry's mother, who was in Europe when the killing occurred, announced upon her return that she would spend a million dollars to save Harry's life, and she hired a press agent to present Harry to the press in the role of the avenger of his wife's honor. She produced a play whose three thinly-disguised characters, Harold Daw, Emeline Huspeth Daw, and Stanford Black, enacted the drama to Thaw's advantage: In one scene Stanford Black knocked down an old blind man who begged to know what had happened to his beautiful daughter. In another a pretty girl sprang from a pie. The curtain came down on a declaration from Harry Daw, made from a cell in the Tombs. "No jury on earth will send me to the electric chair, no matter what I have done or what I have been, for killing the man who defamed my wife. That is the unwritten law."[28]

At the center of it all was Evelyn. Papers printed allegations of a woman who named Evelyn as correspondent in her divorce suit. Gibson's sketch of her as *The Eternal Question*, and photographs of her as a model appeared daily. Earlier articles of an affair between her and actor John Barrymore were reprinted, as were items of her making news at parties in Europe with Harry and the stories of her marriage to the Thaw millions. She was mobbed by both reporters and the public on her daily visits to Harry in prison.

Two weeks before the trial opened, Evelyn's mother, remarried and living in Pittsburgh, announced to the papers that she and her husband would travel to New York with letters in her possession concerning Evelyn, White, and Thaw. She planned to turn them over to the district attorney and testify in order to vindicate Stanford White's name. This plan evaporated, news sources reported, after Mrs. Thaw's attorney visited Evelyn's mother and purportedly paid her $50,000 for the letters. Upon his return to New York, the attorney stated that because of ill health Evelyn's mother had changed her mind about testifying.

When the trial opened in January 1907, the *New York Times* claimed it was "being reported to the ends of the civilized globe" and that all sorts of innovations accompanied this mammoth media event.

Extra seats have been provided for reporters. In the main hall of the building the Western Union Telegraph Company has established a regular office. A great cable of wires comes down from the central skylight and a dozen instruments have been installed. As room has to be provided to-day for the talisman as well as the lawyers, witnesses, and reporters, there will be no chance for the admission of the general public.[29]

Something else signaled a change between the judiciary and the media. For the first time in history, the jurors would be sequestered for the trial's duration.[30] The *Times* interpreted the judge's action:

By those who have followed proceedings in the criminal courts for years it was taken to mean that the judge realizes what strong influences might be set at work to affect the verdict in the case and has determined to allow no opportunity for anyone to approach the jurymen.[31]

At the front of the courtroom at a special table sat four female reporters chosen by their newspapers to cover the trial from the woman's point of view: Winifred Black for Hearst's *New York Journal*; Nixola Greely-Smith for Pulitzer's *New York Evening World*; and, for Hearst's *New York Evening Journal*, Ada Patterson and Dorothy Dix. Upon reading their mawkish copy, Irvin S. Cobb, also reporting for the *New York Evening World*, promptly named them the "sob sisters," a name that has become synonymous with an overly sentimental style of writing.

Prosecuting the case was William Travers Jerome, a popular, honest reformer. Jerome believed that Thaw was insane, but since a not-guilty plea had been entered and a jury selected, it was his job to prove conclusively, in the face of so much adverse publicity about the victim, that Harry Thaw was guilty of a premeditated act of murder in the first degree. In fact, the first lawyers engaged for the defense and the judge wanted an insanity plea entered so that a jury trial could be avoided, but Thaw's mother rejected that option. Thaw's cadre of six attorneys, headed by the suave and courtly Delphin Michael Delmas, had the task of proving that Thaw was perfectly sane before the murder and after, but temporarily deranged when he shot and killed Stanford White.

The prosecution took little time in presenting the bare facts of the case. For the defense, Delmas needed the testimony of Evelyn Nesbit as well as the support of psychiatric experts, or alienists. He placed Evelyn on the stand, dressed in a carefully chosen, subdued navy blue outfit, and guided her through her recitation about how she told Thaw of her ruination by Stanford White. First she talked of the now famous, or perhaps infamous, red velvet swing.

Delmas: You all sat down to luncheon in the studio?
Evelyn: Yes, and pretty soon the man who was with Mr. White got up and

went away. He said he was going away on business. Then Mr. White took me and the young lady (a friend of Evelyn's) upstairs to a room in which there was a big velvet swing. We got in the swing and he pushed it so that it flew way up in the air. The swing went so high that our feet kicked through a big Japanese umbrella.[32]

In later testimony Evelyn stated that following a dinner with White, she had awakened nude in a fully mirrored room with Stanford White beside her.

Delmas: Where was Mr. White, Madam, at the time you regained your consciousness? You say you found that you had been stripped. Did you describe to Mr. Thaw where White was?
Evelyn: Yes, he was right there beside me.
Delmas: Where?
Evelyn: In the bed.
Delmas: Dressed or undressed?
Evelyn: Completely undressed.
Delmas: Did you tell anything more on that occasion to Mr. Thaw than what you have related?
Evelyn: I told him Mr. White came to me again—I was sitting there in the chair. I had not eaten anything and I had not gone to bed. . . . He told me that I must not be worried about what had occurred. He said that everything was all right. He said he thought I had the most beautiful hair he had ever seen. He said he would do a great many things for me. He said everybody did these things; that all people were doing those things, and that is all people were for, all they lived for. He said that I was so nice and young and slim, that he couldn't help it and so did it.[33]

Nixola Greely-Smith reported that "Evelyn Nesbit has laid down everything that womanhood holds precious to save her husband, Harry Thaw."[34] Irvin S. Cobb reported: "Harry Thaw sobbed unrestrainedly as his wife half whispered the story of her degradation."[35]

Delmas introduced Dr. Britton B. Evans to testify to Thaw's mental state following Evelyn's confession. Dr. Evans's description of Thaw's explosive (but temporary) mental condition as a "brain-storm" introduced the term that was to become a permanent part of the language.[36]

In his cross-examination of Evelyn, Jerome attempted to denigrate her by asking questions concerning her posing nude, her possibly having had an abortion, and her reasons for continuing to see White if she was so repulsed by him, as she had testified. Ada Patterson wrote that the "Spaniards of the Middle Ages, geniuses of inventive cruelty, could not have devised tortures more ingenious than the prosecution plied the girl with."[37] When Jerome later produced an affidavit filed by Evelyn after their European trip that accused Thaw of beating her, raping her repeatedly, and using cocaine, Dorothy Dix sadly reported that "at its best, it shows Evelyn Nesbit lying to

Thaw in Paris or lying to White in New York while she lived luxuriously on the money of both and it shows Thaw as completely her dupe or else planning one of the most dastardly and cowardly acts on record, that of getting even with the enemy by dragging a young girl through the mire."[38]

Having cast some doubt on Evelyn's credibility as a witness but not having successfully proved premeditation during her testimony, Jerome, to the surprise of the court and in contradiction of his own case, declared his belief that Thaw was indeed insane and requested the appointment of a lunacy commission. One was appointed, and Harry Thaw was declared sane.

In his summation, Delmas told the jury:

If Thaw is insane it is with a species of insanity that is known from the Canadian border to the Gulf. If you expert gentlemen ask me to give it a name, I suggest that you name it *Dementia Americana*. It is that species of insanity that persuades an American that whoever violates the sanctity of his home or the purity of his wife or daughter has forfeited the protection of the laws of this state or any other state.[39]

The jury returned to the courtroom thirty hours after beginning its deliberations and reported to the judge that they were unable to reach a verdict. It was learned that on the final ballot, seven jurors had voted Thaw guilty of first degree murder while five had voted not guilty by reason of insanity. Shortly thereafter at his second trial, Thaw escaped the death house at Sing Sing when he was found not guilty by reason of insanity. On February 1, 1908, Harry Thaw was delivered to the Asylum for the Criminal Insane at Matteawan, New York.

Irvin S. Cobb later reminisced about the trial:

As I now recall but two benefits—unless you'd include getting a hung jury for Thaw—accrued from the scurvy, sweated smear of pseudo-scientific poppycock which was spread, like batter on a hot griddle, all over the fraud-tinged transcript. For one thing, those former Pooh Bahs of the popular lunatic asylums along our eastern seaboard collected their fat retainers, meanwhile, I suppose, like the Roman augurs in the Forum, avoiding one another's gaze for fear of a betraying giggle; and secondly, the native tongue eminently was enriched by passages of newly coined phraseology. "Brain storm" . . . "Dementia Americana" . . . "Sob Sister.". . . [40] It was a carnival of mayhem and maltreatment. It was a spectacle which always I shall remember.[41]

Harry Thaw spent much of the rest of his life in and out of mental hospitals and made headlines again when a young boy and a nightclub hostess separately accused Thaw of beating them. He died of a heart attack in 1947 at the age of 76.[42]

Evelyn Nesbit did not collect a promised million dollar settlement from her mother-in-law subsequent to her divorce from the heir. The elder Mrs. Thaw gave her $25,000. Evelyn went through a period of destitution; she had a baby who she claimed was Thaw's; she went back on the stage in a ragtime dance production; she married her dance partner and divorced him. She became addicted to drugs and twice attempted suicide. She wrote an autobiography, *Prodigal Days: The Untold Story*. In 1955 she served as writer and technical consultant for the movie *The Girl in the Red Velvet Swing*. In her last interview before her death in 1967 at age eighty one, Evelyn Nesbit said that Stanford White was the only man she ever loved.[43]

NOTES

1. Michael Mooney, *Evelyn Nesbit and Stanford White: Love and Death in the Gilded Age* (New York: William Morrow and Company, 1976), 46.

2. "Murder of the Century," *The American Experience*, WGBH-TV Educational Foundation, Boston, 1995 (one of a series for public service television).

3. Ibid.

4. "The Greatest Love Stories of the Century," *People Magazine*, 26 February 1996, 79.

5. "Murder of the Century," *The American Experience*.

6. Ibid.

7. Ibid.

8. Louis L. Synder and Richard B. Morris, eds., *Treasury of Great Reporting* as reported by Irwin S. Cobb for the *New York Evening World*, 7 February 1907 (New York: Simon and Schuster, 1962), 284.

9. Mooney, *Evelyn Nesbit and Stanford White: Love and Death in the Gilded Age*, 13–19.

10. Ibid., 157.

11. Ibid., 186.

12. Ibid., 157.

13. Ibid.

14. Ibid., 162.

15. Ibid., 75–83.

16. Ibid., 87.

17. Phyllis Leslie Abramson, *Sob Sister Journalism* (New York: Greenwood Press, 1990), 54.

18. Mooney, *Evelyn Nesbit and Stanford White: Love and Death in the Gilded Age*, 29–30.

19. Ibid., 21.

20. "The Greatest Love Stories of the Century," *People Magazine*, 79.

21. Mooney, *Evelyn Nesbit and Stanford White: Love and Death in the Gilded Age*, 93–105.

22. *New York Times*, 26 June 1906.

23. Snyder and Morris, *Treasury of Great Reporting*, 283.

24. *New York Times*, 26, 27, 28, 29 June 1906.

25. *New York Times*, 29 June 1906.

26. Ibid.

27. Mooney, *Evelyn Nesbit and Stanford White: Love and Death in the Gilded Age*,

199, 237.

   28. Ibid., 242.

   29. *New York Times*, 23 January 1907.

   30. Abramson, *Sob Sister Journalism,* 62.

   31. *New York Times*, 24 January 1907.

   32. Synder and Morris, *Treasury of Great Reporting*, 287, as reported by Irwin S. Cobb for the *New York Evening World*, 7 February 1907.

   33. Abramson, *Sob Sister Journalism,* 67–68.

   34. Ibid., 69.

   35. Snyder and Morris, *Treasury of Great Reporting*, 285.

   36. Abramson, *Sob Sister Journalism,* 81.

   37. Ibid., 85.

   38. Ibid.

   39. Ibid., 96.

   40. Irvin S. Cobb, *Exit Laughing* (New York: Bobbs-Merrill Co., 1941), 230.

   41. Ibid., 234.

   42. Abramson, *Sob Sister Journalism,* 128.

   43. Ibid., 132–134.

7

The Case of the Chicago Black Sox
(1921)

"Say it ain't so, Joe."

Lloyd Chiasson Jr.

Baseball is a child's game, a nostalgia, a habit, a noise, a mood, a song. It is a blur of action, a Sunday afternoon under blue skies, a long foul ball, a loud, raucous noise, a close call at home, a double play, a seventh-inning stretch. It is played by grown children, managed by crazy people, umpired by men of impaired vision, attended by aging infants who believe in Peter Pan. Baseball is crowds, hot dogs and beer, and long, lazy afternoons, but most of all, baseball is America. Then suddenly, in one moment, storm clouds fill the horizon and the tempest flourishes. It is 1919, a time of innocence perhaps, but the time when Americans discover that their field of dreams is an illusion.

Everywhere the plea was the same: "Say it ain't so, Joe."

But it was.

The fix was in. The White Sox had thrown the World Series. America's pastime had been betrayed by its most beloved heroes: the great, invincible Chicago White Sox.

But soon, the Black Sox.

Not all White Sox cheated, of course. Depending on who was doing the accusing, nine or eight or five or just two players cheated. But for baseball, particularly baseball in 1919, one cheat was one too many. It is true that some hardliners maintained, and still do, that nobody cheated, that the Cincinnati Redlegs played great, that Chicago played on the up and up, that in baseball, well, anything can happen.[1] But the evidence says that's just not the case.

In the first two decades of the twentieth century, baseball was more than a game; it was, as baseball historian Harold Seymour writes, the national pastime, "occupying a niche just below belief in God."[2] In a period of rapid change, baseball embodied American tradition and values. Dramatic growth in business and industry fostered a massive migration from the rural areas to the cities. At the same time, the greatest influx of immigrants in the nation's history flooded the cities and furthered the need for recreation outlets in urban areas. The harsh reality of city life simply did not match the expectations of these new city dwellers. In addition, industrialization and the growth of big business meant a vast expansion of the capitalistic system that proved detrimental to the common man. Factory work was dangerous, often long, and almost always unregulated. Slums proliferated, corrupt political machines ran burgeoning cities, and the quality of life seemed to decay with each Industrial Revolution "advancement."

In this environment two institutions served as vital links to the traditions of the past and as a means by which immigrants could be acculturated: public schools and baseball.[3] Both nurtured nationalism, but while school was predominantly for the young, baseball was for everyone. Few institutions had deeper roots in America than baseball. It was popular before the Civil War,[4] and by the 1880s it was considered the national pastime.[5] This was a game that had been elevated to a status equal that of Mom and apple pie. In 1910, President William Howard Taft called baseball "a clean, straight game," and summoned to its presence "everybody who enjoys clean, straight athletics." President Theodore Roosevelt acknowledged the "rugged honesty" of baseball.[6]

During this turn of the century love affair, baseball became big business as teams played in almost every major city. Other sports simply lacked the support that baseball enjoyed. Football was an amateur sport limited to a college audience,[7] while boxing and horse racing were subject to various restrictions and legislation from which professional baseball was exempt. In short, by 1919 baseball was clearly The Game.

This is not to suggest that The Game was squeaky clean. Far from it. Stories about fixed games had been around for years. Rumors proliferated that in the 1905 World Series Rube Waddell had been bought. In 1908, the New York Giants' team physician offered umpires Bill Blem and Jimmy Johnstone $2,500 apiece to see to it that the Giants would win the tie-breaker against the Chicago Cubs (which they did).[8] In 1912, the Giants once again were involved when both the management of the Cubs and the Philadelphia Phillies questioned the play of the St. Louis Cardinals against the Giants. As the season wound to an end, the president of the Phillies, Horace Fogel, said that umpire Bill Brennan favored New York and claimed the pennant race was fixed.[9] In 1916 Phillies manager Pat Moran demanded an investigation of the Giants-Brooklyn game that decided the pennant for the Dodgers,[10] and in 1917, rumors circulated that the World Series between the Giants and the White Sox had been fixed.[11]

No player, however, could match the infamous Hal Chase in plain old out-and-out baseball skullduggery. The most jaded ballplayer in history, Chase was to baseball what the Hindenburg was to dirigible sales. He entered the league in 1906, was openly accused of throwing games in 1910, managed a talented Yankees team into sixth place that same year, was sent packing to the Chicago White Sox, then to Buffalo in the Federal League, then on to Cincinnati where it became common knowledge in the league that Chase bet, sometimes against his own team. As a first baseman, he certainly didn't have the control over a game a pitcher or a catcher would have had, but one misstep here, one dropped ball there, one strike-out in a critical situation, and a game could turn. But Chase was a perfectionist if nothing else, so he bribed players. And where there was Hal Chase, there were gamblers. In fact, baseball historians Eliot Asinof and Charles Alexander write that the game was rife with gamblers prior to the 1919 World Series and that they often had influence in the outcome of games.[12] Alexander adds that the willingness of the 1919 Chicago White Sox's players "to collude with gamblers . . . had much to do with official baseball's longtime toleration of Chase and others of his ilk."[13]

So the dark clouds clustered, and in 1919 the storm commenced. In October. In the World Series. In a nine-game series between the overachieving champions of the National League, the Cincinnati Reds, and the White Sox of the American League. On paper it looked to be an easy call: The Sox in a walk. Chicago had arguably the best pitcher in baseball, Eddie Cicotte; the best third baseman in baseball, Buck Weaver; the best fielding, throwing, and hitting player in either league, Shoeless Joe Jackson; and leftovers at the other positions that surely must have looked like filet mignon to the Cincinnati fans.

That's just how the odd-makers saw it. At first. The White Sox opened as hefty 8–5 favorites, then suddenly, inexplicably, the odds dropped to 5–7 against. Although twenty-nine-game winner Eddie Cicotte was starting for Chicago, the odds-makers rated Game 1 as even money. Before the first out, before the first pitch, before the players trotted out on the field, rumors of a fix were afloat. Hugh Fullerton of the *Chicago Herald and Examiner* felt strongly enough to wire every paper carrying his accounts of the games: "ADVISE ALL NOT TO BET ON THIS SERIES. UGLY RUMORS AFLOAT."[14]

Seymour writes that the "lobby of Cincinnati's leading hotel, the Sinton, where the White Sox were staying, was jammed with gamblers, and there was a rush to place bets on the underdog Reds. In other cities the trend was the same."[15] In New York the proprietor of one betting parlor estimated $2 million had been bet on Game 1 alone. "You couldn't miss it," said Jack Doyle, owner of the Billiard Academy. "The thing had an odor. I saw smart guys take even money on the Sox who should have been asking 5 to 1."[16]

Game 1. Redland Park, Cincinnati: The locals hit Cicotte all over the park. Cincinnati wins in a walk, 9–1.

Game 2: Lefty Williams pitches. Cincinnati wins again, 4–2.

As the series heads to Chicago, one question is uppermost in the fans' minds: Can the beleaguered Sox find solace at home? Answer: Thanks to syndicated columnist Ring Lardner, they won't get past Indianapolis.

Sometime quite early in the series, Lardner, a Chicago resident and Sox fan, began to believe the "rumors." Like many others, Lardner was finding it increasingly difficult to believe that the weak-hitting Reds had scored thirteen runs on two of the best pitchers in baseball while the best-hitting team in the game had scored just three times in eighteen innings. After Game 2, Lardner wrote his column with a bottle perched next to his typewriter, an obvious ache in his heart, a tongue in his cheek.

there's a wild rumor going around that Mr. Gleason [Chicago's manager] wants the fourth inning removed for the rest of the Serious, and I don't care which inning they do cut out or maybe even two, but it they eliminate an inning, the Sox maybe will win a game which will merely elongate the Serious so whatever happens we are the losers.[17]

Traveling back to Chicago on the same train as the team, Lardner walked through the players' car, and to the clack clack clack of the wheels, sang:

I'm forever blowin ball games
Pretty ball games in the air
I come from Chi
I hardly try
Just got to bat and fade and die:
fortune's coming my way,
That's why I don't care.
I'm forever blowing ball games,
The gamblers treat us fair. . . .

As Asinof writes in *Eight Men Out*, "Nobody even told him (Lardner) to shut up."[18]

Game 3: Comiskey Park. Dickie Kerr pitches for the Sox and, as Asinof relates it, is so good, there was probably nothing the players "could have done to alter his victory, even it they'd tried." Chicago 3–0.

Game 4: Cicotte pitches again. Cicotte makes two errors which lead to two runs. Final score: 2–0.

Game 5: Williams pitches for the second time. Happy Felsch drops a ball in centerfield which leads to a Redleg rally. Final score: 5–0.

Game 6: Return to Cincinnati and Redland Park: The best game of the series. Although the Sox make three errors and fall behind 4–0, they battle back to win 5–4.

Game 7: The real Eddie Cicotte shows up to play, is brilliant, and wins easily 4–1. The series now stands at four games to three in favor of Cincinnati. Could the series be for real?

Game 8: Comiskey Park. The answer comes quickly. Lefty Williams makes fifteen pitches, gives up three runs, and is pulled by manager Kid Gleason with just one out in the first inning. The rest of the game is a nightmare for Sox fans. Final score: Redlegs 10, White Sox 5.

Asinof writes that on two instances the day before the final game, Lefty Williams was threatened by people representing nervous gambling interests who wanted Cincinnati to have the game in hand before the first inning ended.[19] Sportswriter Hugh Fullerton lent support to this when he reported that on his way to the press box before the game a gambler told him that Cincinnati would win and that "It'll be the biggest first inning you ever saw!"[20]

Although the series was over, the notion that it wasn't played on the up and up lingered. It may have been the persistent rumors. It may have been the see-sawing odds and peculiar betting. It may have been Hugh Fullerton's relentless commentary about something stinking in Chicago besides meat-packing plants. It may have been the final totals: eight games, fifty-three runs scored, thirty-eight by Cincinnati, just fifteen by Chicago.

White Sox owner Charles Comiskey, who certainly suspected and probably knew some players were involved in a fix, followed his lawyer's advice: Take the high ground, offer a reward for information that will never be provided, and let the whole deal blow over.[21]

It almost did. Hugh Fullerton and Hall of Famer Christy Mathewson compared notes at the end of the World Series and found no less than seven questionable plays by the White Sox. Although that winter Fullerton wrote several articles putting forth his concerns, suspicions, allegations, and fears, he met with the same response as a Muslim come to Vatican City to criticize the Pope. *The Sporting News* dismissed the rumors with as glorious a cacophony of hyphenated words as has ever been written. According to the magazine, rumors of a fix were the workings of "a lot of dirty, long-nosed, thick-lipped and strong-smelling gamblers."[22] And Fullerton, the magazine added, "should keep his mouth shut in the presence of intelligent people."[23]

Not until September 27, 1920, was the truth aired. Nearly a year after Ray Schalk had grounded out to end the 1919 World Series, the *North American,* a Philadelphia daily, published a front-page story claiming that the series had been fixed. Not surprisingly, its source was a small-time gambler, Billy Maharg. One day later Eddie Cicotte and Joe Jackson admitted to throwing the series and named as co-conspirators Lefty Williams, Buck Weaver, first baseman Chick Gandil, shortstop Charles "Swede" Risberg, Happy Felsch, and utility infielder Fred McMullin.

By October 1920 the "Black Sox" scandal, as it became known, covered the front pages of newspapers across the country. What followed was a parade of players, managers, gamblers and owners before the Cook County grand jury. And what emerged in bits and pieces was that there had been a fix, that players were involved, that two groups of gamblers had been active participants, that players from other teams—most notably the infamous Hal Chase—knew about the conspiracy and had won a considerable sum on the series. Chase and former player Bill Burns, seven gamblers, and eight White Sox players were indicted. Later five more gamblers were added to that list.[24]

Only when the players testified did muddy waters begin to clear. The idea of fixing the series originated with Gandil, not gamblers. Lefty Williams testified that his wife's life was threatened prior to the last game, and Buck Weaver admitted to knowing about the conspiracy but insisted he received no money and participated in no way.

Nowhere was the public's disbelief more evident than the sport pages of newspapers across the country. For the most part, sports writers generally reacted as disillusioned fans, then recovering from this unseemly lapse, began to imitate news reporters. In short, cynicism dominated commentary and found its way onto the news pages with some regularity. Sports reporters' disgust matched, if not surpassed, that of the average man on the street. Faster than an Eddie Cicotte fastball the stories of the Communist Red Scare sweeping across America were shoved off page 1 and replaced with the Black Sox scandal.[25] Everywhere editorial pages were chock full of commentary about this unthinkable blasphemy. The *Philadelphia Bulletin* wrote that a crooked player was no different that "the soldier . . . who would sell out his country . . . in time of war."[26] The *Grand Rapids Herald* saw the scandal in much the same way. "When cheap leeches strike at this sport of sports, they strike at one of the institutions of the Republic."[27] The *Chicago Tribune*, faced with the horrifying prospect of residing in the same city as the White Sox turncoats, was poetically candid about pitcher Eddie Cicotte:

> I remember, I remember, just back in '17,
> The Sox and Giants battled in the days the game was clean;
> And Cicotte – smiling Eddie – stopped them Giants with his hook,
> And now our good old Eddie confesses he's a crook.
>
> O, somewhere in this favored land the sun is shining bright,
> But the south side's sorely stricken by an overwhelming blight.
> We can stand for honest errors, bonehead plays we somehow brook,
> But heavy are our hearts today – for Eddie is a crook.[28]

Meanwhile, the baseball hierarchy, that is to say the owners, was in the midst of healing long-standing wounds, deep wounds, not the least of which was the World Series scandal. In an attempt to police the owners, bolster public confidence in the game, and rid itself of gambling, the owners named federal judge Kennesaw Mountain Landis to the newly created position of commissioner of baseball. Landis essentially became czar of baseball, a position for which he seemed uniquely suited. As to his stance on the as yet untried players, Landis said: "They are and will remain outlaws."[29]

In a sense, the trial, held in June 1921, was anticlimatic. The trial of eight ballplayers was certainly not molded from the same clay as Lizzie Borden and Harry Thaw's sensational trials. So what if the Sox lost the series? Can't a team lose without being labeled cheaters? So what if the players confessed? So what if the odds, as well as the betting, seemed to make little sense given the records of the teams? Aren't the odds largely determined by who is being bet on, and can't the bets be placed on either team? Just because something stinks doesn't mean it's rotten. It's not like somebody was murdered, right?

Wrong. It was worse. People come and go, but baseball was here to stay. And according to the jury, so too were the players. Verdict: not guilty.

Actually the verdict was as predictable as the series. Somehow Cicotte, Williams and Johnson's grand jury confessions mysteriously disappeared for the trial. Strike 1 for the defense. With no evidence of confessions, the players recanted. Strike 2.[30] Finally the judge's charge to the jury—that the state prove that it was the intent of the players and gamblers to defraud the public and not merely to throw ball games—was so favorable to the defense as to be totally bewildering to the jury. Strike 3, the prosecution headed for the bench.

The evening of August 2, the jury, amid cheering spectators, found the players not guilty. On August 3, newspapers across the country proclaimed, some perhaps not proudly, the news. For the eight players, however, the celebration was pitifully short, for on August 4, newspapers reported the final verdict, Judge Landis's verdict, and that verdict contained no leniency, no room for legal maneuvers, no hope:

[N]o player who throws a ballgame, no player that undertakes or promises to throw a ballgame, no player that sits in conference with a bunch of crooked players and gamblers where the ways and means of throwing a game are discussed and does not promptly tell his club about it, will ever play professional baseball![31]

Angered that Landis could unilaterally toss a court decision in the waste basket, many people blamed the team owners for giving Kennesaw Mountain Landis "carte blanche dictatorial powers" to overturn a not guilty verdict.[32] Some people, rightly or wrongly, blamed Charles Comiskey.[33] It was Comiskey, they said, who alienated his players with a spendthrift attitude that bordered on the comical. Comiskey was the only owner to charge his players for having their uniforms laundered.[34] Comiskey promised his players a bonus if they won the pennant in 1917, and when they did he "rewarded" them with a case of champagne at the victory celebration. It was Comiskey, cheap Comiskey, who watched attendance climb, who benefited from the scheduling of more games, and who still refused to discuss manager Kid Gleason's request in 1918 to reconsider players' salaries.[35] By 1919 the players' paychecks had increased some, but animosities lingered, perhaps as much because of Comiskey's style—or lack of—as with the money. Jackson and Weaver made $6,000 each, Gandil and Felsch $4,000, Risberg and Williams, $3,000. The Reds, however, were much more generous with players' salaries. For example, outfielder Edd Roush made $4,000 more than Jackson and was batting about 50 points less.

It is not difficult to understand how the players may have been a little more susceptible to, and certainly pragmatic about, throwing the World

Series. No doubt a "take the money and run" attitude grabbed hold of some and clouded their judgment. Like dominos they fell. First Gandil, then Cicotte, then Risberg, then McMullin (who overheard Gandil and Risberg and wanted in), then Lefty Williams, then the big hitters in the line-up, Weaver, Jackson and Felsch.[36] On the eve of the series, they gathered to discuss how it would be done. At some point, Weaver decided he could not, or would not, play less than his best. But in knowing and not telling, Weaver's fate inexorably moved from his hands into those of the yet-to-be-named commissioner. Weaver's future turned dark before he realized it.

Unquestionably, the characters to be most pitied in this Faustian morality play were Buck Weaver and Shoeless Joe Jackson—Weaver because he was innocent and Jackson because he wasn't. After Judge Landis's all-encompassing edict, Weaver met with the commissioner. His story was simple: Gandil offered money, and he turned it down. Landis asked Weaver why he didn't inform someone about the fix. This Weaver couldn't answer. At the time Gandil talked money, Weaver had no proof of any wrong-doing. He could tell Landis nothing, and that's what Landis heard from Weaver. This wasn't the answer Landis wanted—one has to doubt that any answer would have sufficed—and Weaver, who desperately wanted to prove his innocence as well as play the game he loved, was denied both.

Thirty-five years later as Weaver walked his neighborhood on the southside of Chicago he died of an apparent heart attack. He was sixty-six. He had never returned to the game he loved.

> Don't bring up Buck Weaver
> Or how he looked that last time you saw him
> Begging a reporter six months out of high school
> To clear his name so he could play again.
> "I'll play for nothing, tell 'em
> Just one season, tell 'em!"[37]

Joe Jackson's story was far different and more difficult to explain. Why did arguably the best natural hitter in baseball risk so much for so little? Jackson had played for ten years, had a .356 batting average, was probably the best fielding and throwing outfielder in the league, and had years left to play. Those seeking a simple answer claimed an illiterate country-bumpkin was a perfect patsy for wily gamblers. However, for ten years Jackson traveled to major league cities—large, industrialized northern cities far removed from his southern upbringing—where he was lauded for his enormous talents. Even someone who couldn't read his press clippings could see his picture in every city he visited. To argue that Jackson somehow failed to appreciate his notoriety, and, it would follow, what he had at stake, is dismally shortsighted. Jackson's motives then, as now, remain a mystery that has become part of the legacy of Shoeless Joe. Unfortunately, it is a legacy darkened by an overwhelming sadness. So much talent wasted. A good name tainted. A great player lost to the game. Although time can dull even the darkest events, the sense of shame remains fresh. Years later Jackson ran a liquor store in his hometown of Greenville, South Carolina. Ty Cobb, a man known for his enormous appetite for alcohol, was passing through town and decided to visit his old nemesis. Cobb ordered a bottle of bourbon, and the two men talked as though they were total strangers. Finally, Cobb simply asked Jackson, "Don't you know me, Joe?" Jackson nodded. "Sure—I know you, Ty. I just didn't think anyone I used to know up there wanted to recognize me again."[38]

Despite the 1919 World Series, despite the trial of those players charged with fixing the games, despite the dictatorial handling of the situation by Judge Landis, golden years were ahead for baseball. In that purgatory between the 1919 series and Landis's decision to excommunicate the Black Sox, an eternal hope that pervaded the baseball community called America persisted. In one sentence, *The Nation* encapsulated what The Game meant to the country: "We do not trust cashiers half as much, or diplomats, or policemen or physicians, as we trust an outfielder or a shortstop."[39] The fire and brimstone of Judge Landis's decision did little to shake America's faith in baseball or in those who played the game. In spite of itself, The Game grew, and a new age, headlined by a beer-bellied, cigar-smoking, easy-going home-run hitter by the name of Ruth, was about to begin.[40]

Bitter memories rarely scrub clean in a day, however. But the same day Judge Landis made his decision to ban the players, a freckled kid with scraggly hair and grass-stained jeans jumped off the front porch of his home, grabbed his glove, bat and ball, and headed for the neighborhood sandlot. In every town and hamlet across America, it was the same. Children playing a child's game. For the fun of it.

NOTES

1. See generally, Victor Luhrs, *The Great Baseball Mystery, the 1919 World Series* (New York: A. S. Barnes and Co., 1966).

2. Harold Seymour, *Baseball: The Golden Age* (New York: Oxford University Press, 1971), 274.

3. Ibid., 6.

4. Steven A. Riess, *Touching Base, Professional Baseball and American Culture in the Progressive Era* (Westport, Conn.: Greenwood Press, 1980), 4.

5. Ibid.

6. Seymour, *Baseball:The Golden Age*, 274.

7. Riess, *Touching Base, Professional Baseball and American Culture in the Progressive Era*, 4.

8. Charles C. Alexander, *Our Game: An American Baseball History* (New York: Henry Holt and Co., 1991), 116–117.

9. Ibid., 117.

10. Ibid.

11. Ibid., 118.

12. See Eliot Asinof, *Eight Men Out* (New York: Holt, Rinehart and Winston, 1963) and Alexander, *Our Game: An American Baseball History*.

13. Alexander, *Our Game: An American Baseball History*, 119.

14. Asinof, *Eight Men Out*, 46.

15. Seymour, *Baseball: The Golden Age*, 294–295.

16. Ibid., 295.

17. Asinof, *Eight Men Out*, 93.

18. Ibid., 94.

19. Ibid., 112–114.

20. Ibid., 115–116.

21. Ibid., 126–129.

22. See Alexander, *Our Game: An American Baseball History*, 116, and Seymour, *Baseball: The Golden Age*, 296.

23. Seymour, *Baseball, The Golden Age*, 296.

24. Alexander, *Our Game: An American Baseball History*, 125.

25. Seymour, *Baseball: The Golden Age*, 276.

26. As reported in Seymour, *Baseball: The Golden Age*, 276.

27. Ibid.

28. Ibid.

29. As reported in Alexander, *Our Game: An American Baseball History*, 126.

30. David Q. Voight, *America Through Baseball* (Chicago: Nelson-Hall, 1976), 70–71.

31. Asinof, *Eight Men Out*, 273.

32. Lee Lowenfish and Tony Lupien, *The Imperfect Diamond: The Story of Baseball's Reserve System and the Men Who Fought to Change It* (New York: Stein and Day, 1980), 100.

33. Alexander, *Our Game: An American Baseball History*, 129.

34. Ibid., 128.

35. Asinof, *Eight Men Out*, 16.

36. Ibid., 16–18.

37. Poem by Nelson Algren as cited in Asinof, *Eight Men Out*, 279.

38. Asinof, *Eight Men Out*, 292–293.

39. As cited in Seymour, *Baseball: The Golden Age*, 274.

40. As cited in Alexander, *Our Game: An American Baseball History*, 129.

8

The Case of John Scopes
(1925)

"In the beginning . . ."

Lloyd Chiasson Jr.

The setting is Rhea County Courthouse, Dayton, Tennessee, July 1925.

For several minutes the lawyer questions the key witness. The questions are short, straightforward; the answers the same. A sparring match tests the best-known trial lawyer in the country and perhaps the most respected politician of the time. It is a battle between giants and the stakes are exceedingly high. Tension envelops the courtroom as though the battle of Armageddon has just started. The spectators, and the press, anxiously await the next word. The moment is at hand:

Darrow: Mr. Bryan, do you believe that the first woman was Eve?
Bryan: Yes.
Darrow: Do you believe she was literally made out of Adams's rib?
Bryan: I do.
Darrow: Did you ever discover where Cain got his wife?
Bryan: No, sir; I leave the agnostics to hunt for her.
Darrow: You have never found out?
Bryan: I have never tried to find out.
Darrow: You have never tried to find out?
Bryan: No.
Darrow: The Bible says he got one, doesn't it? Were there other people on the earth at that time?
Bryan: I cannot say.
Darrow: You cannot say. Did that ever enter your consideration?
Bryan: Never bothered me.
Darrow: There were no others recorded, but Cain got a wife.
Bryan: That is what the Bible says.
Darrow: Where she came from you do not know? All right. Does the

statement, "The morning and the evening were the first day," and "The morning and the evening were the second day," mean anything to you?

Bryan: I do not think it necessarily means a 24–hour day.

Darrow: You do not?

Bryan: No.

Darrow: What do you consider it to be?

Bryan: I have not attempted to explain it . . .

Darrow: Then when the Bible said, for instance, "And God called the firmament heaven. And the evening and the morning were the second day," that does not necessarily mean 24 hours?

Bryan: I do not think it necessarily does.

Darrow: What do you think about it?

Bryan: That is my opinion. I do not know that my opinion is better on that subject than those who think it does.

Darrow: You do not think that?

Bryan: No. But I think it would be just as easy for the kind of God we believe in to make the earth in six days as in six years or in 6 million years or in 6 trillion years. I do not think it important whether we believe one or the other.

Darrow: Do you think those were literal days?

Bryan: My impression is they were periods, but I would not attempt to argue as against anybody who wanted to believe in literal days. . . .

Darrow [later in the questioning]: . . . Now, if you call those periods, they may have been a very long time.

Bryan: They might have been.

Darrow: The creation might have been going on for a very long time.

Bryan: It might have continued for millions of years.[1]

A million years? To most fundamentalists the concept was unthinkable. How could the Creation take a million years? How could William Jennings Bryan say the Creation took more than six days? Perhaps the great Christian leader wasn't so great, wasn't even a Christian, at least not the fundamentalist kind.[2] Throughout the courtroom, amazed spectators awaited the confrontation's climax. For Christians like William Jennings Bryan, it had been a long time coming. Since the beginning of time it had been coming . . .

In the beginning God created the heavens and the earth . . .

And God said, Let the earth bring forth the living creature after his kind, cattle, and creeping things, and the beast of the earth after his kind: and it was

so. . . . And God said, Let us make man in our image, after our likeness: and let them have dominion over the fish of the sea, and over the fowl of the air, and over the cattle, and over all the earth, and over every creeping thing that creepeth upon the earth.

So God created man in his own image, in the image of God created he him; male and

female created he them . . .
And God saw every thing that he had made, and, behold, it was very good. And the
evening and the morning were the sixth day. [*The Holy Bible*, King James Version.]

Long after the universe was created—either millions of years or a little
more than 6,000 years ago—twenty-four-year-old John Thomas Scopes
taught a relatively new scientific theory in his biology class in Dayton High
School in Rhea County, Tennessee. What followed was a battle between
science and theology, between modernism and fundamentalism, between
liberal and literal translation of the Bible, between Genesis and Darwin,
between the greatest trial lawyer in America, Clarence Darrow, and the
nation's best-known fundamentalist, three-time presidential candidate
William Jennings Bryan.[3]
    Scopes's trial commanded the national interest because it pitted what
America was becoming against what America had been. The early years of
the twentieth century saw the dawning of a brave new world filled with
frightening implications and radical change. In the first decade of the
twentieth century the world was turned inside out by three men whose ideas,
to a large degree, would mold the twentieth as the century of science.
Although Charles Darwin's *On the Origin of Species* was first published in
1859,[4] its effect was minimal on an America whose religious landscape was
primarily Protestant and essentially fundamentalist. Social upheaval in the
second half of the nineteenth century laid the foundation for change, but not
until the turn of the century did the theories of other scientists erect a
platform from which "the age of reason" could be launched. Supporting
Darwin's theory that man evolved from lower life forms were Sigmund
Freud's ideas about the id, ego, and super ego. Freud believed man to be an
instinctive animal guided by two basic needs, food and sex, and, since these
needs were natural and instinctive, men were incapable of sin. According to
Freud, man didn't need God, man needed therapy.[5] Confusing matters even
more were Albert Einstein's theories about matter, time, and space,[6] which
certainly must have appeared as crazy to the ordinary man as did the claims
of Copernicus four centuries before that the earth circled the sun and not vice
versa.
    As the world staggered into the new century, it faced a second
Reformation, one that forced even the most religious to somehow fit science
within religion or face the prospect of reinventing religion. In this matrix of
change, fresh ideas flourished. Social Darwinism—the belief that only the
strong survive—became increasingly popular,[7] as did the Social Gospel,
whose proponents asserted that the Church had to be more involved with
social problems because the goals of Christianity and industrial society
clashed.[8] As America became more industrialized, the country changed in
dramatic ways. Cities grew significantly, many burdened by overpopulation.
The urban reform that resulted pitted the political machine representing the
lower classes and the immigrants against the middle and upper classes.[9] At

the same time, immigration boomed. Prior to 1880, the vast majority of immigrants came from Protestant countries in northwestern Europe, and assimilation was smooth. Between 1880 and 1919, about 23 million immigrants flooded the United States, many of whom settled in the industrialized Northeast.[10] These were a new kind of immigrant, however—Catholics and Jews from southeastern and eastern Europe. Italians and Russians came in waves to the eastern seaboard;[11] Orientals, to a lesser degree, settled on the West Coast.[12] Assimilation was often difficult, acceptance slow.[13] A vast transformation was underway, one that was out of control and impossible to stop.

Everywhere in America the theme was change and reform. The big business policies of capitalists like Andrew Carnegie, John D. Rockefeller and J. P. Morgan had effectively destroyed the free marketplace concept, a growing Socialist movement made inroads in both labor and politics,[14] and writers like Emile Zola promoted a pessimistic concept called Naturalism that asserted man had no control over his destiny because of environmental and natural forces.[15] At the forefront of this national metamorphosis were writers determined to spread the seeds of change: Zola (*Nana*), Stephen Crane (*Maggie, A Girl of the Streets*), Frank Norris (*The Octopus*), Upton Sinclair (*The Jungle*), Theodore Dreiser (*Sister Carrie*), and Jack London (*The Iron Heel*).

By 1925, Americans had been introduced to these and other new ideas, and had witnessed vast changes in society. But the Scopes trial clearly embodied in one neat package all the confusing and disturbing forces at work in this new America. But does this adequately explain why the Scopes trial generated so much interest? It certainly was not because of Scopes. It definitely was not because of what was in a biology text. Not even the constitutional issues pushed the engine of this trial. At times, even God and science were shoved into the rumble seat of a Stutz Bearcat being driven by the celebrity of two men who had long been famous for being famous.

As soon as the combatants were announced—Clarence Darrow versus William Jennings Bryan, not God versus monkeys as some joked—the trial attracted the media like a picnic attracts ants. It was the Great Agnostic versus the Great Commoner against a backdrop of science and fundamentalism. In simple terms (and the media all too often view events in simple terms),[16] this promised to be a better fight than the Luis Firpo–Jack Dempsey heavyweight championship two years before. During the trial, an average of 165,000 words a day—a total of 2 million words—were filed by telegraph.[17] According to Darrow, however, the case was not reported as it should have been. "Most of the newspapers treated the whole case as a farce instead of a tragedy, but they did give it no end of publicity. Not only was every paper of importance in America represented, but those of many foreign lands."[18]

Every colorful trial contains similar elements, but few contained as many as the Scopes trial. Perhaps no trial had ever delineated good and evil so clearly, and, depending on one's beliefs, never before were the elements so interchangeable. From beginning to end, Scopes was essentially incidental to the proceedings. On trial was a way of life rapidly descending into distant memory.

Of course, the press was there to record it all, and in many instances, enjoy it all. Laughter from reporters, as well as the spectators, was common throughout the trial, primarily because the ambiguous, larger issues often became secondary to the more tangible struggle at hand: Darrow versus Bryan, science versus religion.

That Darrow would win the battle and lose the war was probably as obvious as it was secondary to the fact that two public figures, one representing the future, the other clinging desperately to the past, were in a titanic battle. This is the stuff of great trials, and what the press covers best. The historic import and social significance were important but could be, and were to a large extent, left to social and religious scholars, to historians and scientists, to school teachers and lawmakers. This gripping, dramatic, simple story was ideal for media coverage. And the timing was perfect. In 1921 the first radio station began broadcasting, and four years later the Scopes trial became the first trial ever to be nationally broadcast[19] and was without question the most "attended" trial in history to that point.

Although events leading to the Great Monkey Trial began in the latter half of the nineteenth century, our story actually begins in 1925. In the spring of that tumultuous year the Butler Bill, which prohibited the teaching of evolution in public schools, was passed by the Tennessee Legislature and signed by Governor Austin Peay, primarily because most elected officials didn't want to vote against a bill if such a vote would insult the electorate by suggesting that voters were descended from a resident of the city zoo. It was easier, and a whole lot more politically expedient, to quote the Bible and pass the plate.[20]

There were those, like the bill's author, John Washington Butler, who believed that "the Bible is the foundation upon which our American Government is built. . . . The evolutionist who denies the biblical story . . . undermines the foundation of our Government."[21] Butler's sentiments reflected those of Fundamentalism, a religious movement formed in the early 1900s but reflected in the beliefs of many Protestants, particularly those who believed in a literal translation of the Bible. Fundamentalism grew in the years prior to the entry of the United States into World War I. After the war it was instrumental in the passage of the eighteenth Amendment—the abolition of alcohol. Next came the movement's biggest challenge of all.

Allan H. Sager summarizes the lofty ambitions of the fundamentalists succinctly:

[T]he psychological climate of the twenties was one in which men were made to feel that the foundations beneath them were tottering, if indeed not crumbling. Fundamentalists sensed that the supreme task before them was the buttressing of the old foundations and that certainly the future of Christianity—if not of humanity—depended upon the spirit and thoroughness with which they accomplished that task.[22]

Working toward the accomplishment of that task were the newly organized Anti-Evolution League of America[23] and the fiery rhetoric of one W. J. Bryan, the most visible fundamentalist in the country. Speaking before state legislatures throughout the country, but primarily in the South, Bryan urged passage of laws prohibiting the teaching of evolution in schools. To Bryan, the issue was simple: Schools teaching evolution were transforming Christian youths into nonbelievers.[24]

The Butler Bill, then, was exactly the kind of legislation that Bryan wanted. Not everyone agreed, however. The constitutionality of such a bill, not to mention the logic, was highly questionable. Enter the American Civil Liberties Union, which advertised for a Tennessee teacher willing to be involved in a test case challenging a law it viewed as a threat to the right of taxpayers to control the separation of church and state, academic freedom, and what is taught in public schools.[25]

A few enterprising Dayton citizens, somewhat on a lark, decided that a challenge to the law might bring positive attention to their town.[26] That it did, but no one—least of all John Thomas Scopes—could have gleaned the national brouhaha that would take place in that peaceful Tennessee hamlet.

As Scopes described it later: "It was just a drugstore discussion that got past control."[27]

It was May 4, just after the Butler Bill became law, that a group congregated at the drugstore of Frank Earle Robinson, chairman of the Rhea County Board of Education. He and Walter White, the superintendent of Rhea County schools, businessman George Rappelyea, and attorneys Sue Hicks and Wallace Haggard began that discussion.

"You been teaching 'em this book?" George Rappelyea, the primary instigator behind the idea, asked Scopes.

The book was George William Hunter's *Civic Biology*. "Yes," said Scopes, who opened the text and showed the group an evolutionary chart. "[Y]ou can't teach biology without teaching evolution. . . . There's our text, provided by the state."

Robinson then showed Scopes the ACLU advertisement for a test case in a Chattanooga newspaper.[28] "Would you be willing to let your name be used?"

"If you can prove that I've taught evolution, and that I can qualify as a defendant, then I'll be willing to stand trial."[29]

Scopes equivocated because of what he viewed as a major flaw in the scheme. He was the high school's football coach and had merely substituted in a biology class. In fact, Scopes admitted to not knowing whether he had actually covered evolution at all. "We reviewed for final exams, as best I remember."[30]

Not a perfect fit, but the friendly salesmen in Robinson's already had the shoes on Scopes. Robinson immediately called the *Chattanooga News*, identified himself, and said: "I'm chairman of the school board here. We've just arrested a man for teaching evolution."[31]

Scopes wrote in his remembrances: "Robinson and the others apparently weren't concerned about this technicality. I had expressed willingness to stand trial. That was enough."[32]

With the defendant in tow, all that remained was the selection of defense and prosecution teams. Bryan essentially selected himself when on May 13 he stated that if Tennessee officials agreed, he would gladly represent the World's Christian Fundamentals Association in the prosecution of the case. And so he joined the prosecution team, even though he had not tried a case in more than thirty years. Bryan's decision started a domino effect on events.[33] Media attention perked (columnist H. L. Mencken quickly dubbed it the Monkey Trial); the case turned into a religious rather than a constitutional battle; and Clarence Darrow, eager to oppose Bryan, volunteered to represent the defense free of charge.[34]

Darrow "probably wouldn't have offered his services if he [Bryan] hadn't entered the case and changed the focus from law to religion,"[35] Scopes later wrote. Although Darrow was anxious to debunk Bryan's fundamentalist views, he, Scopes, the other members of the defense team (Dudley Field Malone, Arthur Garfield Hays, and John Randolph Neal), and ACLU officials agreed that the top priority was to have the law declared unconstitutional. That meant if they lost—and the chances of that looked good—the case would have to be appealed to a federal court.[36]

Darrow, who was sixty-seven at the time of the Scopes trial, was famous both as a defender of the oppressed and as a trial attorney. In fact, whenever there was "a trial of the century," Darrow seemed always to be seated on the left at the defense table. In 1887 he was involved with the defense of the men charged in the Haymarket bombing in Chicago (although he did not represent them), and in 1924 his clients were Leopold and Loeb, who with much media fanfare were charged, convicted and executed for the kidnapping and murder of teenager Bobby Franks.

Darrow's fame also came from his highly unpopular stances on capital punishment (he opposed it and other lesser punishments), and his outspoken, agnostic opposition of fundamentalist dogma, specifically the belief of literal biblical translation.[37] In short, he believed evolution to be scientific fact. Given his adamant opposition to provincial ideas and to what he considered small-minded thinking, you either loved Clarence Darrow or you hated him.

William Jennings Bryan may have been what his critics claimed, "nothing more than a voice," but as historians T. Harry Williams, Richard Current and Frank Freidel wrote, "it was the most beautiful voice in all the long history of American oratory."[38] Bryan gained fame in 1896 as the Democratic nominee for president and for his prosilver oratory—the famous Cross of Gold speech—at that same convention. With one well-timed and emotionally enthralling speech, Bryan won the support of the working man and small businessmen for years to come, and solidified himself as the emotional and spiritual leader of the rural, middle class. Williams wrote that Bryan "did not sense popular opinion, he embodied it. . . . He did not resemble the common man; he was the common man."[39] Unfortunately, urban and upper classes didn't see Bryan as their representative, and so he lost the presidential election that year and also in 1900 and 1908.

Like most well-known men, Bryan had his critics, most of whom agreed he was like a beautifully wrapped, but empty box. He was likened to the Platte River in his home state of Nebraska: a mile wide but only six inches deep.[40] Theodore Roosevelt described Bryan as "an amiable, windy creature who knows almost nothing."[41] Woodrow Wilson considered him "the most charming and lovable of men, but foolish and dangerous in his theoretical beliefs."[42] Bryan's eloquence rested on a foundation of sincerity, however. In short, he truly believed evolution to be scientific hogwash. Given his single-minded proclivity toward the emotional rather than the substantive, you either loved William Jennings Bryan or you hated him.

After the formal indictment of Scopes on April 24, Judge John Raulston scheduled the trial for July 10. This left June as a month of preparation for the defense, for the prosecution, for the media, and for the people of Dayton. When July finally arrived, everyone seemed prepared. No one, however, could have been prepared for what Scopes himself described: "From the beginning to the end . . . Ringling Brothers or Barnum and Bailey would have been pressed hard to produce more acts and sideshows and freaks than Dayton had."[43]

Lewis Levi Johnson Marshall, the "Absolute Ruler of the Entire World, without Military, Naval, or other Physical Force," and Wilber Glenn Voliva, the world's foremost authority on the "flat-earth school of geology," significantly brightened the streets of Dayton.[44] The country capitalists of Dayton were not to be outdone, however, as "monkey business" grabbed hold. The monkey motif was advertised everywhere; cotton apes went on sale along with buttons that read "Your Old Man's a Monkey." One clothing store sign took a humorous approach: "DARWIN IS RIGHT—INSIDE"; the owner of the store, of course, was J. R. Darwin. Hot dog and lemonade vendors walked the streets, booths were set up to hawk books and pamphlets on biology, evolution, religion. Not to be outdone, the Anti-Evolution League set up shop. One sign outside the courthouse proclaimed salvation on sale: "The sweetheart love of Jesus Christ and Paradise Street is at hand. Do you want to be a sweet angel? Forty days of prayer. Itemize your sins and iniquities for eternal life. If you come clean, God will talk back to you in voice."[45]

"Everybody was doing business," wrote Scopes.[46]

Another sign was that of Bryan's far-reaching influence. In his book about the trial, Scopes writes that with the arrival of the Great Commoner three days prior to the trial, the "monkey signs went down and the religious posters started going up."[47] Bryan's early arrival neatly coincided with that of hundreds of newspapermen, most notably H. L. Mencken, about whom Scopes wrote: "His biting commentary on the Bible Belt and the trial itself was one of the highlights of the entire event."[48]

Another prominent media presence was Chicago radio station WGN, whose coverage made the Dayton trial the first remote-control national radio hook-up in history. Not just the people of Dayton would hear this trial.

The eight-day trial began in the sweltering July heat, which somehow seemed appropriate to the case. The tall, gangly Darrow sat relaxed while Bryan waved a palm fan in a futile attempt to stay cool. For the next seven days of the trial, no one did.

Friday, July 10. Day 1: The courtroom is packed. The plodding method of jury selection, however, soon dampens the excitement. To Darrow's surprise, a jury is quickly selected, although three jurors admit that the only book they had read was the Bible.[49]

Monday, July 13. Day 2: There is a short delay as Judge John Raulston waits until the radio hook-up is complete. A. T. Stewart, attorney general for the 18th Circuit and lead counsel for the state, explains that the case is not religious in nature but that the Butler Act simply allows the state to control the allocation of state funds. Lead defense attorney John Randolph Neal counters for the defense, asking Judge Raulston to quash the indictment of Scopes on grounds that the law is unconstitutional.[50] Bryan says nothing and continues to fan himself.

In the afternoon, Darrow continues the defense argument which turns into a brilliant three-hour summation of why the Butler Act is unconstitutional and how it is a threat to both public and private education and to churches. During his argument members of the audience occasionally heckle him but with little effect. On more than one occasion, he directs accusatory comments at Bryan, who resolutely remains silent.[51] Judge Raulston makes no ruling.

Tuesday, July 14. Day 3: Darrow immediately objects to the daily proceedings being opened with a prayer. Bryan slaps down his fan and glares at Darrow. Judge Raulston overrules Darrow's objection. The jury isn't even seated and tension between the defense, prosecution, and judge is already high. Darrow asks that his objection to the prayer each subsequent morning of the trial be recorded. Judge Raulston agrees. During lunch newspaper extra editions hit the streets informing the public that Judge Raulston will not quash the indictment.[52] If this is true, the case will continue. The information leak enrages Raulston. He does not, however, reveal what his decision is. As the day ends, Darrow sits next to Bryan, and they briefly whisper back and forth.

Wednesday, July 15. Day 4: Reporters inform Judge Raulston that in a conversation with a reporter the judge himself inadvertently leaked his decision not to quash the indictment. Raulston's admonishment of the industrious reporter who first reported the news is, understandably, somewhat lacking in vigor. The judge then reads his decision which, of course, validates what was reported the day before. In the afternoon, several witnesses for the prosecution are not in court. Judge Raulston calls a recess to locate them. After the witnesses are found, someone goes to find the jury, many of whom are walking the fair streets of Dayton. In the meantime, the chairs of several attorneys are stolen.[53]

With the indictment sustained, the defense pleads not guilty. The state and defense give their opening statements. The jury is finally sworn in, and the case begins in earnest. Walter White, Rhea County schools' superintendent, is called. Next comes Howard Morgan, a pupil of Scopes. Then Frank Earle Robinson testifies. Satisfied that the witnesses provide sufficient information that Scopes taught evolution, the state rests its case.

The first defense witness is zoologist Maynard M. Metcalf. Before Darrow even begins to question Metcalf, Bryan walks to the stand and stares directly at the scientist. The Great Commoner then quietly returns to his seat. No one speaks. Once Darrow begins to question Metcalf, it quickly becomes evident that the next issue Judge Raulston will be asked to adjudicate will be the admissibility of scientific evidence.

Thursday, July 16. Day 5: Science day. Zoology. Biology. Geology. The argument over admissibility is long, sometimes tedious, and necessarily about science. A big moment finally arrives, however. In the afternoon session, William Jennings Bryan speaks for the prosecution. The courtroom, thinned of spectators after a week of "legalese" ad nauseam, begins to fill once again. The crowd is not disappointed. Bryan attacks the theory of evolution with skill—sometimes garbling his science, but never his presentation. It is filled with humor and emotion and good, old-fashioned William Jennings Bryan. But circumstance victimizes Bryan's timing. What follows is the greatest oratory of the trial. Defense attorney Dudley Malone boldly undercuts each of Bryan's arguments and finishes to loud applause. After adjournment, only Bryan, Malone, and Scopes remain in the courtroom. Bryan, still sitting, sighs, then looks at the defense lawyer and says, "Dudley, that's the greatest speech I ever heard."[54]

Friday, July 17. Day 6: Judge Raulston finally rules on the admissibility of scientific evidence. He explains that because the Butler Act made it unlawful to teach evolution, the testimony of experts will serve no purpose. The motion is denied, which effectively ends the defense's case and brings Darrow into contentious debate with Raulston. The case appears lost except for one fact: Clarence Darrow has not earned the reputation as the best trial lawyer in the country without performing magic tricks at the most opportune moment.

Monday, July 20. Day 7: Scientific affidavits supporting evolution fill the morning. Lunch proves more eventful, however. Plaster found on the ground floor of the courthouse under the courtroom proves the size of the crowd puts too much weight on the courtroom floor. For reasons of safety, Judge Raulston moves the trial to the courthouse lawn. As the crowd surges outside, Darrow addresses Raulston and apologizes for earlier argumentative statements directed at Raulston. Darrow and Raulston shake hands, and the trial continues outside.

The opportune moment: Hays calls Bryan as a witness. Bryan's fan stops in midstroke. A sense of astonishment permeates the crowd. Calling a lawyer involved in the case at hand is unheard of—and is legally questionable. Then Bryan speaks up and asks Raulston if he may call the defense attorneys in return. Raulston agrees, and Bryan walks to the stand.

After seven days the table is finally set, and 2,000 spectators ready themselves on the sprawling courthouse lawn to see who is going to eat crow—Darrow or Bryan.

Although it is a brilliant ploy, calling Bryan to the stand is essentially the only means by which Darrow can topple the fundamentalist foundation upon which the Butler Act rests. Since Bryan is the spokesmen for the fundamentalist movement, and since he was instrumental in getting the antievolution law passed, there is no better witness to call, to question, to discredit.

Darrow starts off slowly, quietly. Bryan answers in the same tone and manner. Then:

Darrow: Do you claim that everything in the Bible should be literally interpreted?"

Bryan: I believe everything in the Bible should be accepted as it is given there . . .

Darrow [later in the questioning]: How long ago was the Flood, Mr. Bryan?

Bryan [after consulting a Bible]: It is given here as 2,348 years B.C.

Darrow [later in the questioning]: Don't you know that the ancient civilizations of China are 6,000 or 7,000 years old, at the very least?

Bryan: No; but they would not run back beyond the Creation, according to the Bible 6,000 years.

Darrow [soon after]: Have you any idea how old the Egyptian civilization is?

Bryan: No.

Darrow [later in the questioning]: Do you know how old the Confucian religion is?

Bryan: I can't give you an exact date on it.

Darrow: Do you know how old the religion of Zoroaster is?

Bryan: No, sir.

Darrow: Do you know they are both more ancient than the Christian religion?

Bryan: I am not willing to take the opinion of people who are trying to find excuses for rejecting the Christian religion . . .

Darrow [later in the questioning]: You never in all your life made any attempt to find out about the other peoples on the earth—how old their civilizations are, how long they had existed on the earth, have you?

Bryan: No, sir. I have been so well satisfied with the Christian religion that I have spent no time trying to find arguments against it.

Darrow: Were you afraid you might find some?

Bryan: No sir. I am not afraid now that you will show me any.... [Bryan seems to lose his temper at this point.] I have all the information I want to live by and to die by!

Darrow [shortly after]: You don't care how old the earth is, how old man is, and how long the animals have been here?

Bryan: I am not so much interested in that ...

Bryan [further into the questioning]: You read that Bible and ask me questions, and I will answer them. I will not answer your questions in your language.

Darrow: I will read it to you from the Bible. "And the Lord God said unto the serpent, Because thou hast done this [Tempted Eve], thou art cursed above all cattle, and above every beast of the field; upon thy belly shalt thou go and dust shalt thou eat all the days of thy life." Do you think that is why the serpent is compelled to crawl upon its belly?

Bryan: I believe that.

Darrow: Have you any idea how the snake went before that time?

Bryan: No, sir.

Darrow: Do you know whether he walked on his tail or not?

Bryan: No, sir. I have no way to know.

[Laughter in the audience.]

Darrow: Now, you refer to the cloud that was put in the heavens after the flood, the rainbow. Do you believe in that?

Bryan: Read it.

Darrow: All right, I will read it for you.

Bryan [to Judge Raulston]: Your Honor, I think I can shorten this testimony. The only purpose Mr. Darrow has is to slur at the Bible, but I will answer his question. I will answer it all at once, and I have no objection in the world, I want the world to know that this man, who does not believe in a God, is trying to use a court in Tennessee ...

Darrow: I object to that.

Bryan [his voice rising to hysterical pitch,[55] comes out of his seat]: ... to slur at it, and while it will require time, I am willing to take it.

Darrow [voice rising]: I object to your statement. I am examining you on your fool ideas that no intelligent Christian on earth believes!

[At this exchange, the crowd rises almost as one, and the voices of both men are drowned out.]

Judge Raulston [jumping to his feet, shouts]: Court is adjourned until 9 o'clock tomorrow morning!

Darrow and Bryan step back, perhaps both in shock over the sudden emotional wave that has washed over the courtroom.[56] Bryan slowly sits down, muttering: "Slurring the Bible . . . slurring the Bible. . . ."[57]

So ends Day 7. The confrontation everyone has so eagerly anticipated has finally taken place. The war will continue tomorrow, of course, but the battle is over. The Great Commoner has been dispatched, publicly and painfully. But as he quickly discovers, neither the public nor the media have any intention of letting his bones bleach in the sun.

As the uproar in the courtroom subsides, people crowd about Darrow. Fundamentalists, however, turn away from Bryan.[58] The crowd quietly disperses, and Bryan is left alone like a broken toy in the attic. Even Darrow, he admits later, feels empathy for him. "I was truly sorry for Mr. Bryan. But I consoled myself by thinking of the years through which he had busied himself tormenting intelligent professors with impudent questions about their faith, and seeking to arouse the ignoramuses and bigots to drive them out of their positions."[59]

Bryan has not achieved his lofty status without developing a bulldog mentality, however. Today is Darrow's. Tomorrow will be Bryan's when once again he takes the stand. But that never happens. In a heated exchange that night, Stewart, the lead counsel for the prosecution, adamantly refuses to allow Bryan to continue testifying or to call Darrow as a witness the next day.[60] Stewart wants no more outlandish exhibitions fueled by egos. No more one-on-one inquisitions. The carnival will be replaced by a straightforward, no-nonsense approach with Stewart quietly finishing what Bryan so confidently started. And the result of Darrow's relentless questioning and Stewart's decision? One journalist covering the trial, Paul Anderson, reported it in the simplest of terms: "Bryan was broken, if ever a man was broken. Darrow never spared him. It was masterly, but it was pitiful."[61]

Tuesday, July 21. Day 8: Secretly, town officials meet with Judge Raulston in an effort to prevent any violence. As the morning session begins, Raulston explains that since Bryan's testimony added nothing pertinent to the issue of the content of Scopes's teaching, the testimony will be expunged from the record. After a short exchange with the judge, Darrow, no doubt as impatient as everyone else to push the case to a higher court, asks Raulston to instruct the jury to find the defendant guilty. The defense, Darrow explains, has "no proof to offer on the issue that the Court has laid down here" and agrees that Scopes taught evolution. The state makes no objection which means Bryan, who has prepared a speech to put right what transpired the day before, has no opportunity to speak before the court. With Bryan effectively silenced, the jury is called and given its charge. Nine minutes later it returns. Scopes is found guilty. The jury, significantly, fixes no fine but Judge Raulston fines Scopes $100.

The Great Monkey Trial is over.

But the drama is not yet complete.

Five days later, William Jennings Bryan dies in his sleep.

The cause of death was officially apoplexy, although many believed it was the bitter defeat and humiliation of the trial. Scopes disagreed. He argued that Bryan was a diabetic, a prodigious eater (some pronounced it overeater), and that the excessive heat during the trial may have eroded his defense system.[62] Whatever the cause of death, Bryan's pretrial statement that it would be a "duel to the death" was all too prophetic.[63] And if such a thing is possible, Bryan's death was well timed. For many, his death was connected to the trial, and he would forever be a hero martyred in a holy cause.

Others felt less magnanimous. The iconoclastic Mencken wrote that Bryan's "last secular act on this globe of sin was to catch flies."[64] Although Darrow offered his regrets, after being asked if Bryan had died of a broken heart because of his questioning, the fiery lawyer replied: "Broken heart nothing; he died of a busted belly."[65]

Eleven months later the Tennessee Supreme Court ruled in *Tennessee vs. Scopes* that under the state constitution any fine of more than $50 must be levied by the jury. The judgment, therefore, was reversed, not on the constitutional issues the defense hoped for but on a technicality. Of course, the case could still be appealed to a federal court except for one minor point: upon the suggestion of the Tennessee Supreme Court, the attorney general entered a *nolle prosequi,* which meant the original indictment was dropped. Now there was nothing to appeal. The case, indeed, had finally ended.

Given its rather inauspicious ending, one is left to wonder exactly what the legacy of the Scopes trial was. For one thing, it probably marked the high point of the fundamentalist movement. Within two years of the trial, antievolution laws had been repealed in ten states that had them. The World's Christian Fundamentals Association never again had the impact that it wielded before and just after the trial.[66] As scientists, writers, and intellectuals mounted attacks against antievolution clatter, the fundamentalist movement began to fizzle.[67]

It would also be pleasant, although perhaps presumptuous, to think that a richer harmony between science and religion emerged from the residue of the trial. It is not unfair to say, however, that the contention that evolution was the methodology and God the ultimate scientist was furthered in the eyes of some observers. The roles of science and religion may have been clarified for those who saw one seeking truth through cause and effect, the other seeking purpose in the quest for Absolute Truth.

It would be unfair to say that the trial had a long-lasting effect on the concept of separation of church and state, particularly in light of a growing conservative movement that presently exists in the United States. It did, however, help immortalize Clarence Darrow and William Jennings Bryan, while the forgotten man, John Scopes, quietly entered graduate school and went on to live a happy and productive life.

And what of the press? Some felt the press had sensationalized the issues.[68] Other were not so sure. Edward Caudill writes that the media was unfair toward Bryan and the issues he laid forth because "the press indulged in its own kind of fundamentalism—faith in the newsgathering process . . .

by being devoted to the process, the press embraced scientific method."[69] Perhaps Michael Williams, writing for *The Commonweal* at the time of the trial, best expressed the role of the press:

The press has made this story. . . . And yet, the newspaper workers at the spot warmly disagree as to the "value" of the story. Some say there is little real public interest in the case. Others consider it the most significant and truly important assignment of their careers. . . . [M]illions upon millions of readers are supposedly following the columns and pages of stuff spread throughout the country by the press. Are the editors right or wrong in this matter? Has the famous news-sense deserted its high priests and adepts: Have these news experts fallen en masse for the skillful publicity work of the Civil Liberties league and of W. J. Bryan? Or is their instinct right? Is the Dayton trial the evidence of the coming of a vast religious issue in this country—a great struggle to be waged in the press, in the political area, and in the courts between Protestant fundamentalists and a most bizarre and incongruous aggregation of "liberal Protestants," "modernists," "scientists" (some of them genuinely deserving the title, and heaps of them mere dabblers and pretenders) and of free speech champions, agnostics, cranks, and "nuts"?[70]

The old warriors would have had an answer to that question.

Darrow: If there is a God, William, he's probably laughing.
Bryan: There is a God, Clarence, and He is.

NOTES

1. *The World's Most Famous Court Trial: State of Tennessee v. John Thomas Scopes [Complete Stenographic Report of the Court Test of the Tennessee Anti-Evolution Act at Dayton, July 19, 1925, Including Speeches and Arguments by Attorneys]*. (New York: Da Capo Press, 1971), 47.

2. L. Sprague de Camp, *The Great Monkey Trial* (Garden City, N.Y.: Doubleday & Company, 1968), 408.

3. For a comprehensive look at the life of William Jennings Bryan, see M. R. Werner, *Bryan* (New York: Harcourt, Brace and Company, 1929).

4. Charles Robert Darwin, *On the Origin of Species by Means of Natural Selection; or, The Preservation of Favoured Races in the Struggle for Life* (London: John Murray, 1859). For a comprehensive look at the debate over evolution and Creationism in schools, see Peter Zetterberg, ed., *Evolution versus Creationism: The Public Education Controversy* (Phoenix, Ariz.: Oryx Press, 1983).

5. A. A. Brill, ed., *The Basic Writings of Sigmund Freud* (New York: Random House, 1938). For brief account of the effects of Freud's writings, see Didier Anzieu, *Freud's Self-Analysis* (Madison, Conn.: International Universities Press, 1986), 579–585.

6. Leopold Infeld, *Albert Einstein: His Work and Its Influence on Our World* (New York: Scribner's, 1958), 112–130. See also Benesh Hoffman, *Albert Einstein,*

Creator and Rebel (New York: Viking Press, 1972).

7. Charles Y. Glock and Rodney Stark, *Religion and Society in Tension* (Chicago: Rand McNally and Company, 1965), 242.

8. H. Richard Niebuhr and Daniel D. Williams, *The Ministry in Historical Perspectives* (New York: Harper & Brothers, 1956), 255, 261–262.

9. Benjamin Parke DeWitte, *The Progressive Movement* (Seattle: University of Washington Press, 1915), 277–298. See also Michael H. Ebner and Eugene M. Tobin, eds., *The Age of Urban Reform: New Perspectives on the Progressive Era* (Port Washington, N.Y.: Kennikat Press, 1977) and William L. Riordon, *Plunkitt of Tammany Hall* (New York: E. P. Dutton, 1963), x–xxii. Introduction by Arthur Mann.

10. Thomas Kessner, *The Golden Door, Italian and Jewish Immigrant Mobility in New York City 1880–1915* (New York: Oxford University Press, 1977), 5.

11. Ibid., 5–6.

12. Lloyd Chiasson Jr., "The Japanese-American Enigma," in *The Press in Times of Crisis*, ed., Lloyd Chiasson Jr. (Westport, Conn.: Praeger, 1995), 140. See also Morton Grodzins, *Americans Betrayed* (Chicago: The University of Chicago Press, 1949), and Bill Hosokawa, *Thirty-five Years in the Frying Pan* (San Francisco, Calif.: McGraw-Hill, 1978.

13. As Grodzins points out in *Americans Betrayed*, assimilation was almost impossible for the Orientals on the West Coast, and they even "retained their Old World subdivisions" which lasted for twenty to thirty years. Kessner writes in *The Golden Door* that the Italian and Jews in New York created their own closeknit communities.

14. The growth and political success of the Socialist Party, the anticapitalism novels such as *The Iron Heel* by Jack London and *Looking Backward* by Edward Bellamy, and the emergence of the Industrial Workers of the World, more commonly known as the Wobblies, highlight the growing socialist trend in the United States during this tumultuous period. For example, Patrick Renshaw points out in *The Wobblies, the Story of Syndicalism in the United States,* that the Wobblies' goal was to unite the working class of the world into one gigantic labor union.

15. William J. Berg and Laurey K. Martin, *Emile Zola Revisited* (New York: Twayne Publishers, 1992), 5–6, 9–13. See also *The Conflict of Naturalism and Humanism* (New York: Teachers College, Columbia University, 1910), 3.

16. Chiasson, *The Press in Times of Crisis*, 221–222.

17. Ray Ginger, *Six Days or Forever* (Boston: Beacon Press, 1958), 191. See also John Thomas Scopes and James Presley, *Center of the Storm* (New York: Holt, Rinehart and Winston), 95–96.

18. Clarence Darrow, *The Story of My Life* (New York: Scribner's, 1932), 249.

19. Sheldon Norman Grebstein, ed., *Monkey Trial* (Boston: Houghton Mifflin Company, 1960), ix.

20. Ginger, *Six Days or Forever?*, 4.

21. Ibid. For an in-depth look at William Jennings Bryan's similar position regarding the marriage of government and Christianity, see Bryan, *In His Image* (London: Fleming H. Revell, 1922),194–247.

22. Allen H. Sager, "Modernists and Fundamentalists Debate Restraints on Freedom," in *America in Controversy*, ed. DeWitte Holland (Dubuque, Iowa: William C. Brown, 1973), 296.

23. Lawrence W. Levine, *Defender of the Faith, William Jennings Bryan: The Last Decade, 1915–1925* (New York: Oxford University Press, 1965), 330. See also de Camp, *The Great Monkey Trial*, 30.

24. Levine, *Defender of the Faith, William Jennings Bryan: The Last Decade, 1915–1925*, 278–281. See Bryan, *In His Image* , 194–247, and de Camp, *The Great Monkey Trial*, 41.

25. Jerry R. Tompkins, ed., *D-Days at Dayton, Reflections on the Scopes Trial* (Baton Rouge: Louisiana State University Press, 1965), vi–vii.

26. Ginger, *Six Days or Forever?*, 18–20. See also Scopes and Presley, *Center of the Storm*, 56–59, and de Camp, *The Great Monkey Trial*, 5–8.

27. Scopes and Presley, *Center of the Storm*, 60.

28. Although Scopes and de Camp differ over the newspaper, their versions of the conversation are identical.

29. Scopes and Presley, *Center of the Storm*, 60. See also de Camp, *The Great Monkey Trial*, 13.

30. Ibid.

31. Ibid.

32. Ginger, *Six Days or Forever?*, 20.

33. Scopes and Presley, *Center of the Storm*, 66.

34. Ibid., 66–67.

35. Ibid., 67.

36. Ibid., 69–70.

37. Darrow's position on man and evolution are revealed in considerable depth by James Edward Sayer in *Clarence Darrow: Public Advocate* (Dayton, Ohio: Monography Series No. 2, Wright State University, 1978), 3, 63–74. Regarding the Leopold and Loeb trial, see Richard J. Jensen, *Clarence Darrow: The Creation of an American Myth* (New York: Greenwood Press, 1992), 21.

38. T. Harry Williams, Richard Current, and Frank Freidel, *History of the United States Since 1865*, 3rd ed. (New York: Alfred A. Knopf, 1969), 224.

39. Ibid., 227. See also Werner, *Bryan*, 56.

40. de Camp, *The Great Monkey Trial*, 37.

41. Ibid. In *Theodore Roosevelt, A Biography*, Henry F. Pringle also quotes Roosevelt on Bryan: "a kindly, well-meaning soul, but . . . cheap and shallow."

42. de Camp, *The Great Monkey Trial*, 38.

43. Scopes and Presley, *Center of the Storm*, 77.

44. Ibid., 99.

45. Ibid., 100

46. Ibid., 98.

47. Ibid., 84, 98.

48. Ibid.

49. See generally John Scopes, "Denouement at Dayton," in *William Jennings Bryan, A Profile*, ed. Paul W. Glad (New York: Hill and Wang, 1968).

50. *The World's Most Famous Trial*, 47. See also de Camp, *The Great Monkey Trial*, p. 240.

51. *The World's Most Famous Court Trial*, 74–87. See also de Camp, *The Great Monkey Trial*, 240.

52. de Camp, *The Great Monkey Trial*, 266–268.

53. Ibid., 285–286.

54. As cited in de Camp, *The Great Monkey Trial*, 343, from an interview with John Scopes on 17 March 1966. See also Scopes and Presley, *The Center of the Storm*, 155.

55. de Camp, *The Great Monkey Trial*, 409.

56. Ibid., 410.

57. Ibid.

58. Scopes and Presley, *Center of the Storm*, 183. See also de Camp, *The Great Monkey Trial*, 410.

59. Darrow, *The Story of My Life*, 267.

60. Although de Camp in *The Great Monkey Trial* and Ginger in *Six Days or Forever?* differ slightly on the discussion that took place that night, there is no disagreement that Stewart felt Bryan had become a hindrance to the case and that any further exchanges with Darrow would be nonproductive.

61. As cited in de Camp, *The Great Monkey Trial*, 413.

62. Scopes and Presley, *Center of the Storm*, 197–199.

63. Jensen, *Clarence Darrow: The Creation of an American Myth*, 88.

64. As cited in Ginger, *Six Days or Forever?*, 193.

65. de Camp, The *Great Monkey Trial*, 440.

66. Ginger, *Six Days or Forever?*, 213.

67. de Camp, The *Great Monkey Trial*, 477.

68. Tompkins, *D-Days at Dayton*, 14.

69. See Edward Caudill, "The Roots of Bias: An Empiricist Press and Coverage of the Scopes Trial," *Journalism Monographs* 114 (July 1989), 15, 33. Caudill writes that the press was not "exploitive" but that it simply preferred one set of facts—those that were scientific and technological—to another set of facts that were more abstract—spirituality and religious dogma.

70. Michael Williams, *The Commonweal*, 22 July 1925, 262, as cited in Tompkins, *D-Days at Dayton*, 200–201.

9

The Case of the Scottsboro Boys
(1931)

"Bigots whose mouths are slits in their faces"

Michael Maher

As it chugged through the pleasant rural hamlets of northern Alabama in March 1931, a Memphis-bound freight carried among its cargo nine young black hoboes. To anyone on the train it would have seemed unlikely that this backwater setting, this slack time, and these impoverished players would soon provide a legal drama that would cause marches on the White House and riots in Dresden, Havana, and Geneva. Who among the hoboes could have known that their plight would eventually inspire a visit from poet Langston Hughes and letters from Albert Einstein, Thomas Mann, President Franklin Roosevelt, and thousands of others across the world?[1]

But as the train pulled into Paint Rock, Alabama, the hoboes found themselves surrounded by an armed posse that had formed to capture them. Earlier in the day the black hoboes had fought with a group of white hoboes and had thrown the whites off the train. The losers had gone to the police, claiming the blacks had started the fight.[2] The Jackson County Sheriff had telephoned Paint Rock and given word to deputize everyone who had a gun and to capture all the Negroes on the train.

The posse did so and bound the blacks together with a length of plow line. They were told they would be charged with assault and attempted murder.[3] But the posse had rounded up some unexpected train occupants: two young white women dressed in coveralls, looking almost like men. After delaying twenty minutes while the sheriff tied the Negroes and loaded them into an open truck, one of the girls told the sheriff she and her friend had been raped by the blacks.

That accusation changed the whole complexion of the day. In those parts, lynching had been considered fitting remedy for black men who raped white women, as it spared the women the painful ordeal of a trial. The incidence of lynching in the South had declined from the outset of the twentieth century from more than 100 a year to less than a dozen per year.

But during the Depression the lynchings increased.[4]

The nine young hoboes were taken to Scottsboro, the county seat, for eventual trial. Thenceforth they would be bound by more than a plow rope. Andrew "Andy" Wright, Leroy "Roy" Wright, Haywood Patterson, Olen Montgomery, Ozie Powell, Clarence Norris, Willie Roberson, Eugene Williams, and Charlie Weems were bound by a common fate as the Scottsboro boys.

This story of the rape soon spread around the county. By late afternoon a large, angry crowd gathered around the Scottsboro jail. The sheriff, fearing a lynching, decided to move the prisoners to another jail that evening. When the crowd cut the wires of the deputies' three cars, the sheriff woke the governor to request help. By 11 p.m. the National Guard was on its way to establish a perimeter around the Scottsboro jail. But by the time they arrived the crowd had dissipated of its own accord.[5] As the *Birmingham News* reported, the girls were not from Jackson County, hence no relatives were among the crowd to demand immediate retribution. The court would decide the fate of the Scottsboro boys.

Jackson County's population of 37,000 was served by two weekly newspapers, the *Progressive Age* and the *Jackson County Sentinel*. The *Progressive Age* reported that "details of the crime coming from the lips of the two girls, Victoria Price and Ruby Bates, are too revolting to be printed." But the *Sentinel* was more explicit, describing how the black "fiends" held the girls while others raped them. Both papers reported that the girls had been physically injured by the defendants—which was later contradicted by the examining physician. In subsequent coverage further false details emerged.

The press reported that most of the defendants had admitted their guilt, but in fact before the trial only one of the Scottsboro boys, Roy Wright, had accused five of the others while maintaining the innocence of himself, his brother Andy, and two friends from Chattanooga. Of these four the *Chattanooga Times* reported they were known to police as the "worst young Negroes in Chattanooga," but none had police records. Before the trial began the *Sentinel* concluded that "the evidence against the negroes is so conclusive as to be almost perfect."

The *New York Times* misreported that the National Guard had prevented a mass lynching at the jail the night of the arrest. But with local indignation boiling from news reports, the guard was necessary to maintain order when the trials began April 6. A crowd estimated by the *Progressive Age* at 7,000 to 10,000 gathered in Scottsboro. The National Guard established a 100-foot perimeter around the courthouse, bolstered by four machine guns at the doors. But by that time the trial was superfluous. As one historian noted, "A fair trial under the circumstances was impossible. The nine Negro boys had already been tried, found guilty, and sentenced to death by the news media."[6]

The Scottsboro boys were represented by Stephen Roddy, a Chattanooga lawyer paid by black civic and church leaders. Roddy, who had been jailed the year before for public drunkenness, showed up at the courthouse at 9 a.m., drunk.[7] He told the judge he was not there as employed counsel, but merely as adviser. He admitted he was not prepared for the trial and was unfamiliar with Alabama law. Only when the judge demanded that someone formally serve as counsel did Milo Moody, a sixty-nine-year-old local attorney, step forward for the defendants. As the trial began, these two attorneys had done no preparation and had talked to the defendants only briefly. The county solicitor said he would demand the death penalty.

Clarence Norris and Charlie Weems were tried first. Weems said that he had never seen the two girls on the train, but Norris implicated all the other defendants, while maintaining his own innocence.[8] In his autobiography, *The Last of the Scottsboro Boys*, Norris omits any mention of this testimony. Subsequent testimony established that Norris was carrying Victoria Price's knife when arrested.

Haywood Patterson was tried individually, and he told the same tale that Roy Wright had told the press earlier: He and his three friends from Chattanooga were innocent, but he had seen the other five defendants rape the two women. He later contradicted himself and denied even seeing the women on the train. He also denied participating in a fight.[9]

In his autobiography, *Scottsboro boy*, Patterson recreates the courtroom scene, omitting any mention of his implicating the other defendants. He admits participating in the fight, but denies seeing any females on the train.[10] Roy Wright testified in Patterson's defense and told the jury that he and the others from Chattanooga were innocent, but he had seen nine other blacks rape the two white women (the number of rapists varied from testimony to testimony). The other two from Chattanooga, Andy Wright and Eugene Williams, denied seeing any rape at all.

Five of the remaining Scottsboro boys were tried simultaneously: Olen Montgomery, Ozie Powell, Willie Roberson, Eugene Williams, and Andy Wright. The ninth, Roy Wright, was tried separately because of his youth.[11] The state sought only life imprisonment.

The trials concluded within four days with convictions and the death penalty for all defendants except Roy Wright. In the latter's trial, Alabama law required that he be tried as a juvenile but the prosecutor wanted swift resolution of the case, so he agreed to seek a sentence of life imprisonment. Nevertheless, seven jurors insisted on the death sentence, which led to a mistrial.

As the trials concluded, the Alabama press was full of praise for the triumph of due process and swift justice.

The Jackson County Sentinel: The defendants received "as fair a trial as they could have gotten in any court in the world."

The Progressive Age: "The people of Jackson County have shown to the world that they believe in Justice, regardless of the color. They proved they were in favor of the law taking its course and giving the defendants a fair trial. Able counsel was provided for them and everything done to see that they received an impartial trial. Our courts have shown the world that they believe in swift and undelayed justice being meted out."

The Huntsville Daily Times: "Personally we believe that each of the Negroes was given a fair and impartial trial, that each had been given his day in court and was given every protection afforded any defendant."

The Birmingham Age-Herald: The people of the United States can be assured that "no reasonable fault can be found with the fairness or the legality of the trials at Scottsboro."

But Alabamans soon discovered that few others shared their local editors' congratulations. The number of defendants and their youth (the oldest was twenty), the near-lynching following the arrest, the lack of adequate counsel, the rapidity of the trials, the angry courthouse crowds, and the severity of the sentences all received wide coverage and appalled many people.

Despite their death sentences, the Scottsboro boys' stories were far from over.

Even before the trials ended, the American Communist Party was declaiming against Scottsboro. The communist house organ, the *New York Daily Worker*, headlined its April 7 story, "9 Negro Workers Face Lynch Mob in Ala. as Trial Opens on Horse Swapping, Fair Day." Its subhead: "Bosses Plan Mass Lynching to Strike Terror at Rising Temper of Masses; Must Answer On May First."

In communist framing, the Scottsboro boys were class-conscious revolutionary workers who were being executed for political reasons. The *Daily Worker* concluded its early coverage of Scottsboro: "This slaughter of Negro young workers is being conducted at the instigation of two notorious white prostitutes who are evidently advertising themselves by claiming that they were raped by the Negroes."

The International Labor Defense (ILD), the legal arm of the party, telegrammed trial Judge A. E. Hawkins, calling the trials a legal lynching and demanding an immediate change of venue, new trials, and dismissal of the defense lawyers. "We hold you responsible for lives of nine workers," the ILD telegram concluded. The *Progressive Age* ran the ILD telegram as a sidebar to its April 9 story on the sentencing.

Involvement by the communists caused the Alabama editors to dig their heels even deeper in defending local justice. "In Alabama the ravishing of women carries with it upon conviction of same the death penalty," wrote the *Huntsville Times*. "And now because the guilty parties at the Scottsboro trial happen to be Negroes, the International Labor Defense has taken upon itself to meddle and to issue threatening telegrams to Judge J. A. Hawkins." The *Times* editorial concluded: "We admire the Judge for his courage and for the expeditions [*sic*] and fair manner in which he proceeded to the trial of these culprits."

Similarly, the *Progressive Age* noted the nationwide interest in the trial and offered that the people of Jackson County would welcome and assist anyone who wished to investigate the fairness of the trial.

So we have nothing but that will bear the closest scrutiny. While we welcome an investigation, we do not relish some of the apparent threats of RED organizations who do not believe in law and order. They serve only one purpose and that is to arouse the fighting spirit of the people and in the end can accomplish no good.

The communists saw the opportunity to win public opinion and many black recruits by positioning themselves as the defenders of the Scottsboro boys. They saw Scottsboro as a gold mine of agitprop, but they wanted all this gold for themselves. Therefore they did everything possible to discredit the National Association for the Advancement of Colored People, which also sought to support the boys in their appeal. The communists portrayed the NAACP as "lickspittles of the capitalist class."

The communists were particularly eager to vilify Negro organizations and black news media, thereby portraying communism as the only friend of the Scottsboro boys. Shortly after the 1931 sentencing the *Daily Worker* headlined a story about black newspapers: "Murderous Frame-up and Death Sentences Ignored By Negro World and Chicago Whip, Soft-Pedalled By the Amsterdam *News*, Pittsburgh *Courier*, Others." On April 15 the *Daily Worker* showed clippings from these papers and began the story, "Concrete Proof of Treacherous Cooperation of Negro Reformists and their Press with Southern Boss Lynchers."

After criticizing the content of black press coverage of Scottsboro, the *Worker* continued:

Also, while scores of working-class organizations and workers' mass meetings are thundering their protests against this ghastly, murderous frame-up, there has been not one word of protest from the National Association for the Advancement of Colored People, the Universal Negro Improvement Association, the Urban League or any of the hundreds of organizations controlled by the Negro reformists who thus as frequently in the past, again expose themselves as traitors to the Negro masses and betrayers of the Negro liberation struggle.

A later story in the *Daily Worker* on April 21 began:

Undeterred by the trechcerous (*sic*) co-operation of the Negro reformists with the southern boss lynchers, the Negro masses are eagerly rallying in a fighting alliance with the white workers to the defense of the nine innocent colored youngsters being railroaded to the electric chair by the southern landlords and capitalists.

When the ILD was grappling with the NAACP over the right to represent the Scottsboro boys' court appeals, the *Worker* quoted Haywood Patterson's father, who in a letter to his son wrote: "You will burn sure if you don't let them preachers alone and trust the International Labor Defense to handle the case."

Despite its strident, hackneyed rhetoric, the communists' defense of the Scottsboro boys resonated with many Americans. The communists organized Scottsboro protest rallies across the country, and these rallies attracted many thousands. They sent the defendants' mothers on road tours across the United States, where the women spoke in hundreds of cities. The communists also organized protests internationally. In the name of the Scottsboro boys, demonstrators smashed U.S. embassy windows in Dresden, Berlin, Leipzig, Geneva, and Havana. The communists sent Roy and Andy Wright's mother to Europe, where she virtually ignored the plight of her sons and delivered standard propaganda about mobilizing the masses and defending the Soviet Union.[12]

The communists also organized letter-writing campaigns. Alabama officials received thousands of letters protesting the Scottsboro decision. Albert Einstein was among the petitioners, as was H. G. Wells, Thomas Mann, Theodore Dreiser, Lincoln Stephens, Upton Sinclair, Sherwood Anderson, and John Dos Passos.[13] Maxim Gorky wrote about the Scottsboro boys in *Pravda*. Langston Hughes visited them in Kilby Prison and read them poetry. Most of the Scottsboro boys ignored him.

Despite the high visibility the communists won for the Scottsboro case, they made few black converts. About 1,300 blacks joined the party during 1931, the peak year for Scottsboro activism. Most lived in the North and most did not remain members long.[14] The communists' attempts to organize Alabama blacks met with even thinner results. Party organizers attempted to form a sharecroppers' union near Camp Hill, but the effort met with disaster when a black man fired on the local sheriff who was investigating the communist activity. The negro was killed and sixty prospective union members were arrested in a highly publicized series of incidents.

Community panic about a communist-inspired black uprising was fanned by the *Birmingham Age-Herald*, which reported that eight carloads of communist blacks from Chattanooga were on their way to Camp Hill to aid the "uprising." This published rumor proved unfounded, but not before defenders mistook a black funeral procession for a convoy of communist insurrection. The communists may not have succeeded in winning converts in Alabama, but they did win the right to defend the Scottsboro boys in legal appeals.

Attorneys for both the NAACP and the ILD showed up in June 1931 to appeal the convictions. The two groups began a tug of war for the boys' allegiance. For a while the Scottsboro boys changed sides regularly, as if they were star athletes vacillating between scholarship offers. NAACP officials charged that the communists would use the Scottsboro boys for purely political reasons—reasons that might be better served by allowing the appeals to fail and the boys to be executed. But eventually the communists outmaneuvered the NAACP by aggressively courting the mothers of the defendants. The communists gave the Scottsboro boys' families, and the boys themselves, monthly stipends. But most important, communist rallies and publicity kept the boys in the public eye.

With celebrity status the defendants' lives actually improved, as they received gifts, cash, and encouragement from many strangers. In his autobiography Clarence Norris recalls the irony of the situation: "We had the death sentence over our heads, but we were eating and dressing better than a lot of men on the outside, including our guards. Good people all over the world were making our lives a lot easier. The letters and money was still coming in from everywhere."[15]

Haywood Patterson was similarly cheered by knowing that he had the support of world opinion:

Talk of our case was heavy all through the world. I heard of a big protest somewhere in Germany; two German trade union men, they lost their lives in it. . . . More big shots all over the world, they put in their names for us, said to let us go: Madame Sun Yat-sen, Romain Rolland, Maxim Gorky. This hollering about us all over the map kept getting me new trials.[16]

The International Labor Defense appealed the Scottsboro boys' convictions to the Alabama Supreme Court. ILD lawyers based their appeal on the lack of adequate counsel, the defendants' inability to win a fair trial amid the hordes of spectators who were hungry for conviction, and the exclusion of blacks from Alabama juries. But in March 1932 the state Supreme Court upheld the convictions, although it allowed Eugene Williams a new trial because he had been a juvenile at the time of his trial.

At this point the Alabama press first began to consider, rather than reject, the glare of world opinion. The *Montgomery Advertiser* endorsed the state Supreme Court's decision, but two Birmingham papers, the *Age-Herald* and the *Post*, allowed that another trial might have allayed the outside world's doubts about the fairness of the Scottsboro trials.

The ILD then took its appeal to the Supreme Court of the United States. Here the issue was constitutional: Upon what grounds in this case could the federal court overturn a state court's decision? Eventually the argument that the Scottsboro boys had been given inadequate counsel, which violated their Fourteenth Amendment right to due process, won the day for the Scottsboro boys. On November 7, 1932, the Supreme Court reversed the Scottsboro boys' conviction and remanded their cases back to the lower court. This was the first time in the country's history that the Supreme Court set aside a state court's criminal conviction. The Scottsboro boys' case, *Powell v. Alabama*, was far from finished making headlines, however.[17]

The new trial was set for March 27, 1933. The site was also moved about fifty miles west of Scottsboro. Playing host to the most attended trial in the country was the rural Alabama community of Decatur.

This time the Scottsboro boys had better counsel. The ILD had agreed with prominent New York criminal attorney Samuel Leibowitz that Leibowitz would represent the Scottsboro boys pro bono, if the communists would downplay their political agitation. Neither side trusted the other, but both had something to gain by the symbiosis.

Haywood Patterson was tried first. Leibowitz began his defense by establishing during jury selection that blacks had been excluded from juries in the region for as long as anyone could remember. One witness who attested to this was Scottsboro resident James Benson, the editor of *Progressive Age*, who explained that blacks had been omitted from juries because no Negro in the county had the required sound judgment and "they will nearly all steal."[18]

Leibowitz cross-examined Victoria Price, showing that her past was tarnished with a conviction for fornication and adultery less than two months before the Scottsboro incident. Leibowitz succeeded in discrediting Victoria Price as unreliable, but his harsh handling of a southern woman may have done more harm than good with the jury.

However, he was able to establish that the physician who examined Victoria Price had found little semen in her, after she had allegedly been raped by at least six men. What sperm cells the doctor had found had been nonmotile, that is, dead. Sperm cells normally live from twelve to forty-eight hours inside the vagina, and the doctor had examined Price within two hours after the alleged rape.

Calling some of the Scottsboro boys as witnesses, Leibowitz established that, at the time of the alleged rape, Willie Roberson was too crippled by syphilis to walk without a cane, and that Olen Montgomery was completely blind in one eye and virtually blind in the other.

Another witness, the train's fireman, said he had seen Negroes emerge from many different points on the train when the posse stopped it at Paint Rock. He also said he had seen the two girls initially try to evade the posse. The defense's star witness, however, caused an audible gasp when she entered the crowded courtroom: Ruby Bates. She had gone over to the side of the defense. She recanted her Scottsboro testimony, saying that in the earlier trial she had merely said what Victoria had told her to say. She said there had been no rape, and she gave the names of two white men that she and Victoria had slept with the night preceding the alleged rape. But Bates withered under cross-examination from the prosecutor. He was able to establish that her fashionable hat and dress had been provided by wealthy New Yorkers who were interested in saving the Scottsboro boys. Further, by recanting her earlier testimony she identified herself as an unreliable witness.

The jury convicted Haywood Patterson and sentenced him to death in the electric chair.

Leibowitz returned for a time to New York, where he told a *Herald Tribune* reporter that the verdict came from "bigots whose mouths are slits in their faces, whose eyes pop out like a frog's, whose chins drip tobacco juice, bewhiskered and filthy." This endeared him little to Alabama editorial writers, who responded in kind to defend their community. Tensions were so high that presiding Judge James Horton postponed the remaining trials. In the meantime the NAACP lost no opportunity to chide the ILD for having failed to defend Haywood Patterson successfully.

The conviction gave the ILD fodder for more public agitation. The group organized a march on Washington. Ruby Bates showed up at the White House arm-in-arm with some of the Scottsboro boys' mothers and their communist sponsors. She told crowds that she had been pressured by the ruling class of white people to tell the false story of rape. Incensed by Bates's selling out to the communists, a *Huntsville Times* editorial called on the Alabama attorney general to charge her with perjury.

When the Scottsboro cases resumed in June 1933, ILD lawyers sought a motion for a new trial. Judge Horton, who had presided over the Patterson trial, opened with a long analysis of the evidence presented in that trial and of the credibility of Victoria Price. He concluded that the evidence did not support a conviction. He overturned the judgment of the jury and granted Haywood Patterson a third trial.

Only the *Birmingham Post* supported Horton's decision. Other editors from across the state dismissed him as having caved in to outside agitators. Horton hoped that dismissing the Patterson conviction would end the Scottsboro cases altogether, but Alabama attorney general Thomas Knight announced he would retry Haywood Patterson as soon as possible. Horton was defeated when he sought reelection the following year.

Judge William Callahan presided over the remaining trials. He made no secret of his contempt for the defendants and their attorneys. He denied the defense motion for a change of venue and overruled a defense motion to quash the Morgan County (i.e., Decatur) venire on the grounds that Negroes had been systematically excluded from juries in the county. Callahan also overlooked evidence that Negro names had been fraudulently added to past jury lists, to give the appearance that blacks had been considered for jury duty. Despite a handwriting expert's testimony that the names had been added post hoc, Callahan said that investigating such fraud would reflect badly on the jury board.

Callahan hurried the defense in jury selection and did not allow Leibowitz to question Victoria Price's character or ask about her activities prior to boarding the train. As the *New York Times* reported, after repeatedly cutting off Leibowitz's questioning, Callahan told the defense attorney, "the more I shut you off the better shape you're in." Callahan would at times offer more objections to Leibowitz's questioning that did the prosecution. After summation by prosecution and defense, Judge Callahan attacked the defense arguments and concluded by instructing the jury only in how they might pronounce the defendant guilty. He gave no instructions for rendering acquittal. Only prompting by Leibowitz forced Callahan to tell the jury how they might reach a "not guilty" verdict.

The jury found Patterson guilty. As Patterson recollected, "When Callahan sentenced me to death for the third time, I noticed he left out the Lord. He didn't even want the Lord to have any mercy on me."[19] Clarence

Norris was also tried and convicted. Leibowitz asked that the remaining trials be postponed, and Callahan agreed. The ILD appealed the Patterson and Norris convictions, but the Alabama Supreme Court again refused to set aside the lower court's verdicts.

In the interim between trials, the communists were caught trying to bribe Victoria Price. An ILD agent had approached her to discuss a price for recanting her earlier testimony. She acted interested, but went to the police. They told her to play along. Eventually two ILD agents were caught with a $1,500 bribe intended for Price. Leibowitz was furious and announced he would resign from the case unless the communists removed themselves entirely from the defense.

The ILD countered that they were firing Leibowitz. But Leibowitz engaged several black ministers to obtain affidavits from the Scottsboro boys indicating that Leibowitz, and not the ILD, was their legal counsel. The ILD relented publicly, but privately struck back by pressuring the Scottsboro mothers. Haywood Patterson and Clarence Norris signed an affidavit in favor of being represented by the ILD. Leibowitz struck back by approaching the defendants again, again getting them to change their counsel back to Leibowitz. But later the Scottsboro mothers came out in favor of the ILD. Eventually Leibowitz and the ILD compromised. Leibowitz would represent Clarence Norris, and the ILD would represent Haywood Patterson. They had work ahead of them, for again the Supreme Court of the United States had agreed to review their clients' cases. After Leibowitz's arguments, the justices ruled that Alabama had acted unconstitutionally in systematically excluding blacks from juries and that local officials had forged the jury rolls to hide this fact. Norris's conviction was reversed and his case remanded back to Alabama. Because of a legal technicality over the date of filing his appeal, the U.S. Supreme Court sent the Patterson case back to the Alabama Supreme Court without actually overturning the verdict.

The *New York Times* editorialized in favor of the Supreme Court decision and asked that Alabama's new governor, Bibb Graves, consider a pardon. Graves did encourage all Alabama circuit judges to ensure that black citizens were accepted on future juries. But no Alabama paper supported the Supreme Court's decision. The *Montgomery Advertiser* pointed to the absence of blacks on many levels of state and federal courts and questioned why the Supreme Court had not invalidated rulings from those courts.

Because the communists had discredited themselves with their attempted bribery, and because Leibowitz had alienated many Alabamans with his statements to the northern press, supporters of the Scottsboro boys formed a Scottsboro Defense Committee in December 1935. The SDC would be the umbrella organization for legally representing the boys. They enlisted Alabama attorney Clarence Watts to handle arguments for the new series of trials that resulted from the Supreme Court ruling. Presiding was Judge William Callahan.

Haywood Patterson's fourth trial, and Victoria Price's eighth, began

January 21, 1936. It was virtually a replay of the earlier trial, with Callahan showing his contempt for the defense and instructing the jury at great length on how to find the defendant guilty. And they did. But to everyone's great surprise, the jury fixed the penalty at seventy-five years in prison, not death.

At a time when Alabamans' attitudes toward the Scottsboro boys seemed to be softening, one of the boys, Ozie Powell, slashed the throat of an Alabama deputy who was transporting him back to jail during a court recess. The deputy recovered, but Powell was shot through the head by another deputy and suffered permanent brain damage, although he lived.

In a written statement to the press, Governor Graves applauded the highway patrol for handling the situation "in an efficient manner." Alabama newspapers commended the police for exercising restraint. But once again Alabamans discovered that the outside world saw the situation differently. The *New York Times* pointed out that Powell was manacled to another prisoner and was sitting in the rear of a car at the time he was shot. The *Times* questioned whether a bullet through the brain was the only way Alabama officials could have dealt with a handcuffed man.

Once again the Scottsboro boys attracted nationwide opprobrium to Alabama. Scores of telegrams protesting Alabama's handling of the Scottsboro boys poured into state officials' offices, as they had many times before. Perhaps to rid themselves of this continuing controversy, Alabama officials began in mid-1936 to discuss compromise with the Scottsboro Defense Committee.

Both sides advanced various proposals: Charges would be dropped for some if others would plead guilty. After offers and counteroffers, the SDC agreed to a compromise, just as Alabama officials retracted the offer and began the third trial of Clarence Norris. He was convicted and sentenced to death in July 1937. But as Andy Wright's trial was beginning, the prosecution said it would not seek the death sentence. He got ninety-nine years. Weems was also convicted and sentenced to a long jail term. Ozie Powell was not tried for rape, only for assaulting an officer. He pleaded guilty and got twenty years. But the state freed the four remaining defendants: nearly blind Olen Montgomery, syphilitic Willie Roberson, and Leroy Wright and Eugene Williams because of their youth at the time of the crime. They had been imprisoned six and a half years. They were freed on the condition that they never return to Alabama again.

The Scottsboro Defense Committee tried to get the Supreme Court of the United States to review the other convictions. But in October 1937 the court declined to review Patterson's conviction. The SDC knew it had no better grounds for appealing any of the other convictions, so it sought clemency from Governor Graves.

The Alabama Supreme Court upheld all the lower court's convictions in June 1938, but Governor Graves commuted Clarence Norris's death sentence to life imprisonment. He seemed on the verge of releasing the remaining prisoners. But the governor's support for the remaining boys was little enhanced when, in a personal meeting about clemency, Clarence Norris told Graves he wanted to kill Haywood Patterson, and Patterson, later the same day, tried to enter the governor's office with a homemade knife hidden in his pants. Despite receiving a personal note encouraging clemency from his friend President Franklin Roosevelt, Graves decided against releasing the remaining Scottsboro boys. In part he feared the political damage that would result.[20]

Finally in November 1943 Weems was released, and in January 1944 Norris and Wright were paroled on the condition they would not leave the state. They left the state. They returned to seek a pardon, but were imprisoned again. Norris was released again in late 1946, along with Powell. Haywood Patterson was never paroled or pardoned, but he escaped from a work crew in 1948 and made his way to Michigan. When he was arrested two years later, the Michigan governor refused to extradite him to Alabama. The final Scottsboro defendant to leave prison was Andy Wright, who was pardoned in 1950.

Having gained freedom, many of the Scottsboro boys had additional brushes with the law. Andy Wright was accused of raping a thirteen-year-old; Olen Montgomery drifted in and out of jail for public drunkenness; Roy Wright killed his wife upon catching her with another man, then killed himself; Haywood Patterson killed a man in a fight and was convicted of manslaughter and sent back to prison.[21] Clarence Norris was arrested several times for possessing an illegal gun; he also stabbed his girlfriend in the throat, but she refused to press charges.[22] The others simply returned to obscurity.

The plot for the "Scottsboro Boys" could have come from Kafka: the unwitting defendants arrested and accused of a crime they probably did not commit; tried and retried, convicted and reconvicted on evidence that appears ever more vaporous, languishing for years on death row while pressure groups and legal bureaucracy machinated to get them out of prison or keep them in. Although they eventually trickled to freedom through parole or escape or legal maneuvering, the Scottsboro boys never established their innocence. Even this lack of closure is Kafkaesque: Only Clarence Norris ever received official pardon, forty-five years after his alleged crime.

As does any drama that captures the public imagination, the Scottsboro trials tell us much about the historical forces that propelled the issue to prominence. These poor black hoboes became internationally known by serving as pawns in a sordid struggle between Alabama apartheid and American communism.

Alabamans in the 1930s seem to have perceived blacks as semihuman: naturally prone to bestial behavior; incapable of the judgment needed for jury service; barely worthy of trial but when brought to trial, undeserving of competent counsel, and guilty until proven innocent. At the time of the boys' trials, the Alabama press viewed not lynching them as a major breakthrough in human relations.

While the Scottsboro boys were on trial for rape, Alabama apartheid was on trial in the court of public opinion. But the chief prosecutor in the latter court was the Communist Party. The communists knew they could get plenty of mileage from serving as the boys' champions. And for a while, they did. On May Day 1931, about 300,000 Americans in 110 cities participated in communist-sponsored demonstrations on the Scottsboro boys' behalf. In Germany the following year, 150,000 attended a rally to hear Roy and Andy Wright's mother.[23]

The Scottsboro era could be regarded as a high-water mark of American communism. Emboldened by the apparent depression-era failure of capitalism, the communists seemed eager to find other issues from which to foment revolution. Racism was such an issue, and their vigorous assault on racism found favor with many Americans.

But the communists failed to consolidate much ground from the Scottsboro cases. Their attacks on the NAACP and their antireligious rhetoric alienated many blacks. Few were fooled by the communists' cynical manipulation of the Scottsboro boys and their mothers. Their strident rhetoric, their disregard for the truth, their bribes and attempted bribes of Ruby Bates and Victoria Price, did little for the communist cause. Indeed, the connection to communism may have done the Scottsboro boys as much harm as good, for the Alabama juries had less use for communists than they did for black people.

The Scottsboro boys were hardly saints, but they were martyrs of a sort. Their struggle provided the news pegs from which world opinion could focus on racism in the South. Without that pressure, change would have come much slower. In a strictly legal sense the Scottsboro cases are credited with expanding the due process scope of the Fourteenth Amendment and with winning for blacks the right to serve on juries.[24] But in a wider social context, press coverage of the Scottsboro boys helped serve notice in the South that such injustice was intolerable.

NOTES

1. D. Carter, *Scottsboro: A Tragedy of the American South* (Baton Rouge: Louisiana State University Press, 1969), 4. In their autobiographies, Scottsboro boys Frank Norris and Haywood Patterson claim the whites started the fight.

2. Ibid., 142.

3. H. Patterson and Conrad Patterson, *Scottsboro boy* (Garden City, N.Y.: Doubleday, 1950), 5.

4. Southern Commission on the Study of Lynching, as quoted in Carter, *Scottsboro: A Tragedy of the American South*, 115.

5. Bernard Ryan Jr., "The Scottsboro Trials: 1931–37," in *Great American Trials*, ed. E. Knappman (Detroit, Mich.: Gale Research, 1994), 351–356.

6. Carter, *Scottsboro: A Tragedy of the American South*, 20.

7. Ryan, "The Scottsboro Trials: 1931–37," *Great American Trials*, 352.

8. Carter, *Scottsboro: A Tragedy of the American South,* 33–34.

9. Ibid., 39.

10. Patterson and Patterson, *Scottsboro boy,* 12–13.

11. Sources differ on Roy Wright's age. For example, Ryan says Wright was 12 at the time of the arrest. Carter and Norris put his age at thirteen; the *Huntsville Daily Times* and Patterson say fourteen.

12. Carter, *Scottsboro: A Tragedy of the American South,* 172.

13. Ibid., 146.

14. Ibid., 167.

15. C. Norris and S. Washington, *The Last of the Scottsboro Boys* (New York: G. P. Putnam's Sons, 1979), 151.

16. Patterson and Patterson, *Scottsboro boy,* 63–64.

17. Robert F. Martin, "The Scottsboro Cases," in *Historic U.S. Court Cases, 1690–1990: An Encyclopedia*, ed. John Johnson (New York: Garland, 1992), 385.

18. Carter, *Scottsboro: A Tragedy of the American South,* 195.

19. Patterson and Patterson, *Scottsboro boy,* 50.

20. Carter, *Scottsboro: A Tragedy of the American South,* 390–396.

21. Ibid., 394.

22. Patterson and Patterson, *Scottsboro boy,* 302.

23. Norris, *Scottsboro: A Tragedy of the American South,* 222–224.

24. Martin, "The Scottsboro Cases," 388.

10

The Case of Bruno Hauptmann
(1935)

"The greatest story since the Resurrection"

Alfred N. Delahaye

Alarmed and angry, Colonel Charles A. Lindbergh Jr. turned to his wife on the night of March 1, 1932, and declared: "Anne, they have stolen our baby!"

They were the adoring masses, reporters, photographers, gawkers, and souvenir hunters who had trampled his privacy and had worshipped him as the Lone Eagle and Lucky Lindy. They had even idolized him as Prince Charming and a Shining Knight.

Three years later a murder trial climaxed a drama that had mesmerized the public. Sometimes called the greatest show on earth, the trial invited superlatives. It was commonly termed the "trial of the century."[1] It was even called the "greatest criminal case in all human history."[2] To H. L. Mencken, it was "the greatest story since the Resurrection."[3]

Lindbergh first inspired journalists to reach for soaring phrases after May 20, 1927. On that date the twenty-five-year-old airmail pilot began the "most famous flight in history"[4] when he took off from New York in an attempt to cross the Atlantic. He had no co-pilot, no navigator, no parachute, not even a radio aboard his little monoplane. He hung in the air for thirty-three hours, twenty-nine minutes, and thirty seconds before landing in Paris to a tumultuous ovation.[5]

A fleet of 1,000 ships in New York Harbor greeted him upon his return. Almost 5 million people witnessed a New York parade in his honor. Former Secretary of State Charles Evans Hughes, addressing a dinner attended by thousands, praised the aviation pioneer for having "displaced everything petty, sordid or vulgar" and for having "kindled anew the fires on our altars."[6] Writer Alexander Woollcott, after noting the world craves a hero as much as earth craves a rain, declared: "Young Lindbergh gave back to mankind its lost self-respect, and it took him to heart."[7] The aviator, slim and photogenic, had become the standard-bearer for both the spirit of exploration and the new technology.

In Mexico, eight months later, he met Anne Morrow, daughter of the wealthy American ambassador to that country. Their romance and marriage became newspaper extravaganzas. She soon joined him in pioneering aviation feats and proved herself a gifted writer. To get away from the admiring hordes, the Lindberghs built a house on a remote 500-acre estate near the village of Hopewell, New Jersey. It was virtually complete when they decided to spend their first Tuesday night there instead of returning to the Morrow mansion in Englewood.

On that damp, windy night, their twenty-month-old son, Charles Jr., was recovering from a cold. At 8 p.m. Mrs. Lindbergh, three months pregnant, and nurse Betty Gow tucked him in his crib on the second floor. Next to his skin was a flannel shirt the nurse had sewn only minutes earlier. Two hours later she checked on the child, only to find his crib empty. Lindbergh instructed the butler to call the police and ordered his wife and three servants to touch nothing.

He soon noticed an envelope on a radiator grating. Police found no fingerprints on it. But a note inside warned the Lindberghs not to notify the police or the public and to have $50,000 ready. It bore symbols and a unique identifying misspelling of signature—"singnature."

Less than half an hour after the child's disappearance, radio stations began broadcasting the news and newspapers began replating. Scores of police and newsmen soon arrived. Lindbergh warmly welcomed the first reporters, believing publicity would speed the return of his child. Through them he could appeal to the kidnappers and notify them of his son's special diet. The press was both friend and foe, he realized, for publicity could also jeopardize his son's life. Within twelve hours after the kidnapping, the *New York Daily News* had a dozen reporters on the scene.[8]

Police found on the ground a homemade ladder built in three sections, a chisel, and a footprint. They found smudged footprints inside the nursery. Was the crime an outside or an inside job? Was it the work of professionals?

Shocked and excited, the public occasionally lapsed into hysteria. Throughout the country men and women carrying an infant were sometimes stopped and held until they proved the identity of their child. Although Little Lindy had curly blond hair, parents of toddlers with dark hair were sometimes under suspicion.[9] In the weeks ahead false leads and a servant's suicide (seemingly for personal reasons) would bedevil investigators and create headlines. Evalyn Walsh McLean, a Washington socialite and owner of the Hope diamond, was swindled out of $100,000 by a confidence man promising he could return the child.[10]

Dr. John F. Condon, a retired educator, garrulous and eccentric, wrote a letter on March 5 to the *Bronx Home News* offering himself as intermediary between Lindbergh and the kidnappers. On March 9 Condon received an envelope addressed to him. It contained a note and another envelope, and, ultimately, the unique kidnapping signature. Misspellings suggested German authorship.

Condon, accepted by the Lindberghs as their go-between, sometimes communicated with the ransom demander by inserting ads in newspapers and signing them "Jafsie," his initials being J. F. C. During many bizarre developments, Condon received a garment the child was wearing at the time of his disappearance. At one point, Condon, without the money, met with the extortionist, who identified himself as John. Incredibly, they talked for an hour in the dark while seated on a park bench.

On April 2, Condon handed over $50,000 to John in a Bronx cemetery after authorities had earlier recorded the serial numbers. Lindbergh, who had driven Condon to the cemetery rendezvous, heard a voice say, "Hey, Doctor!" A note in exchange for the ransom said the child was on a twenty-eight-foot boat named "Nelly" near Elizabeth Island. No such boat could be found.

A week later an alert teller spotted the first of many ransom bills to turn up. They had been deposited two days after the ransom payment. On May 12 a truck driver, having stopped a few miles from the Lindbergh home to answer a call of nature, discovered the body of a half-buried child about fifty feet into the woods. It was that of Charles Jr., dead of "a fractured skull caused by external violence."

In June, Congress, responding to public outrage, passed a law making kidnapping, in effect, a federal crime.[11] Then for more than two years investigators plotted the appearance of ransom bills, generally in the Bronx. Psychologists offered their theories, handwriting experts their analyses.

Arthur Koehler, "a Sherlock Holmes of wood," came from Wisconsin to fathom every secret held by the ladder found at the scene. He detected unique marks made by planer knives. He determined the exact number, placement, and speed of the knives. When 1,598 planer mills on the East Coast were asked if they had such a machine, twenty-five said yes. Koehler soon found the one mill he sought. He was optimistic when he traced a lumber shipment made to a Bronx company three months before the kidnapping, disappointed when told no sales records were kept.[12]

The Roosevelt administration inadvertently assisted the investigation by recalling gold certificates. Almost two-thirds of the ransom had been paid in gold notes. Henceforth they would stand out, making detection by tellers more likely. When the flow of ransom notes slowed or stopped, the suspicion was that press publicity had precipitated caution.

On September 15, 1934, a driver stopped for gasoline in upper Manhattan. An attendant accepted a $10 gold certificate, knowing it was technically illegal and possibly counterfeit. He wrote the license number on the bill; a bank teller checked it for a ransom-bill match; and on September 21 the *New York Daily News* printed a two-inch-high headline: LINDBERGH KIDNAPER JAILED.[13]

The suspect was Bruno Richard Hauptmann, thirty-five, a Bronx carpenter who had entered the country illegally after serving prison time in his native Germany. He steadfastly asserted his innocence. After extradition proceedings, New Jersey prosecutors could charge Hauptmann with first-degree murder under the state's antiquated law only if the child's death was linked to burglary—perhaps the theft of the baby's clothing.[14] Guards were not permitted to speak to him as he awaited trial in a little jail cell. A light glowed down on him twenty-four hours a day, emphasizing his triangular face, blue eyes, small mouth, and pointed chin.

Also under a twenty-four-hour watch as the trial neared was Hauptmann's wife, Anna, for the couple and the *New York Journal* had entered into an agreement which the newspaper was determined to enforce: It would pay Hauptmann's legal defense costs, and the Hauptmanns would give interviews only to Hearst reporters.[15]

The news media, lawyers, and the rural New Jersey town of Flemington, the county seat, had challenging preparations to make. Communication facilities suitable for a city of 1 million had to be installed.[16] Many of the 2,700 residents rearranged the furniture in their homes to accommodate visitors who refused to commute from Trenton. Flemington newcomers included many of the nation's best-known writers, reporters, and broadcasters: Edna Ferber, Kathleen Norris, Fannie Hurst, Ford Maddox Ford, Damon Runyon, Walter Winchell, Adela Rogers St. Johns, Arthur Brisbane, Alexander Woollcott, Dorothy Kilgallen, Sheilah Graham, Joseph Alsop, Boake Carter, and Gabriel Heatter.

Photographs in the courtroom, the judge decreed, could be taken only when he was not on the bench. Only four photographers would be permitted in the courtroom at one time. A precedent-setting cooperative darkroom was set up in a former bakery two blocks away to provide copies of courtroom pictures. Five major newsreel companies jointly agreed to operate a single sound motion-picture camera in the courtroom. Broadcasters had to rely on microphones outside the courtroom.[17]

Even before jury selection, the press introduced the major players:

Judge: Justice Thomas Whitaker Trenchard, seventy-one, in his fifth seven-year term as a New Jersey Supreme Court justice; patient, grandfatherly, and wise.

Lead prosecutor: Attorney General David Wilentz, thirty-nine, in his first criminal case of any kind and privately opposed to capital punishment; self-possessed, poised, and brilliant.

Lead defense attorney: Edward J. Reilly, fifty-two, "the Bull of Brooklyn," with an astonishing record of acquittals, most of them in murder cases; flamboyant, impressive, and effective. (A crimson drawing of the kidnap ladder ornamented his letterhead, even though he insisted his client had nothing to do with the ladder).[18]

On January 3, 1935, the complete, official story[19] began to unfold in "the most heavily covered trial in history."[20]

Week One. About 500 people wedge themselves into a courtroom designed for 200. Eight men and four women are chosen for the jury in slightly more than a day. Their names, occupations, and photographs receive wide dissemination. Jurors remain sequestered across the street at Flemington's only hotel where dozens of reporters sleep, work, eat, and drink. Trudging between courthouse and hotel, they hear crowd comments.

Wilentz begins by summarizing the events leading to Hauptmann's arrest and the discovery of ransom money hidden in his garage. "Where did you get it?" the prosecutor asks rhetorically. "Why, a partner of mine, an associate of mine, a friend of mine—now dead—gave it to me," he answers in a voice brimming with irony. In the witness chair Anne Lindbergh identifies and fingers her child's sleeping garment. The grief of Mrs. Lindbergh needs no cross-examination, the defense declares.

From the witness chair, Charles Lindbergh declares he heard, and ignored, on the night of the crime what could have been the noise of a falling ladder outside. The voice he heard calling "Hey, Doctor" from the cemetery was Hauptmann's, he testifies. Defense attorney Reilly, in his usual morning coat, striped trousers, and spats, asks Lindbergh if he is armed. "No," he answers. (Reporters had noticed and reported on the first day a pistol in a shoulder holster under Lindbergh's jacket, prompting rumors he intended to kill Hauptmann.)

Still under questioning, Lindbergh says he cannot recall the family's little fox terrier barking on the night of his son's disappearance—nor his son crying. It was possible but improbable that someone could have used the stairs to remove the child without him and his wife knowing it. It is inconceivable, he testifies, that the mastermind of the crime might have both placed the ad in the *Bronx Home News* and answered it himself. The colonel more or less acknowledges that in every important development thereafter Dr. Condon acted alone and unseen. "You believe the defendant is guilty?" Reilly asks. "I do," Lindbergh answers.[21]

(Trial coverage statistics prove staggering: about 700 reporters, photographers, communications workers; seventy-four columns of type and pictures in the *New York Evening Journal* in a single day; the news media collectively churning out a million words a day; the AP transmitting about 55,000 words of trial transcript daily.[22] Flemington becomes the destination for movie stars, socialites—and hucksters selling miniature ladders. On Sunday, January 6, three-mile-an-hour traffic clogs Flemington's roads. Sightseers number 60,000.)

Week Two. With nurse Betty Gow in the witness chair, the defense establishes that she, two other servants, and her boyfriend knew of the Lindberghs' change of plan that kept them at their new home on the night of the kidnapping. Several questions concern who telephoned whom and why, one implication being that Gow's boyfriend telephoned to determine if the coast was clear. Sarcastically, Reilly asks why a supposedly devoted nurse did not look in on the child for two hours.

Then follow four police witnesses. They concede they did not measure a footprint carefully or make a plaster cast of it. One testifies no fingerprints could be found on the ladder. Another says he did not check the bottom rung for mud as evidence the ladder had been used. Reilly objects to admitting the ladder as evidence: It has been bandied from hand to hand, taken apart, put back together again, one rail sawed in two, a new strip added to hold it together—it cannot be said to be the same ladder found on the Lindbergh grounds. Reilly's assistant offers another argument: It cannot be introduced until it has been traced through every person who possessed it from its discovery to the present. The trial of the century promises to become boring. And the judge defers ruling on the ladder issue.

To counter the defense argument of no connection between Hauptmann and the ladder, Reilly calls a frail, eighty-seven-year-old man who says he saw a car with a ladder in it speeding toward the Lindbergh place on the day of the crime. Pointing a shaky finger, he identifies the driver as Hauptmann. (At this moment, courtroom lights dim, flicker out, and flash on again, as if an electrocution is taking place.) Reilly asks for a description of the man in the car. The witness remembers only glaring eyes and a very red face. (Reporters usually describe Hauptmann's face as pale, almost cadaverous.) Meanwhile the news wires have a bulletin: The defendant has been positively identified and placed near the scene of the crime on the day of the crime.

The prosecution calls a police lieutenant to testify. Using a strong ladder propped in a parallel position to the crude ladder, he says, he easily climbed through the nursery window. The defense attorney is astonished to learn that the test was conducted while the shutters and the window were wide open. During the test, the top rung of the ladder was more than thirty inches below the window sill, according to the officer's testimony. In beginning his descent, he held on to the casing with one hand, the sill with the other. How could he do that while holding a bundle? Flushed, the witness admits his experiment omitted a bundle.

The night before "Jafsie" will testify, hundreds of people desperately wait outside the courthouse. About 600 humans somehow sardine themselves into the courtroom the next morning. For two and a half years, Condon has talked freely to the press. Asked where he lives, the seventy-four-year-old replies: "In the most beautiful borough in the world, the Bronx." His recitation of his degrees seems to take forever.

The old man testifies to having handed the ransom money to John. Who is John? Enunciating, he answers: "Bruno Richard Hauptmann." Evening papers gain a headline: "Jafsie Identifies Hauptmann." His sole motive as an intermediary, Condon says, was the safe return of the baby, not the capture of the kidnapper. Wilentz asks Condon to state the description of John he gave the police two years ago. He does, and it fits Hauptmann.

Reilly explores various Condon statements that appeared in newspapers and then tries to exploit Condon's refusal or inability to identify Hauptmann in a police line-up soon after the defendant's arrest. Condon says he made an "identification" but no "declaration of identification." In the manner of teacher addressing pupil, Condon declares: "I want you to know, Counselor, that identification is purely a mental process after the senses have distinguished; declaration is when I tell it to others." Reilly insists that identification means picking out a person, something Condon has not done until now. Reilly also establishes that Condon was not invited to be a witness at Hauptmann's extradition hearing.

Next, a treasury agent testifies that not one ransom bill has turned up since the prisoner's arrest. Emphasis then shifts to the first of eight handwriting experts and to giant enlargements representing the defendant's handwriting and 14 ransom notes.

Week Three. During monotonous, repetitive testimony, the prosecution's experts declare Hauptmann the author of the ransom notes. For the first time, no one need fight to get a courtroom seat. Next, the court considers the time, place, and manner of the infant's death. The physician who performed the autopsy testifies that a blood clot indicated the fracture occurred while the baby was alive. Neither exposure nor choking were possible causes.

The defense claims that the body was perhaps that of a child from a nearby orphanage. But a St. Michael's representative testifies that no children were missing or unaccounted for in May 1932. "There is no dispute," Reilly concedes. A defense assistant angrily strides out of the courtroom.

At last, the prosecution turns to $14,600 of ransom money found in Hauptmann's garage. A federal investigator outlines details about bills found in the garage. Hauptmann rises and shouts: "Mister, Mister, you stop lying!" Guards force him back to his chair. Another witness tells of Hauptmann's inability to explain satisfactorily Condon's address and phone number found penciled on a trim board inside a closet in his home. Reilly makes the point that Hauptmann had no attorney present after his arrest and was never told of his constitutional right not to answer police questions.

Week Four. A treasury intelligence agent testifies that in the thirty months after April 2, 1932, the Hauptmanns came into almost $50,000 of unaccounted-for funds. Although Hauptmann regularly invested in Wall Street and experienced ups and downs, he sustained a net loss.

Finally, the judge admits the ladder in evidence. At last, Koehler, the wood expert, can testify. (This is after learning in court that the Bronx lumber firm he had visited did indeed have sales records; had he not been misinformed and had he checked them out, Hauptmann might have been arrested nine months sooner.) Koehler tells of a ladder rail matching a half-length floor board in Hauptmann's attic. Jurors and spectators study vastly enlarged photographs on display. Koehler soon connects the unique imprint patterns of Hauptmann's plane to those on the ladder rungs and a rail. Koehler even gives a planing demonstration. And he says he had no trouble fitting the disassembled ladder in Hauptmann's car.

When the prosecution rests, the defense moves for acquittal: The prosecution failed to prove the crime took place in Hunterdon County, so the court lacks jurisdiction. No evidence proves that a deliberate, premeditated murder was committed. Hauptmann could not be charged with murder resulting from statutory burglary because theft of a sleeping garment does not fit the New Jersey burglary definition. Only inconclusive testimony placed Hauptmann near the crime scene. Even if he did write the ransom note found in the nursery, that does not prove he was there.

The prosecution offers counterarguments. The judge denies the defense motion. The trial continues.

A local lawyer, not Reilly, presents the opening statement for the defense. He promises proof that Hauptmann obtained his money honestly, that he was elsewhere at the crucial times, that the police bungled the case. He warns the jury not to expect the vast number of witnesses the prosecution called; the defense doesn't have the money, and New Jersey has Hauptmann's funds tied up.

Reilly rises: "Bruno Richard Hauptmann, take the stand." With the approval of both sides, a guard follows him and stands behind the witness chair—a routine measure to prevent any disturbance.

Reilly takes him through much of his life: army service at seventeen, combat on the Western Front, grim times in postwar Germany, conviction of an "offense," hiding aboard ship to reach the United States, marriage two years later. Finally, the testimony centers on Isidor Fisch, Hauptmann's friend and investment partner, who sailed for Europe on December 6, 1933, and died of tuberculosis in Leipzig on March 29, 1934. Among the items Fisch left in the care of Hauptmann, the defendant testifies, were two suitcases and a shoe box. In time a roof leak completely wet the box, causing him to discover drenched gold notes inside.

Testimony shifts to his whereabouts at critical times and to the crude ladder. He denies building it, proudly announcing, "I am a carpenter." He is asked to come down and inspect it. "Looks like a musical instrument," he volunteers. Later, Reilly guides the witness through his accounting records, his dealings with Fisch, and police interrogations after his arrest. Police beat him, the witness declares, and threatened him with no sleep. They dictated statements for him to write, requiring him to misspell certain words, such as "singnature" for signature.

Reilly turns the witness over to Wilentz. The prosecutor asks about Hauptmann's climb up a ladder to a second-floor window in Germany to break into the home of an eminent citizen, about subsequently holding up two women pushing baby carriages, about a parole violation. Holding Hauptmann's little accounting book, the prosecutor asks about unique misspellings in the carpenter's own handwriting.

(Poor ventilation in the crowded courtroom and long work days cause at least two dozen members of the "news army" to be down with influenza from time to time. Some reporters with eighteen-inch-wide table space have their backs to the judge.[23] Several New York newspapers hire airplanes to make deliveries to New York, but motorcycles make better time. A Philadelphia paper installs a darkroom in its trimotored plane.[24])

Week Five. The prosecution quickly gets an admission from Hauptmann that he did not tell his wife about finding and hiding almost $15,000. Pressing on, Wilentz asks Hauptmann about his tendency to transpose letters in words and then produces a Hauptmann check with seventy misspelled as "senvety." Noting that the defendant had bought Curtis-Wright Aviation stock, Wilentz asks him to spell Wright. "W-r-i-h-g-t," he responds. Wilentz fires back: "Just like in the ransom notes—h-g-t in *light*?" Objection—and the question goes unanswered. Next Hauptmann admits he wrote "boad ride" in his account book. Thus, six months before Condon received the "Board Nelly" note, Hauptmann spelled boat with a *d*? Yes.

Later Wilentz accuses Hauptmann of spending lavishly while unemployed, but the defendant insists his investments were yielding well. Hauptmann never knew he was spending ransom money, Reilly contends, and so never used disguises or changed his license plate.

Anna, on the witness stand, tells Reilly she trusts her husband completely and never saw the Fisch money box on a top shelf because she never looked there.

Week Six. Continuing, Reilly suggests that Condon actually handed the ransom money to Fisch and that Fisch flashed large wads of money after April 1932. A series of witnesses testify about Fisch and about Hauptmann's whereabouts at certain times. Wilentz discredits the alibi witnesses, one of whom admits to using three different last names, another to having been in a mental institution about five times. Hauptmann shakes his head as the witnesses harm his case. (Wilentz is so successful because, as soon as a witness speaks his name and address, New Jersey and New York police search records, make phone calls, and send cables.[25])

The pace changes when a lumberman-nurseryman produces boards to show an exact match of grains, even though the boards came from separate trees. His examination of the ladder rail and the wood taken from the defendant's attic convinces him that they are different boards. A mill owner offers similar testimony. Finally, the defense rests, and a parade of rebuttal witnesses begins. Anne Lindbergh accompanies her mother, who testifies about servants.

Week Seven. Reilly has much to tell the jury in his summation: Lindbergh was stabbed in the back by disloyal servants. Hauptmann, a Bronx resident, knew nothing about the Lindbergh house. The dog didn't bark, the baby didn't cry. How could a stranger enter the nursery, climb out of a window in the dark while holding a twenty- or twenty-five-pound baby, and maneuver down a rickety ladder? The kidnapping could not have been the work of one man; it had to have been the work of a gang—and the ladder was a plant. Dr. Condon did everything alone. The closet board is "the worst example of police crookedness that I have ever seen." Hauptmann is "absolutely innocent of murder."

Wilentz gets his turn: The evidence is not circumstantial but positive. The Lindbergh murder could only have been the work of an egomaniac who thought he was omnipotent. Hauptmann used the chisel to knock the child into insensibility in the nursery. (In his opening statement, he had said the child died when the ladder broke and the kidnapper fell.)

Suddenly, a spectator in clerical black rises and says someone confessed the crime to him. Judge Trenchard instructs the jury to disregard the scene. Using the latitude New Jersey law permits a judge when instructing a jury, Trenchard sorts out the evidence and the testimony, indicating what has been established and what the jury must decide. It must acquit the defendant or find him guilty. A "guilty" verdict will mean the death penalty, but the jury may decide "guilty with a recommendation of life imprisonment."

The jury deliberates eleven hours and fourteen minutes. Meanwhile, members of the press poll themselves, and none find Hauptmann innocent.[26] The courthouse bell tolls, a traditional signal that a jury has a verdict. Locked doors separate those in the courtroom from everyone outside. The window shades are drawn. The foreman announces the verdict: "Guilty." A throng outside cheers. Then follow fourteen months of appeals and rejections and even a thirty-day reprieve. Steadfastly declaring his innocence, the condemned man refuses lucrative offers to confess or tell his story and thus provide for his wife and child. On April 3, 1936, he is electrocuted.

The trial represented a logistical triumph for newspapers and newsreels. But Associated Press newsmen, desperate to transmit the verdict the instant it was announced, filed an erroneous bulletin. In violation of court orders and AP policies, they arranged for a secret radio to transmit the coded verdict from the courtroom to a receiver in the courthouse attic. A mix-up caused the wire service to report "guilty and life" shortly *before* the verdict of "guilty and death" was in. The accurate verdict went out at 10:46 p.m., immediately after the foreman announced it. But the false flash stood for eleven minutes, long enough for millions to be misinformed.[27]

Hearst's Metrotone News dispatched two newsreels well in advance—one "conviction," the other "acquittal"; the appropriate reel was ready in 107 theaters in fifteen cities minutes after the verdict. Similarly, many newspapers preset more than one headline.[28]

In assigning Adela Rogers St. Johns to the trial, William Randolph Hearst said: "We cannot endure the kidnapping of our children. In this trial, I am sure we can produce a flame of nationwide indignation that will deter other criminals."[29] Before and during the trial, Damon Runyon was neutral about Hauptmann's guilt or innocence,[30] but St. Johns told Hearst toward the end of the trial, "I know he is guilty."[31] NBC's legal department insisted to no avail that Walter Winchell, totally convinced of Hauptmann's guilt, not tilt his broadcasts against him.[32]

Reilly was on the radio more than once, sometimes asking anyone with information to come forward. One radio station called in actors to enact the day's proceedings from hastily prepared texts. During the trial, newsreel companies got in trouble with the judge by showing courtroom sequences in theaters around the country.[33] Obtrusive cameras at the trial resulted in the creation of a joint committee of lawyers and newspapermen; it, in turn, brought about Canon 35 of the American Bar Association which banned cameras in courtrooms.[34] The trial precipitated a free press-fair trial debate which the Sam Sheppard case intensified three decades later.

Throughout the trial Wilentz held evening press conferences in Trenton; Reilly was generally available in Flemington to answer questions. After the verdict, Reilly termed the press unfair, believing that from the beginning it took the side of the state, the popular side, and thus sold more papers. He praised the reporters, but denounced their editors and publishers. He liked the publication of Q-and-A testimony, but objected to the use of daily interviews with a lawyer temporarily turned newspaperman. Overall, he said, he had no complaint about "the big things." Wilentz found press coverage of his side not only fair but also generous and flattering.[35]

A Brooklyn editor said, "I believe a story of such sustained interest cannot possibly be overplayed."[36] But journalists, lawyers, and laymen offered widespread criticism that the trial had been "hippodromed," historian Frank Luther Mott concluded. "The recess statements of counsel to the press were especially censured as 'trial by newspaper,' " Mott wrote.[37]

In a long editorial, *Editor & Publisher* faulted newspapers, radio, and newsreels for their part in "degrading the administration of justice." It cited commercialization, libel, and irresponsible and unprecedented conduct, although "the vast majority of newspapers can, of course, plead not guilty." Regular staff men and women, on the whole, did magnificent work, it decided. "The whole exhibition calls for action by decent members of the bench and bar," the editorial pleaded, "for upon their shoulders rests the responsibility for the conduct of the judicial process."[38]

Sidney W. Whipple, writing in 1939, cited preliminary skirmishing between the state and the defense as having developed into a battle of publicity and propaganda as the time for the trial approached.[39] A *New York Times* editorial after the verdict offered this conclusion: "To the general public, as evidently to the jury, there was no question that Hauptmann had a fair trial."[40]

Decades after the conviction, writers continued to analyze the trial. After three years of research, writer Anthony Scaduto in 1976 declared the Hauptmann trial and execution possibly "the most terrifying example in American history of the defects in our system of criminal justice and of the arrogance of police power." Authorities invented and suppressed evidence, he concluded.[41]

In 1985 Ludovic Kennedy, an Englishman whose previous books concerned British miscarriages of justice, indicted the law and the press for not affording Hauptmann protection. He cited leading questions, hearsay evidence, testimony offered and accepted without corroboration or proof, and a mass of evidence that would have cleared Hauptmann but that was suppressed or destroyed. Newspapers, with no judicial curbs on them,

Kennedy wrote, branded Hauptmann as the kidnapper and murderer from the moment of his arrest.[42] "The Crime of the Century," according to a 1996 Home Box Office television movie bearing that title and based on Kennedy's book, was not the Lindbergh kidnapping but the Hauptmann execution.

Kennedy, to some extent, echoed Condon, who, writing in 1936, said Hauptmann from the time of his arrest "was being tried in the newspapers." That was part of the reason he refused to pick Hauptmann out in the police line-up and "rebelled against the whole disorderly atmosphere."[43]

Forty years after the trial, Wilentz said the prosecution's case had been overwhelming and honest.[44] In a 1987 book, Jim Fisher agreed with the prosecutor. Fisher called the police investigation thorough and its errors relatively harmless. Investigators and prosecutors did not fabricate or suppress evidence, he declared, and Hauptmann received a fair trial. In his opinion, Hauptmann, without the aid of accomplices, "murdered the baby in cold blood for the money."[45]

The Hauptmann trial, like the John Kennedy assassination, left a legacy of unanswered questions. Millions of words and thousands of facts continue to be analyzed more than sixty years later. Two books published in the 1980s, in the view of one observer, "titillate a new generation of readers" and "offer ludicrous theses."[46]

When 23,000 pages of police documents were made public in 1985, a lawyer for Hauptmann's widow argued that they and 30,000 pages of FBI files not used in the trial demonstrated "a smorgasbord of fraud" against Hauptmann.[47] In 1991 at age ninety-two, Anna Hauptmann continued to plead for the case to be reopened.[48] The Hauptmann case has been cited to support and to discredit the death penalty.

Justice may be in great peril in sensational cases when pressures on law enforcement and the judicial system are at their most intense.[49] Investigators, judges, lawyers, and media professionals—all fallible humans—are themselves judged during and after a sensational trial. A verdict on their performance and fairness is rarely explicit or final, and so the Hauptmann case goes on and on.

Hauptmann predicted it would. To the governor of New Jersey he said: "They think when I die, the case will die. They think it will be like a book I close. But the book, it will never close."[50]

NOTES

1. Adela Rogers St. Johns, *The Honeycomb* (Garden City, N.Y.: Doubleday & Company, 1969), 287. St. Johns credits Damon Runyon with being the first to use the phrase.

2. John F. Condon, *Jafsie Tells All!: Revealing the Inside Story of the Lindbergh-Hauptmann Case* (New York: Jonathan Lee Publishing, 1936), vii.

3. Jim Fisher, *The Lindbergh Case* (New Brunswick, N.J.: Rutgers University Press, 1987), 270.

4. St. Johns, *The Honeycomb*, 289.

5. Ibid., 289–290.

6. Ibid., 290–291.

7. Joseph Hennessey, ed., "The Hauptmann Case" in *The Portable Woollcott* (New York: Viking Press, 1946), 572.

8. Anthony Scaduto, *Scapegoat: The Lonesome Death of Bruno Richard Hauptmann* (New York: G. P. Putnam's Sons, 1976), 33–35.

9. Ibid., 35.

10. Ibid., 406.

11. Walter S. Ross, *The Last Hero: Charles A. Lindbergh* (New York: Harper and Row, 1964), 228.

12. George Waller, *Kidnap: The Story of the Lindbergh Case* (New York: The Dial Press, 1961), 191–193, 196–201, 205–207.

13. Ludovic Kennedy, *The Airman and the Carpenter: The Lindbergh Kidnapping and the Framing of Richard Hauptmann* (New York: Viking, 1985), 13.

14. Waller, *Kidnap*, 272–274.

15. Sidney B. Whipple, *The Lindbergh Crime* (New York: Blue Ribbon Books, 1935), 315.

16. *New York Times*, 2 January 1935.

17. "Public Avid for News of Trial," *Editor & Publisher*, 12 January 1935, 5.

18. Geoffrey C. Ward, "Cols. Lindbergh and Mustard," *The American Heritage*, April 1944, 20–22.

19. Trial information is largely from Waller, *Kidnap*, 251–494; information from other sources noted when significant.

20. Richard Kluger, *The Paper: The Life and Death of the New York Herald Tribune* (New York: Alfred A. Knopf, 1986), 253.

21. "Hauptmann," *Newsweek*, 12 January 1935, 8.

22. *Editor & Publisher*, 12 January 1935, 5, 31.

23. Helen Scott Mann, "Working Press Works Hard at Trial," *Editor & Publisher*, 19 January 1935, 7, 41.

24. "Flemington: 11,500,000 Words, Words, Words, Words, Words," *Newsweek*, 16 February 1935, 35–36.

25. Whipple, *The Lindbergh Crime*, 309–310.

26. St. Johns quoted by Joan Saunders Wixen, "I Covered the Lindbergh Kidnapping," *Modern Maturity*, April-May 1982, 35–38.

27. Oliver Gramling, *AP: The Story of News* (New York: Farrar and Rinehart, 1940), 398–405

28. "Verdict in Newsreel," *Editor & Publisher*, 16 February 1935, 4.

29. St. Johns, *The Honeycomb*, 288.

30. Ibid., 305, 308

31. Ibid., 326.

32. Neal Gabler, *Winchell: Gossip, Power, and the Culture of Celebrity* (New York: Vintage Books, 1994), 210.

33. Kennedy, *The Airman and the Carpenter*, 256.

34. James Russell Wiggins, *Freedom or Secrecy* (New York: Oxford University

Press, 1964), 230.

35. "'Press Unfair,' Reilly Charges; Newsmen 'Grand,' Says Wilentz," *Editor & Publisher,* 16 February 1935, 4.

36. "Trial Overplayed? Editors Differ," *Editor & Publisher*, 9 February 1935, 5, 31.

37. Frank Luther Mott, *American Journalism* (New York: The Macmillan Company, 1947), 703.

38. "Hippodroming," *Editor & Publisher*, 16 February 1935, 24.

39. Whipple, *The Lindbergh Crime*, 231.

40. *New York Times*, 15 February 1935.

41. Scaduto, *Scapegoat*, preface.

42. Kennedy, *The Airman and the Carpenter*, 4–5.

43. Condon, *Jafsie Tells All!* 225–226.

44. Ibid., 480.

45. Fisher, *The Lindbergh Case*, 5.

46. Geofrey C. Ward, "Cols. Lindbergh and Mustard," *American Heritage,* April 1994, 20–22.

47. "Lindbergh Kidnapping's Final Victim," *U.S. News & World Report*, 4 November 1985, 11.

48. Bernard Ryan Jr., "Bruno Richard Hauptmann Trial: 1935," in *Great American Trials: From Salem Witchcraft to Rodney King*, ed. Edward W. Knappman (Detroit, Mich.: New England Publishing Association, 1994), 386–391.

49. "We Cannot Be Sure," *The Nation*, 9 April 1977, 420.

50. Scaduto, *Scapegoat*, 484.

11

The Cases of Alger Hiss and the Rosenbergs
(1949, 1951)

"I said, would you open your mouth . . ."

Joseph McKerns

Illuminating the sky with a light brighter than a thousand suns, the explosion of atomic bombs over Hiroshima and Nagasaki marked both an end and a beginning. Hailed as a harbinger of peace, a savior of lives, and a weapon of freedom, "The Bomb" was also an omen of death, a destroyer of worlds, and a tool of aggression. V-J Day, August 15, 1945, marked the dawn of a new day of world peace, international cooperation, and national prosperity. As the shadows of day slip too soon into the darkness of night, so too did the bright prospects of V-J Day soon fade into the long, dark night of the cold war. Fear replaced confidence in the public's outlook on the future: fear of war, fear of annihilation, and an overarching fear of global Communist aggression and subversion. At a time when to "name" something was to make it so in the public's mind, the role played by the American press in the national obsession with Communist infiltration and subversion is central to the period. No two instances better capture this national hysteria and the press's role in fostering it than the espionage cases of Alger Hiss, and Julius and Ethel Rosenberg.

However, the national hysteria that provided the backdrop for both cases was not initiated by them. Rather, by the time Alger Hiss faced members of the House Un-American Activities Committee (HUAC) to answer allegations that he was a Communist, the hysteria was already full blown and feeding on itself. The wartime cooperation between the Soviet Union and the United States had dispelled long-held suspicions about Communist Russia among many Americans, and it appeared that differences between the two nations would be resolved following their shared victory over Germany and Japan. This was not to be. Within months of Japan's surrender, the two military giants became involved in a series of confrontations that spawned the tension between East and West that came to be called the cold war. These confrontations took several forms, sometimes rhetorical, sometimes diplomatic, at times political or economic. There were even outbreaks of "hot" wars fought by surrogates such as the Chinese, Koreans, or popular liberation fronts in many emerging nations. The American news media reported this fearful march of events that seemed to push the world closer to the ultimate confrontation—World War III.

The postwar era of good feelings between East and West died with the refusal of the Soviet Union to remove its troops from the Eastern European countries it had liberated from German occupation. One by one, Communists assumed control of the governments in these liberated countries. By March 15, 1946, only seven months after the end of World War II, Winston Churchill, Britain's wartime prime minister, declared that an "Iron Curtain" had fallen across Central Europe that was every bit as formidable as Nazi Germany's "Fortress Europe" in 1940. Then, in rapid succession, confrontation followed confrontation. In April 1946, the United States and the Soviet Union clashed over Turkey; then in August, it was a Communist-led civil war in Greece.

In March 1947, the Truman Doctrine declared that the United States would do whatever was necessary to protect the nations of the world from further Soviet infiltration and subversion. That summer, the Truman administration adopted a policy of "containment" toward the Soviet Union and its expansionist tendencies. In March 1948, the democracies of the West signed the Brussels Pact that pledged the United States to respond to an attack on any of the other pact members as if it were an attack on America itself. By June 1948, it seemed that Americans would be called on to honor that pact with military action when the Soviet Union began its blockade of the Berlin corridor in an attempt to force the Allies to abandon West Berlin. Then, in the midst of this global tension, Alger Hiss, a former State Department official, was called by HUAC to answer accusations that he was a Communist sworn to obey the Kremlin in Moscow, and perhaps even a spy for the Soviets.

THE ALGER HISS CASE

On March 21, 1946, one week after Churchill's "Iron Curtain" speech, the Truman administration enacted a Loyalty Program requiring all government employees, from the president down to the local post office worker, to swear that they were "not now, nor ever have been, a member of the Communist Party, or any other organization seeking to overthrow the established government of the United States." Failure to take the oath cost employees their jobs. With this program, the Truman administration, and the Democratic Party joined the Republican Party in launching a bipartisan campaign to associate dissent with treason. Soon after, similar oaths were required of state and local government employees, and eventually even many in the private sector were asked "to take the oath."[1]

To many in the federal government in 1948, Alger Hiss seemed an unlikely spy for anyone, let alone the Russians. It was just too improbable. Hiss was "a man groomed for national leadership." A graduate of the Johns Hopkins University and the Harvard Law School, Hiss was then serving as president of the prestigious Carnegie Endowment for International Peace. He had been a prominent Washington figure through the war years, was an ardent New Dealer, and had served in the State Department where he was responsible for Far East Affairs. In 1945, he was the secretary-general of the conference that organized and founded the United Nations. He was well mannered, eloquent, and elegant of dress; the cream of his generation and social class. When Whittaker Chambers accused Hiss of being a Communist before the House Un-American Activities Committee, few in government and the news media believed he would be "shown to be susceptible to subversion for a foreign power." But before it was over, the college-educated generation of the 1930s and 1940s would define itself according to how it felt about Whittaker Chambers and Alger Hiss.[2]

If Hiss was Dr. Jekyll to many who knew him, then surely Whittaker Chambers was Mr. Hyde. Both men were of the same generation, both products of the same social class, both had similar academic pedigrees. However, for as slim, elegant, and polished as Hiss was, Chambers was short, chunky, powerfully built, and untidy. His necktie was always twisted and his dark baggy suits littered with the ashes of his cigarettes. When he was subpoenaed before HUAC in 1948, Chambers was the foreign editor of *Time* magazine, personally picked for the job by Henry R. Luce, the magazine's founder and editor-in-chief, who was impressed with Chambers intellectual powers and his strident anti-Communist zeal. But his "life" as a *Time* editor was only one of several Chambers led since his days at Columbia University.

In the late 1920s, Chambers joined the Communist Party and became a freelance journalist and translator. He began to help edit the *Communist Daily Worker* in 1927, then became news editor in 1929. Also, he taught journalism classes in the Communist Party's "Workers School." In 1931, he joined the staff of *The New Masses* and became an editor in 1932. In addition to his party work, Chambers translated the first version of *Bambi* from French into English. He joined *Time* as a writer in 1939 and held several minor editorial positions prior to being named foreign editor in 1945. In the meantime, Chambers left the Communist Party and renounced his loyalty to it. Luce appreciated Chambers's dramatic writing style as well as his anticommunism. Chambers also fit Luce's plan to use conservative editors to offset his correspondents, whom he believed were too liberal, and maybe even sympathetic to communism. As foreign editor, Chambers performed as Luce intended. He translated his strident anticommunism into practice by rewriting or heavily editing reports from correspondents he felt were not anti-Soviet enough. The foreign news section of *Time* bore his heavy imprint, and his editing of some of *Time's* best correspondents was harsh and merciless. Many at *Time* despised him and thought him overimaginative and a liar.[3]

Volumes of speculation have been written about the type of man Chambers was. It is clear there was both an artistic and melancholy bent to the man. His response to the subpoena to appear before the House Committee, for example, was couched in elegant, emotional verbiage:

What I felt was what we see in the eye of a bird or an animal that we are about to kill, which knows that it is about to be killed, and whose torment is not the certainty of death or pain, but the horror of the interval before death comes in which it knows that it has lost light and freedom forever. It is not yet dead. But it is no longer alive.[4]

When he did appear on August 3, 1948, Chambers told HUAC that Hiss was a Communist and that he had been involved in espionage. Two days later Hiss denied the accusations in an appearance before HUAC. The two went back and forth, each appearing several times before HUAC, in private and public sessions, together and alone, but the result was the same. Chambers accused, Hiss denied. At times their dialogue, as well as the manner in which they acted, seemed written by Albert Camus and edited by Kurt Vonnegut Jr. A prime example is Hiss's questioning of Chambers before the House Un-American Activities Committee.

Senator Richard Nixon: Sit over here, Mr. Chambers. Mr. Chambers, will you please stand? And will you please stand, Mr. Hiss? Mr. Hiss, the man standing here is Mr. Whittaker Chambers. I ask you now if you have ever known that man before?
Hiss: May I ask him to speak? Will you ask him to say something?
Nixon: Yes. Mr. Chambers, will you tell us your name and your business?
Chambers: My name is Whittaker Chambers.

[At this juncture, Hiss approaches Chambers.]

Hiss: Would you mind opening your mouth wider?
Chambers: My name is Whittaker Chambers.
Hiss: I said, would you open your mouth. . . .
Hiss [later in the testimony]: Would you ask him to talk a little more?
Nixon: Read something, Mr. Chambers. I will let you read from—
Hiss: I think he is George Crosley, but I would like to hear him talk a little longer. [Hiss had earlier testified before HUAC that Whittaker Chambers had never stayed at his residence, but that a man by the name of George Crosley—a man with, as Hiss remembered, "notably bad teeth"—had rented a flat from him and had perhaps spent one night at his house.]
Hiss [later in the testimony]: Did you ever go under the name of George Crosley?
Chambers: Not to my knowledge. [In later testimony, Chambers would

be asked if his front teeth were in very bad shape in 1934. His answer: "Yes. I think so."]

Hiss: Did you ever sublet an apartment on Twenty-ninth Street from me?

Chambers: No; I did not. . . .

Hiss: Did you ever spend any time with your wife and child in an apartment on 29th Street in Washington when I was not there because I and my family were living on P Street?

Chambers: I most certainly did.

Hiss: You did or did not?

Chambers: I did.

Hiss: Would you tell me how you reconcile your negative answers with this affirmative answer?

Chambers: Very easily, Alger. I was a Communist and you were a Communist [In his autobiography, *Witness*, Chambers wrote: "I answered very quietly, from the depth of my distress."].

Hiss: Would you be responsive and continue with your answer?

Chambers: I do not think it is needed.[5]

In their defense of Hiss, his supporters in the press and in government relied on conspiracy theories and accusations that Chambers had perjured himself. Chambers's supporters pointed to Hiss's close associations with New Deal radicals and with the wartime policy of Soviet-American entente as corroboration of his guilt. From beginning to end, however, it was man against man, word against word, all against the tedious backdrop of congressional hearings with endless questioning and vague responses.

Between the accusations, however, it was politics as usual. With a presidential election less than three months away, Republicans in Congress, and in the news media, used Hiss's presumed treachery as a means of accusing the Democratic administration of condoning communism in government. Liberals viewed the assault on Hiss as a spearhead of a conservative attempt to discredit the New Deal and the foreign and domestic policies of the Roosevelt and Truman administrations. Many of those who served in the New Deal were called Communists by the press, but stories linking Hiss to the Communist Party appeared as early as 1939. In 1946, the *Christian Science Monitor* wrote that, "More than one Congressman, whenever the subject of leftist activity in the State Department is mentioned, pulled out a list of suspects headed by Mr. Hiss."[6]

The Soviet blockade of Berlin produced ominous headlines in the nation's press in the summer of 1948. The world seemed on the brink of World War III when Whittaker Chambers appeared before a public session of the House Un-American Activities Committee to admit that he had been a Communist, and that he believed others, including Alger Hiss, still were. HUAC's reputation had been tarnished since its 1947 motion picture industry hearings, and it had come under severe criticism from leading newspapers, such as the *New York Times*, the *Washington Post*, and the *New*

York Herald Tribune, for its brutal "witch-hunting" tactics. On the day of Chambers's first appearance, committee chairman J. Parnell Thomas was not able to attend because he was being investigated for accepting kickbacks from his employees. All of the committee's members, including Democrats, opposed Truman administration policies, and seemed to have difficulty differentiating between Communist activities and New Deal programs. Originally created in 1938 to investigate all political extremism, it seemed interested only in exposing the liberal-left faction of the Democratic Party as Communists in 1948. However, the stream of headlines detailing the Hiss-Chambers hearings throughout August helped to restore its credibility in the press.[7]

The *New York Herald Tribune* called the hearings "a matter of serious public consequence." Once a critic of HUAC, the *Herald Tribune* now urged the committee to "Get to the Bottom" of the Hiss-Chambers relationship. The general tone of the press coverage of the hearings, especially among Republican newspapers, was to accentuate the accusations against Hiss, and to underplay his response. The day after Chambers named Hiss as one of a group of people he knew were Communists, newspapers across the United States headlined the story as *"Time* Editor Charges Carnegie Endowment Head Was Soviet Agent," even though Chambers had actually never singled out Hiss in the manner implied in the headline. News stories relating the testimony of Chambers, Hiss, and others sometimes read like spy fiction instead of news. Newspapers played up sensational witnesses, regardless of plausibility of their testimony, but failed to report as thoroughly the testimony of boring witnesses, or of those who replied to attacks against them. Most newspapers also carried the most trivial, or illogical musings, speculations, and predictions of the committee's members. Hiss lost what favorable press he had when he admitted to having known Chambers years earlier after he failed to admit this when first given the opportunity. In addition, Hiss's credibility was hurt by the intense coverage given to the hearings by the *Communist Daily Worker*. "Un-Americans Plot to 'Get' Hiss on Perjury," the paper reported on August 26.[8]

Time's coverage of the Hiss-Chambers hearings is the most interesting. Prior to his first appearance before HUAC, Chambers told Luce that he had been a Communist and wondered if Luce wanted him to resign. Luce said no, that testifying was a patriotic act. However, Chambers did not reveal to Luce that he was also involved in espionage. Chambers remained with *Time* throughout the hearings until December 1948 when he resigned after his spy role became public. During the hearings, Luce placed *Time* and *Life* in league with the Republican Party's efforts to portray Hiss as the fruit of a Democratic administration that was soft on communism and had sold out China to the Russians. *Time* repeatedly emphasized and exaggerated Hiss's role at the Yalta Conference of 1945, which Luce considered a crime. Also, *Time* played up Hiss's relationship with Secretary of State Dean Acheson, whom Luce viewed as having abandoned China to the Communists. *Time* even coined a word to describe American Communists: "Comsymps."[9]

Richard Nixon, a member of HUAC and a first-term congressman from California, stole the spotlight in the Hiss-Chambers hearings. He had close relationships with several correspondents from leading newspapers, including Bert Andrews, a Pulitzer Prize–winning reporter for the *New York Herald Tribune*, who acted as Nixon's adviser and sounding board. Nixon was considered the most reliable source on the committee, and he received a large share of the headlines nationwide. The hearings made Nixon a national figure, and he rode that to a Senate seat in 1950 and the vice presidency in 1952.[10]

Throughout the Hiss-Chambers case, and especially during the critical months between the beginning of the HUAC hearings in August 1948, and Hiss's indictment for perjury by a federal grand jury in December 1948, Alger Hiss's actions appeared to confirm his guilt, at least in the eyes of the press. Hiss's aristocratic manner and intellectualism did not endear him to the "working press." Most reporters believed he was at least guilty of perjury long before his conviction. But more important, because Hiss did not act to defend himself in a way that the press expected an innocent man should act, the press concluded that he must be guilty. This is best illustrated by press reaction to Hiss's libel suit against Chambers in the fall of 1948. During a closed session of HUAC on August 17, 1948, Hiss dared Chambers to repeat his accusations in public where he would not be protected by the congressional blanket of immunity from libel. On August 27, on *Meet the Press*, a national public affairs program on NBC radio, Chambers did just that. Hiss failed to file a libel suit until September 27, and in the month that elapsed, he was pilloried by the press, including newspapers that had been sympathetic to his case. One of those friendly papers, the *Washington Post*, editorialized: "Mr. Hiss himself has created a situation in which he is obliged to put up or shut up. . . . Each day of delay in making it known that he will avail himself of the opportunity Mr. Chambers has afforded him does incalculable damage to his reputation." The *New York Daily News* put it bluntly: "Well, Alger, where's that suit?"[11]

Hiss also seemed to be constantly on the defensive, having to react to revelations of what seemed to be startling information when revealed by government witnesses, but often was something he himself could have admitted to without compromising his innocence. One example was his admitting, after first denying, that he knew Chambers as early as the 1930s. Another instance involved a story the *Baltimore Post* published a few days before Chambers's appearance on *Meet the Press*, which revealed to startled readers that Hiss and Chambers had both held title to a farm in Westminster, Maryland. The paper failed to mention that each owned the property at different times, but it did offer groundless speculation that the farm was used as an underground Communist hideaway. That farm would figure prominently in Hiss's final downfall in the press's eyes, that is, the infamous "Pumpkin Papers," five rolls of microfilm of State Department documents that Chambers said he hid inside a pumpkin on his farm in Westminster. Some of the documents appeared to bear Hiss's signature, thus implicating him. On December 6, 1948, four days after Chambers surrendered the microfilm, HUAC investigators and the Justice Department reconvened a grand jury.[12]

December 1948 offered the nation's news media an orgy of information emanating from four separate, and simultaneous, investigations into the Hiss-Chambers case: Hiss's libel suit, ongoing HUAC hearings where Richard Nixon took center stage, the federal grand jury probe, and an investigation by the State Department. The press was impatient for results. An editorial in the *Atlanta Constitution* charged the attorney general of the United States, the Justice Department, and the FBI with "dereliction of duty" in their failure to follow up on leads in the case. The paper insisted that those responsible for the stolen State Department documents receive "full prosecution." The *Washington Post*, in an editorial entitled, "Let's Have the Facts," denounced the four separate investigations as a "four-ring circus." On December 15, 1948, Alger Hiss was indicted by the federal grand jury for perjury during his testimony before HUAC. The indictment was hailed by the media, but few papers raised any questions regarding the possibility of perjury charges against Chambers even though several instances clearly raised questions about his veracity.[13]

Hiss's long awaited trial began on May 31, 1949, and ended on July 8 with a hung jury and no verdict. Indignation was widespread among the nation's news media, who placed the blame squarely on the shoulders of Judge Samuel H. Kaufman. Demands for a congressional inquiry were made, and for days afterward Richard Nixon made page 1 by criticizing Judge Kaufman for his "obvious and apparent prejudice" against the prosecution. Newspapers also seized on a report that during the pretrial proceedings, the foreman of the jury had expressed a belief in Hiss's innocence, but that Judge Kaufman failed to dismiss him. However, most papers failed to note that Kaufman offered to dismiss the foreman on a motion from the prosecution. But the motion was never made. The *New York Herald Tribune* zealously questioned jurors looking for evidence to back up its criticism of Judge Kaufman. The *Chicago Tribune* reported that the FBI was opening an investigation of the four jurors who voted for acquittal, but when approached by the Associated Press for confirmation of the investigation, FBI spokesmen had "no comment." Jurors reported receiving threatening phone calls after the story appeared.[14]

In the four months between Hiss's first and second perjury trials, the tension of the cold war rose, and its drama was played out on the nation's front pages and airwaves. Congress ratified the NATO treaty, which committed the United States to defend Western Europe against Communist aggression; on September 24, President Truman announced that the Soviet Union had successfully exploded its first atomic bomb, thus shattering Americans' confidence in their military superiority. Three weeks later, *Life* magazine published an article that asked, "Can the Russians Deliver the Bomb?" It was accompanied by a photograph taken on September 16, 1920, after a bombing on Wall Street. No one was ever arrested for the crime, but *Life's* photo caption said, "In 1920 Reds Exploded Bomb in Wall Street, Killed 30, Wounded Hundreds." On October 14, 1949, a federal jury convicted eleven Americans for violating the Smith Act as Communist Party leaders. By the time Hiss's second trial began on November 17, 1949, *Time* and *Life* magazines made it clear to their readers that all Democrats, not only Hiss, were on trial.[15]

Hiss's lawyers argued that the trial should be relocated from New York to Vermont because of the "unprecedented volume" and "extraordinary virulence" of the coverage of the first trial. The defense reported having difficulty getting witnesses to agree to testify in Hiss's behalf because of the critical treatment witnesses received in the first trial. Hiss's attorneys also alleged that FBI agents paid "visits" to defense witnesses in an attempt to intimidate them. The New York press was held up as an example of the prejudicial coverage given the first trial such as its publication of evidence excluded from trial, editorials critical of character witnesses, numerous interviews with jurors, wide publicity given to newspaper and congressional attacks on Judge Kaufman, and publication of the names of jurors who voted for acquittal. The request for change of venue was denied. During the second trial the *New York Journal American* published the names and addresses of all the jurors. The subtle tone of *Time's* coverage of the second trial seemed intended to influence readers' impressions about Hiss's guilt long before the verdict was rendered. For example, *Time* referred to the prosecuting attorney, in a clearly affectionate way, as "Tom" Murphy, while it undercut the credibility of defense witness Dr. Carl Binger by captioning a picture of him as, "Psychiatrist Binger Assumes Professional Air." Dr. Binger was a key defense witness in an attempt to portray Chambers as a "psychopathic personality" and a liar. While testifying, a *New York Times* article stated that Dr. Binger had made "pro-Communist remarks" after a speech in England. The remarks the *Times* referred to involved a response to a question in which he pointed to the hysteria about communism in the United States as a state of neurotic anxiety spreading throughout the country. On January 21, 1950, to no one's surprise, the jury found Alger Hiss guilty of perjury. He was sentenced to five years in prison.[16]

The mystery surrounding the Hiss case didn't end with Hiss's conviction. It was widely revisited with the death of Whittaker Chambers on July 9, 1961. Initial reports cited the cause of death was a heart attack. Many people, however, believed Chambers committed suicide. They pointed to the fact that three days after the death, the body was cremated, preventing forever any opportunity to gather evidence contradicting the cause of death. It is plausible that Chambers committed suicide, that he had been depressed because events had not turned out as he might have hoped, that his honor had been questioned, that he was considered by some to have been the villain in the Hiss case. It is interesting to note that in referring to the questionable way that Walter Krivitsky died [either killed by the Soviet secret police or committed suicide because the secret police were after him], Chambers wrote in his autobiography that "Any fool can commit murder, but it takes an artist to commit a good natural death." As author and psychoanalyst Meyer Zeligs points out in *Friendship and Fratricide*, "Chambers, by his own admission, was weary of life and waiting for death in order to find peace of mind. But to end his life, and to let the world know that he had, would have been tantamount to an admission of his guilt."[17] Something else added to the mystery: Chambers's death came twelve years, to the day, after the end of the first Hiss trial.

THE ROSENBERGS'S CASE

The "bugaboo" of communism and the national state of anxiety it fed was notably abated with the conviction of Alger Hiss. If anything, Hiss's conviction for perjury seemed to confirm what Republican politicians charged and daily headlines implied: that the United States was a besieged nation, threatened by a powerful enemy abroad whose minions plotted to betray the country from within. Since 1946 it seemed that seldom did a week pass by, or at times a day, without a front-page headline revealing another Communist threat to American security at home or abroad. The press' objective style of reporting the news led to its treatment of stories as discreet events, with little or no attempt to place those events into an interpretative context. The cold war was "hot" news, and the more threatening the news, the bigger the play it received. Whether or not any or all of the "Communist-threat" incidents were interrelated, the sheer volume and prominence of the stories about those events left an impression in the public's mind that there was a very definite connection.

Within a month of Hiss's conviction, the British spy, Klaus Fuchs, was arrested for supplying the Soviet Union with atomic bomb secrets, and a little known U.S. senator from Wisconsin, Joseph R. McCarthy, made a speech in Wheeling, West Virginia, in which he announced that he had a list of more than 200 names of Communists in the State Department. Less than five months after Hiss's conviction, on June 6, 1950, North Korean troops, supported by Communist China and the Soviet Union, invaded South Korea, initiating the Korean War. A few weeks later, on July 17, Julius Rosenberg, a thirty-two-year-old civilian engineer from New York City was arrested and accused of belonging to a "spy ring" that supplied atomic bomb secrets to the Soviet Union in 1945. His wife, Ethel, was arrested on August 11 on similar charges. Because objective journalism treats what public officials say as news, their statements most often are reported, not as opinions, speculations, or points of view, but as facts. From their arrest through their trial, before any legal verdict was rendered, Julius and Ethel Rosenberg were deemed "spies" or "Soviet agents," not "alleged" or "accused" spies, in headlines on the front pages of the nation's press, because public officials said they were spies. In appeals following their convictions, attorneys for the Rosenbergs complained that their clients were victims of "inflammatory trial-by-newspaper" coverage. They maintained that FBI director J. Edgar Hoover, and other officials in Washington, D.C., and New York, created widespread hostility against their clients before the trial. In statements and press releases about the arrest of the Rosenbergs, Hoover and FBI spokespersons framed the case as a simple, neatly packaged cloak-and-dagger story.[18]

During World War II, Julius Rosenberg was a civilian engineer employed by the Army Signal Corps in New York City, who was fired in 1945 because of his Communist affiliations. He was supposed to have become involved with Morton Sobell and Harry Gold in espionage activities. Gold was a chemist from Philadelphia who was linked to British spy Klaus Fuchs following Fuchs's arrest in England in 1950. In 1943, Ethel Rosenberg's younger brother, David Greenglass, was inducted into the army and stationed at the Los Alamos atomic bomb facility as a machinist. Julius and Ethel were said to have recruited Greenglass into their spy ring in order to obtain atomic bomb secrets to pass along to the Russians. A government informant, Elizabeth Bentley, who was a former Communist and who had figured prominently in leading HUAC to subpoena Whittaker Chambers in 1948, gave the FBI information that led to the arrest of David Greenglass. Greenglass, in turn, led the FBI to the Rosenbergs. Following Julius Rosenberg's arrest on July 17, 1950, Hoover described him to the press as "another important link" in the Russian spy network. Specifically, what Julius, and later his wife Ethel, were charged with was "conspiracy to commit espionage," not with "espionage," and with recruiting Ethel's brother, David Greenglass, into the spy ring that also included Morton Sobell and Harry Gold. However, headlines the day after the arrest more closely reflected Hoover's framing rather than the technical accuracy of the charge. For example, the *Chicago Tribune* wrote: "FBI Seizes Fourth American as A-Bomb Spy;" the *Atlanta Constitution* said: "New Yorker Arrested on Spy Charge;" the *Washington Post*: "FBI Seizes 4th Man on A-Spy Charges;" and the *New York Herald Tribune* stated: "New Yorker Seized as Atom Spy, Linked to Fuchs."[19]

The *New York Times* coverage of the arrest of Julius Rosenberg failed to mention that he entered a plea of not guilty when he was arraigned in federal court within hours of his arrest. The *New York Daily News* scored an interview with Ethel Rosenberg on the morning following the arrest. The newspaper stated, in appallingly subjective terms, that she denied being "wife and sister to suspected traitors." The story described the Rosenbergs's apartment as "barren" with only a few pieces of furniture, but it did note that among the books the Rosenbergs owned were titles such as *Stalin Must Have Peace* and *Battle Hymn of China*. When Ethel Rosenberg was arrested on August 11, 1950, newspapers reported that officials said there was "ample evidence that Mrs. Rosenberg and her husband have been affiliated with

Communist activities for a long time." Headlines reporting the arrest clearly reflected an official point of view: "Plot to Have G.I. Give Bomb Data to Soviet Is Laid to His Sister Here," "Mother of Two Seized as Atom Spy Ring Link;" and "FBI Arrests Woman as Atomic Spy."[20]

The Rosenbergs's trial opened on March 7, 1951, in federal court in New York City and concluded on March 30 when the jury returned a verdict of guilty after only fifteen days of testimony. The case seemed to be simple, straightforward, "open-and-shut." Critics of the trial have since charged that the Rosenbergs's attorney botched their defense by conceding too much questionable evidence to the prosecution and by failing to challenge vigorously the government's attorneys and witnesses. Nevertheless, news coverage of the trial clearly reflected a presumption of guilt long before the verdict was announced. In *Time's* coverage of the trial, the Rosenbergs were repeatedly referred to as "spies" without any qualifying terms such as alleged or suspected. In the most damaging testimony of the trial, the prosecution produced as evidence a "replica" of a cross-section sketch of the atomic bomb dropped on Nagasaki. Newspapers described it as a "copy" of a free-hand sketch that David Greenglass gave to Julius Rosenberg in September 1945. The *New York Herald Tribune* called the sketch an "exact" copy. Few publications, including *Time*, gave much space to Julius's denials or his version of Greenglass's testimony. The Rosenbergs's use of their Fifth Amendment privilege was reported in the press with a clear implication that it was invoked selectively to hide the truth. The *New York Times* even went so far as to say that the questions that Ethel Rosenberg refused to answer were really "harmless" and that she would have answered them if she were innocent.[21]

Events occurring outside of the courtroom also seemed to weigh heavily in the case, at least in terms of press coverage and treatment. For example, during the testimony of Ruth Greenglass, the Rosenbergs's sister-in-law and wife of David Greenglass, William Perl—a college classmate of both Julius Rosenberg and Morton Sobell—was arrested on perjury charges stemming from his testimony to a grand jury in the summer of 1950 that he did not know the Rosenbergs or the other spy ring suspects. Many papers linked the two events together and displayed them prominently on their front pages, often times side-by-side. For example, the day following Perl's arrest, the *New York Times* ran two front-page stories, above the fold, with these headlines: "Columbia Teacher Arrested Linked to 2 on Trial as Spies"; and "Greenglass Wife Backs His Testimony as Theft of Atomic Bomb Secrets." On March 28, 1951, the day before the Rosenberg jury met to deliberate the verdict in the case, the New York *Times* carried stories with these ominous cold war headlines: "Acheson Exhorts Americans to Meet Soviet Peril Now"; "U.S. Power Must 'Frighten' Enemy, Wilson Asserts"; "Danger of Atom Bomb Attack is Greatest in Period Up to This Fall, Expert Asserts"; "Red China Rejects M'Arthur's Offer"; and "Ferrer Denies He Is Red."[22]

Throughout the trial, the prosecution characterized the Rosenbergs as "traitors" even though they were never charged with treason. In his opening statement at the trial, chief prosecutor, Irving Saypol, whom *Time* referred to as "the nation's number one legal hunter of top Communists," set the tone when he linked the Rosenbergs's affinity for communism to "treason." Headlines reporting his remarks the next day followed Saypol's line, for example,—"Three Accused as 'Traitors' in Spy Trial;" and "Trio on Trial for Spying to Serve Russia." Saypol repeated this theme of treason again in his summation of the case to the jury before it retired to deliberate a verdict.[23]

The theme of "treason" was repeated in newspaper stories and editorials published the day after Judge Irving Kaufman sentenced the Rosenbergs to die in the electric chair. The *New York Mirror* wrote: "Atom spy traitors Julius and Ethel Rosenberg, their chalk white faces frozen into grimaces of incredulity, yesterday heard themselves condemned to death for passing wartime A-bomb secrets to the Soviets." Editorials in the *Mirror* and other Hearst newspapers spoke approvingly of the death sentences: "The importance of the trial cannot be minimized. Its findings disclosed in shuddering detail the Red cancer which the government is now forced to obliterate in self-defense. The sentences indicate the scalpel which prosecutors can be expected to use in that operation." The *Atlanta Constitution* said the sentences "marked the end of our soft treatment of those who are disloyal. . . . Let other traitors be warned. . . . And let us not forget every Communist is a potential espionage agent pledged to lie and steal to accomplish the direction of the Kremlin."[24]

While in prison, Julius wrote letters criticizing the "liberal press" and split it into two camps, progressive and capitalist. On December 3, 1952, he wrote a letter to his lawyer, Manny Bloch, that revealed critical insight, a considerable amount of truth, and a distrust of the inevitable marriage of business interests and the media:

On this the fortieth day left to live, I want to talk about some of the servants of the abattoir, such as pen hirelings of big business. As you know, it takes large sums of money to own a newspaper and it depends on advertising and the revenue needed to keep on operating. Through control of the technical means in the newspaper business such as: newsprint, paper, the large news services, and by the very practical lever of paid advertisements, which is tantamount to a mortgage, the first brothers control, and in the main, dominate the editorial and news slanting policies of the so called "free press."[25]

Julius, however, also seemed resolute to the political fervor cresting about him. In a letter to Ethel, he wrote, "We must be realists. The political climate has not cleared up and a great fear is paralyzing many former liberals and progressives into silence. I'm still optimistic but I'm prepared for any eventuality."[26]

The *Daily Worker* printed a letter by the Rosenbergs:

We do not want to die. We are young and yearn for a long life. Yet, if the only alternative to death is the purchase of life at the cost of personal dignity and abandonment of the struggle for democracy and ethical standard, there is no future for us or a legacy we can leave our children or those who survive and follow us. For what is life without the right to live it? Death holds no horror as great as the horror of a sterile existence, devoid of social responsibility and the courage of one's convictions.[27]

And, then, inescapably, their last, final day arrived.

The Rosenbergs skipped their last meal to spend time together in a "condemned cell." At 8 p.m. Julius was taken to the death chamber. As John F. Neville writes in *The Press, the Rosenbergs, and the Cold War*, "Three wire services reporters, Bob Considine, International News Service; Relman Morin, Associated Press; and Jack Wolilston, United Press; watched him enter. He was clad in a brown t-shirt, white pants, and slippers." Meanwhile, Rabbi Irving Koslowe read the 23rd Psalm. Then Julius was strapped into the chair, a mask was placed over his head, and he was electrocuted. Twelve minutes had elapsed.

Ethel was next. "She moved slowly and wore a dark green print dress. Rabbi Koslowe read the 50th and 23rd Psalms. Ethel's serene expression surprised and discomfited even the veteran reporters. Before being strapped into the electric chair, she thrust out a hand at prison matron Helen Evans. Rosenberg pulled Evans toward her and kissed her on the cheek while being strapped into the chair."

The switch was thrown, and Ethel joined her husband. Almost. "To their great surprise both physicians detected a heartbeat. They held a 'whispered conference' and then informed the Warden that Ethel Rosenberg was still alive. Denno ordered two more surges of electricity be sent through the prisoner's body. Ethel Rosenberg was pronounced dead at about seventeen past eight. She was the first American woman to be electrocuted by federal order."[28]

Although there was no direct link between the Hiss case and the Rosenbergs's trial, their proximity in time left an impression that they were part of a flow of cold war episodes of Communist intrigue and Soviet subversion of the United States both at home and abroad. In the press, the cold war and communism was treated as one big story with many parts, but the whole added up to an image of a nation besieged by enemies outside and by traitors within. The Hiss case provided Richard Nixon a springboard to national fame as a Communist hunter and defender of freedom, which catapulted him to a Senate seat, the vice presidency, and eventually the White House. It gave a sense of plausibility to Senator Joseph McCarthy's red-baiting claims of Communists-in-government and launched his four-year reign of terror. McCarthy's tactics never produced a single piece of evidence supporting his claims, but his wanton trampling of basic constitutional rights left the mark of his name on the era. The Rosenbergs were treated by the press as proof that the international Communist conspiracy was very real and very close to home. The actions and words of those who criticized the government's or the press' behavior in either the Hiss or Rosenbergs cases were portrayed as "disloyal." And the press helped to make it clear that "disloyalty" was tantamount to "treason." Dissent was not tolerated. To diverge from the consensus view, to be a member of a vocal minority that refused to accept the majority viewpoint created a national political environment in the 1950s that was closeminded and oppressively conservative. It also did something else. It set the stage for society's convulsive, and often times violent, reaction to the antiwar and civil rights movements of the 1960s.

NOTES

1. James Aronson, *The Press and the Cold War* (Boston: Beacon Press, 1973), 51; see also Victor S. Navasky, *Naming Names* (New York: Viking Press, 1980); David Caute, *The Great Fear: The Anti-Communist Purge Under Truman and Eisenhower* (New York: Simon and Schuster, 1978).

2. Allen Weinstein, *Perjury: The Hiss-Chambers Case* (New York: Alfred A. Knopf, 1978), xvi; see also David Halberstam, *The Powers That Be* (New York: Alfred A. Knopf, 1979), 80.

3. Weinstein, *Perjury*, 344; Halberstam, *The Powers That Be*, 80–81; W. A. Swanberg, *Luce and His Empire* (New York: Charles Scribner's Sons, 1972), 196–197 and 222.

4. Meyer A. Zeligs, *Friendship and Fratricide: An Analysis of Whittaker Chambers and Alger Hiss* (New York: The Viking Press, 1967), 4.

5. See Whittaker Chambers, *Witness* (New York: Random House, 1952), 610–611; Zeligs, *Friendship and Fratricide;* Aronson, The Press and the Cold War.

6. Swanberg, *Luce and His Empire*, 197; see also Weinstein, *Perjury*; Morton Levitt and Michael Levitt, *A Tissue of Lies: Nixon v. Hiss* (New York: McGraw-Hill, 1979), 267.

7. Weinstein, *Perjury*, 3–4, 58.

8. Ibid., passim; Aronson, *The Press and the Cold War*, 76; *Communist Daily Worker*, 26 August 1948.

9. Swanberg, *Luce and His Empire*, 284–288.

10. Halberstam, *The Powers That Be*, 260–261; Aronson, *The Press and the Cold War*, 51–52; Levitt and Levitt, *A Tissue of Lies*, 23–25; Weinstein, *Perjury,* 27.

11. Halberstam, *The Powers That Be*, 261; Levitt and Levitt, *A Tissue of Lies*, 20.

12. Chambers, *Witness*, 709; Weinstein, *Perjury*, 276–286.

13. Weinstein, *Perjury*, 280–281; *Atlanta Constitution*, 11 December 1948; *Washington Post*, 9 December 1948.

14. Aronson, *The Press and the Cold War*, 56–57; Levitt and Levitt, *A Tissue of Lies*, 145; *Chicago Tribune*, 10 July 1949.

15. *Life*, 10 October 1949; Aronson, *The Press and the Cold War*, 57.

16. Aronson, *The Press and the Cold War*, 56–57; Swanberg, *Luce and His Empire*, 287; Levitt and Levitt, *A Tissue of Lies*, 161; Weinstein, *Perjury*, 471.

17. Zeligs, *Friendship and Fratricide*, 431.

18. John F. Neville, *The Press, the Rosenbergs, and the Cold War* (Westport, Conn.: Praeger, 1995), 19–29; Michael Schudson, *Discovering the News: A Social History of the Newspaper* (New York: Basic Books, 1978).

19. Neville, *The Press, the Rosenbergs, and the Cold War*, 20; *Chicago Tribune*, 18 July 1950; *Atlanta Constitution*, 18 July 1950; *Washington Post*, 18 July 1950; *New York Herald Tribune*, 18 July 1950.

20. Neville, *The Press, the Rosenbergs, and the Cold War*, 23; *New York Times*, 12 August 1950; *New York Herald Tribune*, 12 August 1950; and *San Francisco Chronicle*, 12 August 1950.

21. Neville, *The Press, the Rosenbergs, and the Cold War*, 38–46.

22. Ibid., 40–42; *New York Times*, 15 March 1951; Caute, *The Great Fear*, 66; *New York Times*, 28 March 1951.

23. Caute, *The Great Fear*, 63; Neville, *The Press, the Rosenbergs, and the Cold War*, 36, 48; *Atlanta Constitution*, 8 March 1951; *Chicago Tribune*, 8 March 1951.

24. Neville, *The Press, the Rosenbergs, and the Cold War*, 35, 50–51; Aronson, *The Press and the Cold War*, 59; *New York Daily Mirror*, 6 April 1951; *Atlanta Constitution*, 6 April 1951.

25. Neville, *The Press, the Rosenbergs, and the Cold War*, 84.

26. Ibid., 74.

27. Ibid., 75.

28. Ibid., 133.

12

The Case of the Chicago Seven
(1969)

"'The pigs are coming, the pigs are coming'"

Arthur J. Kaul

Jerry Rubin: "I did not walk out on the trial . . . I like being here. It is interesting . . ."
U.S. Judge Julius J. Hoffman: "That is the best statement I have heard during the trial. You said you enjoyed being here."
Jerry Rubin: "It is good theater, Your Honor." [1]

U.S. District Judge Julius J. Hoffman, seventy-four, peered from his wood-paneled bench on the twenty-third floor of the Federal Building in Chicago on October 29, 1969, and told marshals to remove Black Panther Party chairman Bobby Seale, thirty-two, from his courtroom and "deal with him as he should be dealt with in these circumstances." Ten minutes later, Seale returned to the table where seven other defendants sat, his ankles shackled to a gray steel folding chair, his arms handcuffed, and a white muslin cloth tied around his mouth to silence his outbursts against the judge. "I want my right to speak on behalf of my constitutional rights," Seale's muffled voice shouted through the gag." "I don't think you accomplish your purpose with that contrivance," the judge told marshals.

Again, Seale was removed from the courtroom, returning after a brief recess with ten inches of white adhesive tape over the gag. "Let me cross-examine the witness," he said after working the tape loose. "I still want a right to cross-examine the witness."[2] The next day, Seale's gag came off during a scuffle with marshals, and the militant black leader shouted to the judge: "You fascist dog!" Defense attorney William M. Kunstler protested the gagging, saying it was "impossible for us as human beings to go on like this with a black man in chains."[3] Meanwhile, outside the Federal Building picketing demonstrators wearing gags carried placards saying "Free Bobby, Power to the People."[4]

The five-month trial of the "Chicago Eight" for conspiracy to cross state lines with intent to "incite, organize, promote and encourage" riots at the August 1968 National Democratic Convention in Chicago became the "Chicago Seven" trial on November 5, 1969, when the judge convicted Seale of sixteen counts of contempt of court, sentenced him to four years in prison, and severed his case from the other seven defendants.[5] Yet, the chaining and gagging of Bobby Seale became emblematic of "the most important political trial in the history of the United States."[6] Artists' drawings of the militant black dissident found their way into newspapers and television news broadcasts across the nation. The defendants and their attorneys used the courtroom to stage a counterculture guerrilla theater that transformed a federal court into a circus of protest against racism and the Vietnam War.

The federal grand jury indictments for conspiracy against the eight defendants grew out of confrontational and volatile moments in the civil rights and antiwar movements of the 1960s. Urban violence that erupted in the summer of 1967 prompted Congress to pass antiriot provisions attached to the 1968 Civil Rights Act that became law on April 11, 1968. Chicago's law-and-order reputation emerged a week after the April 4, 1968, assassination of Martin Luther King Jr. when Chicago's blacks rampaged through the streets, looting stores and starting fires. Eleven days later, Chicago mayor Richard J. Daley called a press conference at which he disclosed his orders to "shoot to kill" any arsonist and "shoot to maim" looters.[7]

Anti–Vietnam War activists planned demonstrations at the Democratic National Convention in August 1968 and unsuccessfully sought parade permits from the city administration. The longtime Democratic mayor was determined not to let the convention be disrupted. Chicago became an armed camp by the time the convention opened, the mayor defending his actions by telling CBS correspondent Walter Cronkite that he had "reports and intelligence on my desk" of plans to "assassinate" presidential contenders. *Chicago Sun-Times* columnist Mike Royko observed that the city had completed "the most massive security arrangements in the history of American politics," a "defensive force" of 25,000 that included 12,000 Chicago policemen on twelve-hour shifts, the mobilization of 5,000 Illinois national guardsmen, and 6,000 specially trained army troops in combat readiness north of the city.[8]

The preparations didn't help.

Millions of Americans watched the nationally televised Democratic Convention in Chicago erupt into violence when police retaliated against both peaceful and provocative antiwar demonstrators on the city streets. Chicago attorney Daniel Walker's investigative team later concluded that "police violence against media representatives" was "plainly deliberate" [at times it appeared reporters were arrested, attacked, and sometimes mugged by the police.] and law enforcement's "indiscriminate" and "unrestrained" attacks against demonstrators constituted "a police riot."[9] On March 20, 1969, five months after publication of the "Walker Report," a federal grand jury indicted protest organizers and participants for conspiracy to promote riots. In addition to Bobby Seale, then being held in a federal prison in California charged with unlawful flight to avoid prosecution for the slaying of a former Black Panther, the grand jury indicted:

> Rennard "Rennie" C. Davis, twenty-nine, a founder of Students for a Democratic Society (SDS) and a project director for the demonstrations during the convention of the National Mobilization Committee to End the War in Vietnam (MOBE).
>
> David Dellinger, fifty-three, the pacifist chairman of MOBE and editor of *Liberation* magazine who had served prison terms for failure to register for the military draft.
>
> John Froines, thirty, an assistant professor of chemistry at the University of Oregon and a member of MOBE's convention staff.
>
> Tom Hayden, twenty-nine, a founder of SDS who helped draft its "Port Huron Statement" in 1962 and later made trips to Hanoi, was co-director of the convention project.
>
> Abbott "Abbie" Hoffman, thirty-one, a founder of the Youth International Party ("Yippies") who led demonstrations at the convention.
>
> Jerry Rubin, thirty-one, co-founder of the Yippies and project director for the 1967 March on the Pentagon who was serving a forty-five-day jail sentence in California for participating in a sit-in at the University of California at Berkeley.
>
> Lee Weiner, thirty, a Chicago community organizer, then a teaching assistant in the sociology department at Northwestern University and a member of the mobilization committee staff.

The trial opened on September 24, 1969, amidst demonstrators outside the Federal Building chanting "Hey, hey, Richard J., how many skulls did you crack today." *New York Times* correspondent J. Anthony Lukas viewed the trial as a continuing engagement in the "Battle of Chicago," a resumption of the "struggle between the young dissenters and constituted authority" that erupted during the convention a year earlier. The first prosecution under the riot provisions of the 1968 Civil Rights Act held dual significance as an "important test of the limits of radical dissent in America," he wrote, and as "an event in the radical movement itself" to further demonstrations against war and racism.[10] A spokesman for the defendants called the trial "a combination of Scopes trial, revolution in the streets, Woodstock festival and People's Park, all rolled into one."[11] Indeed, three months before the trial, Hayden proclaimed: "We need to expand our struggle to include a total attack on the courts. . . . There is no reason for us to become submissive at the courtroom door."[12]

The tone of the trial was set the first day when Judge Julius J. Hoffman found four defense attorneys in contempt for their failure to appear in court and ordered their arrest. Defense attorney Leonard I. Weinglass argued that three of the attorney's had been hired only to prepare pretrial motions and the fourth was detained at a trial in New York City. All four lawyers earlier had sent telegrams to the court withdrawing from the case. Government prosecutor Thomas Foran complained that the absent lawyers' conduct was "irresponsible and unprofessional." The judge agreed, saying: "My wishes are that a lawyer respect the court. You cannot withdraw from a case in my court by telegram." Two days later, two of the lawyers had been taken into custody and stood before Judge Hoffman, prompting defense attorney Kunstler to protest: "I've never heard of trying a case with two counsel in custody." The judge ordered the two attorneys jailed over the weekend, but an appeals court released them on bail.[13]

Five days after the trial's raucous opening, nearly 150 lawyers from around the country, including a thirteen-member faculty delegation from Harvard Law School, arrived at the Federal Court building to protest the judge's actions. A contingent of lawyers filed a friend-of-the-court brief that criticized the judge's actions as being "a travesty of justice [which] threatens to destroy confidence in the entire judicial process." "I have no desire to damage the professional careers of young lawyers," Hoffman told the four defense lawyers, then abruptly vacated his own contempt order.[14] When defense attorney Kunstler moved for a mistrial on grounds that the judge was prejudiced, Hoffman denied the motion. Kunstler complained that the judge's "intimidation" was making the defense "try this case while fearing." "You'll always have to fear in this courtroom when you make allegations like these over your signature," the judge said.[15]

Black Panther Bobby Seale's on-going argument with the judge over his legal representation led to his conviction for contempt. Seale repeatedly insisted from the trial's outset that he wanted to be represented in the case only by West Coast lawyer Charles R. Garry, who had defended the Black Panthers in other cases. Garry was about to undergo gall bladder surgery when the conspiracy trial began and was not available for Seale's defense. The judge refused a motion to delay the trial to allow Garry to recover and participate in the case. Instead, Judge Hoffman insisted over Seale's protests that Kunstler was his attorney. On September 26, Seale submitted a handwritten motion to the court:

I submit to Judge Julius Hoffman that the trial be postponed until a later date when I, Bobby G. Seale, can have the "legal council [sic] of my choice who is effective," Attorney Charles R. Garry and if my constitutional rights are not respected by this court then other lawyers on the record here representing me, except Charles R. Garry, do not speak for me, represent me, as of this date 9-26-69. I fire them now until Charles R. Garry can be made chief counsel in this trial.[16]

If his request was denied, Seale said, then he would "see the Judge as a blatant racist." Hoffman denied the motion and refused to let Seale represent himself in his own defense. A month later, on October 27, after numerous caustic outbursts and courtroom scuffles, Hoffman ordered Seale to be seated. "You represent the corruptness of this rotten Government," Seale shouted to the judge. Later he told the judge: "You begin to stink . . . oink, oink." When the judge ordered federal marshals to make him sit down, Seale shouted: "I demand my constitutional rights! Demand! Demand! Demand!"[17]

When he was found guilty of sixteen counts of contempt of court on November 5, Seale objected, again calling the judge a "racist," a "fascist," and a "pig." After Hoffman read the contempt citation, he asked the Black Panther if he had anything to tell the court. "What kind of crap is this," Seale asked. "All this time I ask to speak in behalf of my constitutional rights and you won't let me. Now after reading all this stuff, you say I can speak. Is this a court? It must be a fascist operation." Seale continued: "I'm not in contempt of court. I know that I, as a human being, have a right to stand up in court and ask for my constitutional rights. I'll continue to ask for my rights as a black man living in the scope of racist, decadent America."[18] When marshals led him from the courtroom, spectators raised clenched fists and shouted, "Right on, Bobby."[19] The Chicago Eight became the Chicago Seven.

Defense attorneys asked for a mistrial, claiming that testimony about Seale's activities at the Democratic convention had tainted the jury, thus preventing the remaining seven from getting a fair trial. The motion was denied. "A glorious chapter in jurisprudence is not being written in Chicago," a *New York Times* editorial commented, calling the Chicago Seven trial proceedings a "farce."[20] Judge Hoffman continued to frustrate defense efforts to plead their case. His refusal to allow the defense to bring a "White Panther" defense witness from a Michigan prison set the stage for another angry protest. "That's an arbitrary denial," David Dellinger muttered. When Judge Hoffman demanded to know who uttered the remark, Dellinger jumped up and yelled: "It's David Dellinger and he says it's an arbitrary denial when you say who is a necessary witness! It's just like Bobby Seale said, this is a fascist court!" Yippie leader Abbie Hoffman added: "Is the Government going to present our defense as well as our prosecution? We can't respect the law when it's a tyranny."[21]

Government prosecutors rested their case on December 5, 1969, after presenting fifty-four witnesses—policemen, special investigators, undercover agents, and informers—fourteen movies and three tape recordings during fifty working days that sent the typed trial transcript to 9,315 pages. The Chicago Seven and their defense attorneys now faced two major strategy options: (1) move for a directed verdict of acquittal on grounds that the government had failed to prove conspiratorial intent to incite riots or (2) mount a costly and lengthy defense to vindicate themselves and to present their generation's alternative culture, lifestyle, and political ideals to the public. A taste of that alternative cultural style was contained in a pamphlet distributed during the Democratic National Convention:

Disobey your parents. . . . Burn your money. You know life is a dream and all our institutions are man-made illusions, effective only because you take the dream for reality. Break down the family, church, nature, city, economy, turn life into an art form and theater of the soul. What is needed is a generation of people who are freaky, crazy, irrational, sexy, angry, irreligious, childish and mad. People who burn draft cards, burn high school diplomas, college degrees. . . . People who lure the youth with music, pot, and acid. . . . Burn your houses down and you will be free.[22]

On the first day of the defense, Tom Hayden told the press that the Chicago Seven and other radicals were striving for "the creation of a new society in the streets . . . with its own natural laws, structures, language and symbols. . . . Chicago, 1968, will be recreated in the courtroom," he said.[23]

The Chicago Seven staged street theater in Federal District Court, with a parade of defense witnesses drawn from the counterculture. Folksinger Phil Ochs was called to the stand to perform a rendition of his protest song "I Ain't Marchin' Anymore" accompanied on a guitar that attorneys had submitted as a defense exhibit. The judge sustained the prosecution's objection to the guitar, permitting the singer to recite lyrics about how the old lead the young to war and death, about how they want the young to fight and kill and then do it all again, about how it's always the young to die. As Ochs concluded, "[B]ut I ain't marchin' anymore."[24]

The judge later refused to let twenty-two-year-old Arlo Guthrie sing his folk anthem, "Alice's Restaurant." "No reflection on your professional capacity—just a matter of law," the judge remarked. At a news conference outside the court, Guthrie said of the trial: "It's like Perry Mason. The good guys are in trouble. The bad guys have the evidence. But the good guys are going to win—like they always do."[25]

The testimony of beat poet Allen Ginsberg prompted *New York Times* correspondent J. Anthony Lukas to write: "Allen Ginsberg, the poet, met Julius Hoffman, the judge, today and the result was a total lack of communication."[26] Ginsberg entered the courtroom wearing a psychedelic tie and bright sport shirt with his folded hands under his chin in a Hindu greeting gesture. Ginsberg testified that he had attended a "be-in" in San Francisco with defendant Jerry Rubin. When Judge Hoffman asked the poet "What is a be-in?" Ginsberg described it as "a gathering of young people aware of our planetary fate, imbued with a new consciousness, a new planetary lifestyle . . . emphasizing life rather than competition, acquisition and war." Ginsberg described a news conference in New York in February 1968 where he gave a speech and chanted. The poet then launched into a courtroom performance of the Hare Krishna mantra: "Hare Krishna, Krishna Hare Krishna, Hare Rama. Hare Rama, Ram. Ram. Hare. Hare." Government prosecutor Thomas A. Foran objected that the mantra had "no materiality to this case." "But it has a spirituality to this case," Ginsberg countered. Judge Hoffman sustained the objection.

Judge Hoffman: The language of the United States District Court is English. I don't even know what that language was.
Ginsberg: It's Sanskrit.
Judge Hoffman: Well, we don't allow Sanskrit in the Federal Courts.

The judge recessed court for the day when the poet started to play a harmonium to accompany his chant. The next day, Ginsberg took the witness stand and tried to calm a boisterous dispute between the judge and a defense attorney with a booming Hindu incantation of "om." Government prosecutors repeatedly objected to "oms." When Ginsberg again began chanting "oms," the chief government prosecutor jumped to his feet to object: "I had no objection to the two 'oms.' I just didn't want it to go on all morning." The objection was sustained.[27] Defense attorneys asked Ginsberg to recite his long poem, "Howl," to the court, and the poet obliged. He described how the best young minds were ruined by madness as they dragged "themselves through the Negro streets looking for an angry fix. . . ."

After more than five minutes of recitation, the poet boomed a line into the ear of the judge, who leaped to his feet and put his hand on his head in a expression of horrified astonishment.[28]

Chicago mayor Richard Daley spent about three hours in the witness stand on January 6, 1970. Government prosecutors successfully thwarted defense attorneys' attempts at interrogation, objecting to twenty-six straight questions during a twenty-minute period. The judge upheld every objection. The mayor uttered only a few hundred words during testimony, certainly not enough for the defense to show the mayor as a "hostile" witness. The judge denied the defense argument: "Nothing in the witness's behavior indicates that he is hostile. His manner has been that of a gentleman." Defense attorney Kunstler asked to present an "offer of proof" of what the defense would have proved with the mayor's testimony. With the jury out of the courtroom, Kunstler's "offer of proof" asserted: "There was a conspiracy, overt or tacit, between Mayor Daley and the Democratic Administration of Lyndon B. Johnson to prevent or crush any significant demonstrations against war, poverty, imperialism and racism and in support of alternative cultures at the 1968 Democratic National Convention."[29]

The day before Daley testified, the Chicago Seven handed to newsmen their own "indictments" of the mayor, accusing him of using the "facilities and power of his office" to "rob, steal, denigrate, repress, and murder the people of the City of Chicago and elsewhere."[30]

Some observers saw the February 4, 1970, court session as the most tumultuous of the five-plus month trial. Judge Hoffman revoked the bail of David Dellinger and ordered him sent to the Cook County jail after the defendant shouted vulgarities at a government witness. "Never in my 50 years in court have I heard so much obscenity as I've heard during this trial," Judge Hoffman said. "You've never been a defendant here and had to sit and

154 The Press on Trial

listen while witnesses lie about you," defense attorney Kunstler retorted. Assistant U.S. attorney Richard C. Schultz stormed to the lectern objecting to Kunstler's remarks. "Schultz, you're a Nazi jailer," Abbie Hoffman shouted. When marshals came to escort Dellinger from the courtroom, Abbie Hoffman scuffled with them. "Leave him alone," Hoffman's wife, Anita, shouted. Rennie Davis, Jerry Rubin, and two other defendants shouted vulgarities. "You brought this on, Your Honor," Kunstler told the judge. "This is what happened in Chicago. Your action is entirely vindictive." Abbie Hoffman shouted to the judge: "You're a disgrace to the Jews, runt! You should have served Hitler better!" Marshals threw the defendant into a chair, finally managed to take Dellinger to jail, and cleared the courtroom.[31]

The trial of the Chicago Seven ended as it began—in contempt. After the jury filed out of the courtroom to begin deliberations on February 14, 1970, Judge Hoffman convicted four defendants of contempt of court for "numerous acts that add up to a total disregard for the conduct of this trial." David T. Dellinger was found guilty of thirty-one counts and sentenced to two years, five months, and sixteen days in prison; Rennie Davis, twenty-three counts and sentenced to two years, one month, and fourteen days; Tom Hayden, eleven counts and sentenced to one year, two months, and fourteen days; and Abbie Hoffman, twenty-four counts and sentenced to eight months.

Hayden told the judge: "You see around you proof that your system is collapsing." "This court is in contempt of human life, dignity and justice," Dellinger said. "You want us to be like good Jews, going quietly to concentration camps while the court suppresses the truth. It's a travesty of justice. The record condemns you, not us."

Said Rennie Davis: "You represent all that is old, ugly and bigoted in this country and I'll tell you that the spirit you see at this defense table will devour you."

Abbie Hoffman told the judge: "When decorum is repression, the only duty free men have is to speak out. We can't respect an authority we regard as illegitimate."[32]

The next day, Judge Hoffman convicted two defense attorneys and the three other defendants for contempt and ordered prison sentences. Attorney William M. Kunstler was convicted on 24 counts and sentenced to 4 years and 13 days in federal prison; Attorney Leonard I. Weinglass, 14 counts and sentenced to 1 year 8 months and 3 days. The defendants' sentences were: Jerry Rubin, 15 counts and 2 years, one month, and 23 days; John Froines, 10 counts and 6 months and 15 days; and Lee Weiner, 7 counts and 2 months, 18 days. In two days, the judge dispensed 15 years, 9 months, and 116 days in prison for 159 counts of contempt of court. Outside the courtroom, demonstrators chanted "Two, four, six, eight, jail Hoffman, smash the state."[33]

The jury of ten women and two men deliberated for forty hours, returning its verdict at 12:20 p.m., February 18, 1970. The seven defendants were acquitted of conspiracy to incite a riot during the 1968 Democratic

National Convention. Five defendants—Dellinger, Davis, Hayden, Hoffman, and Rubin—were convicted of individual acts of promoting a riot and two defendants—Froines and Weiner—were acquitted on all counts. Judge Hoffman rejected a motion for bond pending an appeal of the convictions. "From the evidence in this case, from their conduct in this trial," he said, "I conclude that these are dangerous men to be at large." At a postverdict news conference, a spokesman for the Chicago Seven issued a statement drafted by the defendants:

This outrageous verdict results from the unholy combination of an unconstitutional law, a Daley prosecutor and a hostile authoritarian judge. . . . Everyone who opposes the war against Vietnam—and everyone who advocates the liberation of black people—everyone with long hair and a free spirit—everyone who condemns the existence of poverty here and throughout the world—all have been found guilty by this verdict.[34]

Two days later, Judge Hoffman imposed the maximum sentence of five years in prison and fines of $5,000 each plus "the costs of prosecution." The prison terms were to run concurrently with sentences imposed for contempt of court. The judge again refused bail. David Dellinger told the judge: "All prisoners, we must realize, are political prisoners. The bank robber I talked to yesterday was only trying to get his in the ways he thought were open to him." Rennie Davis turned to Prosecutor Thomas A. Foran. "I'm going to turn his kids into revolutionaries," he said. "We are going to turn the sons and daughters of the ruling class into Vietcong." "I know those guys up there better than you do," Abbie Hoffman told the judge, pointing to portraits of American presidents on the wall. "Hell, I grew up only a few miles from Sam Adams's place, from the bridge which Paul Revere rode across on his motorcycle yelling 'The pigs are coming, the pigs are coming.'" Jerry Rubin offered the judge a copy of his new book, _Do It!_, with an inscription that read: "You radicalized more young people than we did. You're America's top Yippie."[35]

The Chicago Seven took the sixties protest movement off the streets and into the courtroom, staging a bizarre guerrilla-style theater of anarchy and absurdity in the halls of justice. Their antics and stridently incendiary rhetoric succeeded in making everyone look silly. Their ideological clownmanship transformed formidable problems of the human condition—poverty, racism, and war—into jokes that everyone could all the more easily ignore. These privileged members of the American middle class viewed themselves as victims and political prisoners, caught in the juggernaut of an unjust and illegitimate system. And they laughed about it. For the poor, the degraded, and the dispossessed, poverty, racism, and war aren't the least bit funny.

NOTES

1. Jason Epstein, *The Great Conspiracy Trial: An Essay on Law, Liberty and the Constitution* (New York: Random House, 1970), 283–285; John Schultz, *Motion Will Be Denied: A New Report on the Chicago Conspiracy Trial* (New York: William Morrow, 1972), 37–83.

2. *New York Times,* 30 October 1969.

3. *New York Times,* 31 October 1969; 1 November 1969.

4. *New York Times,* 31 October 1969.

5. *New York Times,* 6 November 1969.

6. *New York Times,* 24 September 1969.

7. Mike Royko, *Boss: Richard J. Daley of Chicago* (New York: E. P. Dutton, 1971), 164–165.

8. Ibid., 178, 187.

9. *New York Times,* 24 September 1969; *Rights in Conflict: The Violent Confrontation of Demonstrators and Police in the Parks and Streets of Chicago During the Week of the Democratic National Convention of 1968. A Report Submitted by Daniel Walker, Director of the Chicago Study Team, to the National Commission on the Causes and Prevention of Violence* ["Walker Report"] (New York: Bantam Books, 1968), 1–7, 317; Arthur J. Kaul, "The Unraveling of America," in *The Press in Times of Crisis,* ed., Lloyd Chiasson Jr. (Westport, Conn.: Praeger, 1995), 175–176.

10. *New York Times,* 24 September 1969.

11. Ibid.

12. James W. Ely Jr., "The Chicago Conspiracy Case," in *American Political Trials,* ed., Michael R. Belknap (Westport, Conn.: Greenwood Press, 1981), 280.

13. *New York Times,* 25 September 1969, 27 September 1969.

14. *New York Times,* 30 September 1969.

15. Ibid.

16. Ely, "The Chicago Conspiracy Case," 272.

17. *New York Times,* 28 October 1969.

18. *New York Times,* 6 November 1969.

19. Ibid.

20. *New York Times,* 7 November 1969.

21. *New York Times,* 27 November 1969.

22. Epstein, *The Great Conspiracy Trial,* 310.

23. Ibid., 306-307.

24. *New York Times,* 12 December 1969.

25. *New York Times,* 16 January 1970.

26. *New York Times,* 12 December 1969.

27. Ibid.

28. Ibid.

29. Ibid.

30. Ibid.

31. *New York Times,* 5 February 1970.

32. *New York Times*, 15 February 1970.
33. *New York Times*, 16 February 1970.
34. *New York Times*, 19 February 1970.
35. *New York Times*, 21 February 1970.

13

The Case of Charles Manson
(1970)

"Plump, white rabbits"

Robert Dardenne

California, the make-believe land of milk and honey, attracted thousands of America's children in the 1960s. They roamed its cities and highways, sleeping in crash pads and fields looking for better lives and maybe a better world. They left duties and responsibilities to seek enlightenment and simple pleasures through sex, drugs, and rock 'n' roll, finding a mystic or guru along the way.

Hopeful but naive, these "plump, white rabbits,"[1] so the story goes, loved, danced, sang, and wore flowers in their hair. But by 1967, they had already attracted wolves, hungry for a good feed. The wolves took advantage, selling bad dope, stealing, raping, and honing the ugly edge of violence that sheared innocence from flower power.

A thirty-two-year-old ex-convict and petty thief, just out of prison and amazed at the free love world outside, found the late sixties California a paradise made for a man with his lusts, ambitions, talents, and morals.

Charles Manson was a wolf. But one with extraordinary appetites. He blossomed among the flower children into a predator father figure who collected lost and damaged souls and mentally stripped them of their pasts. He formed them into his "family" and imbued them with his upside down value system—no sense makes sense, love is death, death is life, guilt is sin.

Ultimately, they became the puppets in his horror show, as Manson orchestrated "perhaps the most inhuman, nightmarish, horror-filled hour of savage murder and human slaughter in the recorded annals of crime."[2]

Neither the press nor the public could comprehend what happened, or why. How could a diminutive penny-ante con man develop into a cult leader of young people, many from upper-class backgrounds? How could he influence them to senselessly butcher strangers, to carve messages on flesh, write slogans in blood on the walls, without a glimmer of remorse?

A reactive press could provide little insight. It reported facts, but was ill-equipped to deal with the complexities that would lead to the truth of what happened, and in the end, like the unsuspecting public it served, was surprised and shocked by each new twist. Reflecting its own white, middle-class mindset, and focusing on the odd and sensational, of which the murders and following trial provided an abundant supply, the press could do little more than follow the authorities on a wild chase through the depths of human cruelty and one of the longest, most flamboyant and bizarre trials in California history.

Called a cult leader, guru, evil Pied Piper, and con man who failed at everything he tried, Manson was a mixture of megalomania and self-pity, seeing himself at times as Jesus Christ or Satan or "a half-assed nothing who hardly knew how to read or write," a man who "couldn't hold on to my wives, was a lousy pimp, got caught every time I stole, wasn't a good enough musician to hit the market, . . . and resented every aspect of family life."[3] Blaming his mother for a childhood of neglect and abuse, he described his early life as one of rejection, pain, and sadness. This background gave him insight into the troubled, needy, impressionable young people he attracted through cunning and some strange charisma.

He brought to them a piecemeal philosophy born in jails and prisons. It combined mysticism, hypnosis, Eastern religions, the Bible, the Beatles, and "The Process," a radical Scientology offshoot whose adherents worship both Christ and the devil. Manson "deprogrammed" his followers using sex, suggestion, repetition, isolation, drugs, and a love that most who study cults recognize as distorted.[4] He repeatedly insisted that parental bonds, restrictions, and values be rejected, stripping away the past to the "pure," resulting in a blank mind he recreated in his own twisted image.

Charles "Tex" Watson, a significant figure in the horror that followed, said this brainwashing was greatly enhanced by drugs, particularly LSD,[5] which Manson frequently dispensed, apparently taking smaller doses himself.[6] What came to be called his "Family" comprised insecure, vulnerable people finding an acceptance, affection, and freedom among each other. Most had rejected their families and normal society before meeting Manson, who turned that rejection into hatred.

Mary Brunner, twenty-three, slim, red-haired, and educated, was charmed so much by the man playing his guitar outside the university library where she worked that she took him to live in her apartment.[7] On a foray from Brunner's apartment, Manson happened upon a slight, brown-haired, freckle-faced, obviously distraught young woman sitting on a curb at Venice Beach. He listened to her story and sympathized. At odds with a domineering father, she saw in Manson an understanding and accepting figure. Lynette Fromme left with Manson to join Brunner as Manson's second steady companion. Watching his women live without dissension, Manson made a decision that would have devastating consequences. "I wanted," he said, "my own little circle,"[8] and he set about collecting lost children for purposes he probably did not understand himself.[9] "Everybody should have a father like

Charlie," one of his devoted women once said. Manson thought so too, often telling a sexual partner to imagine him as her father. Said Manson to one of the female members of the family: "Forget your daddy. I'm your daddy. Doesn't this feel too good to be wrong?"[10]

Many things felt good to Charles Manson during those days: "I was living," he noted, "a fantasy come true."[11] He, Brunner, and Fromme met eighteen-year-old Patricia Krenwinkel, who after four days of sex with Manson, left her job and supposedly her last paycheck to follow him.[12] Later in the Haight, eighteen-year-old Susan Denise Atkins, having left her troubled home, having been arrested, and having drunk her way through numerous lovers, found in Manson whatever it was she sought. After "dancing with him and making love, after sensing and seeing the power of his mind, I knew I would go with him if he asked me."[13] He did, and she went, joining the ever widening circle.

Manson moved his young people frequently, replenishing his supply of "young loves" through "personal magnetism" and a "constant process of selection" that attracted those who "thirsted for a leader."[14] Like a weird mirror, he reflected each person's desires and needs. Because "deprogramming" didn't always take, Manson relied on Bobby Beausoleil and Paul Watkins to procure his young women.[15] Beausoleil, for example, brought in Catherine Share and Leslie Van Houten. Manson orchestrated the group's sex, forbidding his women from having sex with those out of favor.[16]

But for a man who collected so many women, Manson didn't like them much. He told several people women were good mainly for sex,[17] but they also absorbed his abuse, and satisfied his need to dominate. They cleaned, gathered food from garbage bins, cooked, sewed, stole, and eventually killed for him. At the trial, they wanted to die for him. His mother remembered him as a "charming little boy who never worked or fought for what he wanted, but let others, usually women, do it for him."[18]

Even by far out sixties' California standards, the Manson circle of females was unusual and attracted attention, not all of which he liked. They frequented "The Spiral Staircase," a Topanga Canyon house that drew an odd crowd of knowns and unknowns seeking chemical and sexual fulfillment. One night, with "the girls" in the house and Manson on the Family bus preparing to wash himself, Susan Atkins had a vision. "Charlie was there, alone. He was dressed in a long white robe. I immediately knew that he might be God himself; if not, he was close to him."[19] Manson washed her feet, and she washed the feet of a man behind her. Atkins saw God that night just as many Manson followers would see Jesus Christ, the "messiah come again."[20] Manson had already seen himself as Christ when he experienced an LSD crucifixion. He later said he may have "implied" he was Christ.[21]

As it turned out, the "deep spiritual moment" on the bus quickly became a sex circus involving more than a dozen people,[22] an orgy that intensified Manson's bad vibes about the Spiral Staircase and illustrated the fragility of his control over his circle in places of easy access. He needed a home for his family, an isolated one; he needed money and lots of it; he had plans.

Not only did his circle grow, but his odd charm and clever, cunning doggedness appealed, at least temporarily, to important people in Hollywood. For awhile he moved his group into the luxurious home of the Beach Boys' Dennis Wilson, and he briefly held an advisory position on a film never produced.[23] Having learned to play the guitar in prison, this "moderately talented amateur"[24] wrote songs that still appear on albums of various groups, including the Beach Boys. Talent scout Gregg Jacobson, fascinated with the "'whole Charlie Manson package,' songs, philosophy, life style,"[25] introduced him to producer Terry Melcher and arranged a recording session. Manson counted on success in part to spread his word,[26] but his career dreams ended in acrimony. He blamed many people, including Melcher.

In August 1968, Manson found as much a home as his Family would ever have. The group settled in Chatsworth, California, in the northwest of the San Fernando Valley at the Spahn Movie Ranch, a B Western movie set consisting of several buildings, false fronts and a riding stable. Several ranch hands worked for blind, eighty-year-old George Spahn, who Manson kept happy with young women, particularly Fromme, who cooked, cleaned, and had sex with him. The early days at the ranch, from which Manson banned watches and calendars, were filled with drugs, sex, and games of make-believe.[27] At times the Manson group traveled to the Death Valley area to the virtually inaccessible Myers and Barker ranches. Desolate and inhabited mostly by miners and those escaping civilization, the area fitted Manson's needs, increasingly fueled by paranoia about police and race wars. Stories and rumors of the group's activities at the Spahn, Barker, and Myers ranches include everything from fun and games to rituals, sacrifice, and other violence.[28]

The lost hope of Manson's music career, his bitterness toward Wilson and Melcher, a galling snub by Wilson's agent, and real or imagined affronts by the Hollywood establishment embittered Manson. And the Beatles' "White Album," released in December, somehow fed his fantasies of violence. Also, his circle faced growing police pressure. Although several, including Manson, were arrested for drug and other offenses, they nonetheless dramatically increased their criminal activity, stealing cars and credit cards, dealing drugs, and creepy-crawling houses (burglarizing while inhabitants slept). Manson talked more about his vision of Apocalypse, using his interpretations of the Bible, particularly from Revelations, and now of the Beatles, whom he considered prophets speaking to him, the fifth prophet, through their music. Manson told many people about Helter Skelter, a violent uprising resulting in temporary rule by blacks, whom he thought incapable of governing. This would lead them to seek help from Manson, who with his followers would live out the race war in a "bottomless pit" in the desert awaiting their destiny. Manson also talked about a catalyst, some kind of murderous act or acts to set off a holocaust-like race war.[29] In the end, a charged-up Manson increased his racist, death-oriented rhetoric. He preached fear and hatred; he obsessed about gore and pain, hanging and cutting, stabbing and slitting throats, killing "rich pigs," and even killing each other.

As Watkins testified, "Death was Charlie's trip."[30] Soon, death was everybody's trip. Either Watson screwed up a drug deal[31] or Manson attempted a burn,[32] setting up a confrontation between an armed Manson and Bernard "Lotsapoppa" Crowe, black, almost 300 pounds, and out $2,400. On July 1, 1969, Manson shot Crowe in the stomach and stole his leather jacket, out of which was born the baseless story that Manson killed a Black Panther, a story that intensified the fear and hatred at Spahn Ranch as a tense and frightened Family prepared for retribution. The Family didn't know that Crowe lived, but it wouldn't have mattered.

As Manson's obsession with knives, swords, killing, and torture worsened, fear of revenge by blacks necessitated a retreat to the desert. They desperately needed money. A common story is that Manson, believing Family acquaintance Gary Hinman had money, sent Beausoleil, Brunner, and Atkins to get it. With Hinman refusing to cooperate even after Beausoleil bashed him with a gun butt, Beausoleil summoned Manson, who, brandishing a sword, cut a deep, ugly gash in Hinman's face. Some say the slash severed an ear that Atkins or Brunner tried to sew back on with dental floss. As usual, Manson left, leaving others to kill.

Beausoleil beat Hinman "horribly,"[33] and as he lay moaning in pain, Hinman signed over his cars. Late in the third day of torture, Beausoleil stabbed him in the chest and smothered him with a pillow.[34] On the wall, someone wrote "POLITICAL PIGGY" in Hinman's blood.

Manson's circle finally found that bottomless pit, one from which it never ascended. The grotesque Hinman murder set the tone for some of the most bizarre, horrendous, and unusual murders in history. Police quickly arrested Beausoleil driving one of Hinman's vehicles, and afterward, the blur of conflicting stories and chaos centered around a maniacally obsessed and paranoid leader. Manson, throughout the book written in his name and virtually in all of his public utterings to this day, denies responsibility for almost everything that happened in his life, as he did for the gore that followed. He claimed the "girls" decided to throw doubt on Beausoleil's arrest by committing similar murders while he was in custody.[35] Prosecuting attorney Vincent Bugliosi effectively argued, backed by many witnesses, that Manson "zombies" butchered those victims to ignite the bloody race war, Helter Skelter.[36] Watson said their motives were the race war, money for the move to the desert, and Beausoleil.[37]

For whatever reasons, selected members of the Manson Family soon would participate in a bloodbath inflicting more than 160 stab wounds in killing and mutilating at least eight people—Sharon Tate, Abigail Folger, Voytek Frykowski, Jay Sebring, Steven Earl Parent, Leno LaBianca, Rosemary LaBianca, and Donald Jerome "Shorty" Shea. On the night of

August 8, 1968, Watson, Atkins, Patricia Krenwinkel, and Linda Kasabian, all claiming to have been controlled by the man they believed to be Jesus Christ, drove to 10050 Cielo Drive in Benedict Canyon to a house once occupied by Melcher and Candace Bergen, but then leased to Roman Polanski. Watson shot Parent four times as they entered the grounds. Kasabian stayed outside as Watson, saying, "I'm the devil, and I'm here to do the devil's business,"[38] and the other two shot, clubbed, and stabbed Frykowski; shot, stabbed, and hung Sebring; stabbed Folger; stabbed and hung the eight-and-one-half-month pregnant Tate, who was begging and pleading for her life and that of her male child. Killed last, "she had to watch the others die."[39]

Everyone except Kasabian could have stabbed all the victims. One account said everyone stabbed Tate,[40] although Atkins eventually denied it.[41] Watson admitted stabbing everyone and even cutting Parent.[42] Apparently the murderers wanted to mutilate the bodies, to gouge out the eyeballs and squash them on the walls, but didn't take the time.[43] They wrote "PIG" on the front door in Tate's blood. Manson claimed he visited the scene, removing fingerprints and leaving a pair of eyeglasses to confuse police.[44]

Calling the murders messy, Manson said he'd show his charges how to do it right. The next night he took Kasabian, Watson, Atkins, Krenwinkel, Steve Grogan, and Leslie Van Houten on a seemingly random drive seeking victims. Pictures of children saved one family, an unanswered rectory bell saved a priest Manson was going to kill and hang upside down at the altar,[45] and a green light saved a man who drove off when the light changed. With more specific directions from Manson, Kasabian drove to 3301 Waverly Drive, near Griffith Park in the Los Feliz section of Los Angeles. Manson likely entered the residence alone and tied up Leno and Rosemary LaBianca with leather thongs from around his neck. Watson claimed he went in with Manson.[46] Either way, Manson again left before the murders, telling Watson, "Make sure the girls get to do some of it, both of them."[47] Watson plunged a bayonet many times into the bound Leno LaBianca; Krenwinkel stabbed him eleven times with a large two-tined fork, leaving it protruding from his belly. Watson buried a butter knife in his neck and Watson or Krenwinkel carved the word "WAR" on his belly. Meanwhile, Van Houten held the bound and hooded Rosemary LaBianca while Krenwinkel stabbed her. Watson finally killed her with the bayonet, then told Van Houten to stab her too, which she did, later saying she liked it.[48] Before leaving the house, they showered and had a bite to eat. Krenwinkel wrote "HEALTER SKELTER," misspelled, on the refrigerator door and someone wrote "RISE" and "DEATH TO PIGS" on the walls.

Several weeks later Steve Grogan and others killed Spahn ranch-hand Donald "Shorty" Shea in a Family affair and buried his body in an isolated spot on the ranch. Grogan revealed the site to police years afterward to prove he didn't cut off Shea's head, as was widely believed. One author called it "the most sickening of their crimes. . . . They tortured him and, during the torture, tampered with his mental state, as if they were conducting experiments."[49]

Six days after the LaBianca killings, more than 100 police raided Spahn Ranch and arrested Manson and twenty-five followers for auto theft.[50] When the charges didn't hold, police released everyone, and Manson returned the Family to Spahn for the final move to the desert.

Meanwhile, press coverage of the Tate murders stressed drugs, hippie lifestyles, and the glamor and quirkiness of L.A. culture, coloring the gruesome murders in garish Hollywood neon. "Live freaky, die freaky," the *Los Angeles Times* quoted someone as saying.[51] These bloody murders in the heart of glitz with characters too incredible to be real would be unambiguously sensational even if the press wasn't traditionally inclined to ferret out the bizarre and different.

For here was Sharon Tate, beautiful star of *The Fearless Vampire Killers* and pregnant wife of the director of *Rosemary's Baby*, brutally slashed to death with her former lover, an internationally known hair stylist to the stars prone to kinky sex; and a coffee-fortune heiress who worked in the ghettos and her lover, a Polish, drug-using playboy. The other victim was a kid working two jobs who chose the wrong time to try to sell a clock radio to the groundskeeper.

Police and eventually the press treated the Tate killings separately from the Hinman and LaBianca murders despite obvious parallels. Police "solved" Hinman's murder by arresting Beausoleil, the Tate killings likely resulted from a busted drug deal or lunatic spasm of drug-induced violence, and some addled copycat butchered the LaBiancas. Fear fueled rocketing sales of firearms and unbridled paranoia in Los Angeles after the August murders. The media reported on three and a half months of police leaks and speculation about gambling, drugs, Hollywood orgies, black magic, glitzy weirdos, and the mob. The Tate coverage insinuated that the victims' self-indulgent and deviant lifestyles brought about their own destruction. One article knowingly stated that the "Tate-Polanski crowd picked up tough strangers" and played rough games that often ended "in brutal murders when the games get out of hand."[52] Live freaky, die freaky.

This smug coverage resulted partly from the press' inability to seriously, consistently cover nonmainsteam cultures, its inability to see them in any way but different, other, and alien, unworthy of anything but ridicule. The August 17 wire service account of Woodstock, for example, focused on the "mud, sickness and drugs." One person was quoted, "I don't know, man. This thing is just one big bad trip."[53] This world was virtually incomprehensible to the middle-class, largely white press, which, however, was fascinated with the word "hippie," and used it as a term of derision and amusement assigned indiscriminately to anyone and anything associated with the counterculture. The term was terribly misused when applied to Manson and his followers, who gruesomely inverted the hippies' "peace and love" to war, hate, and death. Yet most of the press seemed incapable of trying to understand the hippie culture and certainly incapable of understanding how a Charles Manson could so efficiently and devastatingly operate within it.

As of yet, the press knew little of Manson, who, now in the desert, attracted more attention from authorities with his dune buggy forays and thieving ways. Manson burned a $30,000 Inyo county-owned Michigan Articulated loader in September,[54] resulting in a raid on the remote Barker Ranch in which police arrested everyone including Manson, who was hiding in a tiny bathroom cabinet. Police later learned from Kitty Lutesinger, who escaped from Manson's circle and was pregnant with Beausoleil's baby, that Atkins and Brunner were present at Hinman's murder.

Although police had many murderers in custody, they hadn't connected Manson's circle to Tate or LaBianca. Atkins, arrested in the raid and now charged in Hinman's murder, blew open the case by providing cellmates with nauseating details of the Tate murders. She admitted telling a sobbing Tate: "Look, bitch, I don't care about you. . . . You're going to die, and I don't feel anything about it."[55] She shocked her cellmates by telling them the stabbing "felt good" and that she "just kept stabbing" until Tate "stopped screaming." With Tate's "blood spurting out," it was better than "a climax."[56]

As if that wasn't enough, Atkins said she tasted Tate's blood, prompting Bugliosi to call her a "vampira" in court.[57] She denied all this later, saying she lied to feel important.[58] Atkins also told cellmates about plans for skinning Frank Sinatra and selling objects made from his skin (so everybody could have a piece of Frank), cutting Tom Jones's throat as he climaxed during sex with her, and sexually mutilating Elizabeth Taylor and Richard Burton. Unable to contain such horror, the cellmates gave authorities their case.

Atkins, who eventually testified before a grand jury, initiated the case's most sensational news coverage when she sold her story for publication in the European press, although on December 14, 1969, the *Los Angeles Times*,[59] the *Miami Herald*,[60] and other U.S. newspapers published it. Her story also appeared as a book during the trial. The Atkins's accounts—so horrible they disgusted cellmates and literally sickened a grand juror—varied from telling to telling, but provided dispassionate details about the murders. They defined the event and its coverage throughout one of the longest criminal trials in California history and led to charges against Manson, Krenwinkel, Atkins, Watson, and Kasabian for the Tate murders and Manson, Van Houten, Watson, and Krenwinkel for the LaBianca murders.

All except Watson, who was fighting extradition from Texas, were tried together. Atkins backed out of a deal with the state, but prosecutors granted immunity to Kasabian, who did not kill at the Hinman, Tate, or LaBianca houses. Bugliosi said Manson sent out "three heartless, blood-thirsty robots" and "one human being," the "little hippie" Linda Kasabian.[61] As star witness she underwent weeks of grueling testimony, yet was compelling and effective. Still, Atkins's story remains at the core of the convictions.

Because the explosion of local, national, and world publicity, defense attorney Paul Fitzgerald said the defendants could never get a fair trial in California even with the jury sequestered. He was probably right. Some of the underground press saw Manson as a political martyr (although by several accounts, Manson, when asked about "fellow" political revolutionary Bobby Seale, said, "Who's he?"). *Life* magazine published a full spread of photos,[62] *Rolling Stone* put him on the cover as "the most dangerous man alive,"[63] and television, covering him daily, participated in the investigation. One Los Angeles TV station, using Atkins's story as a guide, found in a ravine the bundle of clothes worn by the murderers during the Tate killings.

The timing of the Manson trial in mid-1970 was also critical to the manner in which it was reported, as well as how it was adjudicated. The trial occurred five years after the Warren Commission report blamed the press and police for releasing incriminating evidence. Then the Supreme Court of the United States overturned Sam Sheppard's murder conviction because of prejudicial pretrial publicity, citing the judge's inability to keep order and control information. In 1968, the Reardon report urged judges in appropriate cases to close pretrial hearings, issue gag orders, and enforce order through contempt citations. Judges in the Tate/LaBianca proceedings issued a restrictive gag order and cited virtually every attorney, some more than once, with contempt. Yet nothing could even slow publicity in this case.

At one point Judge William Older interviewed each juror as to the impact of a *Los Angeles Times* front-page headline ("NIXON DECLARES MANSON GUILTY"), which Manson held up in court. Nixon told reporters in Colorado that Manson was "guilty, directly or indirectly of eight murders without reason."[64] William Farr, a reporter for the *Los Angeles Herald-Examiner*, eventually served time in jail for refusing to reveal sources for the story he wrote about Atkins' celebrity hit list.

Criminal proceedings brought forth massive amounts of information, too complex for the press to rationally organize yet too rich to ignore. Speculation, rumor, and actions by principals in the proceedings focused media attention on the bizarre moments, of which there were many. Manson, repeatedly trying to assume his own defense, ended up with an obstructionist lawyer virtually unanimously seen as ineffective. Manson constantly interrupted proceedings by shouting, chanting, turning his back on the judge, assuming a crucifixion pose, and singing, actions often parroted by the three women defendants and that led to frequent removals from the courtroom. Manson insulted and struck his own attorney and leaped over the defense table to attack the judge with a pencil, after which he shouted, "In the name of Christian justice, someone should cut your head off."[65] He carved an X in his forehead, "Xing" himself out of society, as did the women defendants and loyal followers camped outside the courtroom at Temple and Broadway. Bugliosi called defendant Atkins a "little bitch" in court after she grabbed and tore his notes. The defense, after listening to months of prosecution testimony, shockingly rested its case without calling a witness, at which point the defendants insisted upon testifying. Defense attorneys said they would refuse to question the three female clients, who wanted to incriminate themselves to free Manson. But Manson surprisingly testified, and with the jury absent denied responsibility for the murders.[66] Defense attorney Ronald Hughes disappeared near the end of the trial and was later found dead from causes still unknown.

Even with this, reporters often exaggerated. Sharon Tate's breasts were not cut off, the victims were not otherwise sexually mutilated, Shorty Shea was not decapitated and chopped into bits, and the district attorney did not slug Susan Atkins in the courtroom. Roman Polanski, distraught by coverage of his dead wife, called a press conference and tearfully denied reports that she was into black magic, orgies, and drugs.[67] Press competition, enthusiasm, and tradition make it impossible to avoid mistakes and tempting to exaggerate and sensationalize, but criticism often results from the press' proclivity to present information as unassailable fact, as truth, even when that truth depends largely on perception.

Facts deceive and truth is illusive. The police, press, and participants in a trial of this complexity get information wrong. People lie and exaggerate for their own purposes and authors write about people and events in light of their own perceptions and needs. Never sure about even who and how many people followed Manson, neither the press nor police could be sure how many murders Manson and his followers committed. Manson has said it was more than the nine for which he was tried, and Bugliosi, among others, said it was up to forty.[68] Convictions and ensuing death penalties resulted largely from the testimony of Kasabian, an accomplice who as a member of the circle freely engaged in their sex and took LSD at least fifty times.[69] Details of the killings came largely from Atkins, whose drug appetite matched or exceeded Kasabian's and whose lurid accounts of the crimes in which she participated vary significantly.

Given the differences not only in the vast coverage of the time, but in articles, books, and broadcasts, the Tate/LaBianca murders show clearly the fragility of truth and the power of the human mind to interpret what it sees. So long as news media are competitive, profit-oriented, and organized through convention and routine to seek out traditionally defined news, they will forever attract the same criticisms. The press, uncomfortable with these issues, remains ill-equipped to confront them.

"Manson" has come to represent evil. He has repeatedly said, conveniently, that he is merely what others make him, a reflection of their own evil, an evil that still exists. Hundreds of people, searching for something missing from themselves, continue to seek him out. "Now I ask you," he said, "is my charisma, my power, my love or my madness drawing those people to me?"[70]

What sickness is it that keeps sending me kids and followers? It's your world out there that does it. I don't solicit any mail or ask anyone to come and visit me. Yet the mail continues to arrive and your pretty little flowers of innocence keep showing up at the gate. Hell, they don't know me. They only know what your world has projected and won't let go of.[71]

That his evil is really ours projected through him is cheap justification for brutality and conscienceless destruction of human life and consistent with his lifelong inability to accept responsibility for his actions. It is also a damning statement. The press will always report stories about an evil man who kills by remote control, wonder how it can happen, and ask how he attracts so many damaged souls. But for all its coverage and analysis of the Manson murders, however, the press fails to report on why society produces so many damaged souls.

NOTES

1. Ed Sanders, *The Family: The Story of Charles Manson's Dune Buggy Attack Battalion* (New York: Avon Books, 1971), 40.

2. Vincent Bugliosi, with Curt Gentry, *Helter Skelter, The True Story of the Manson Murders* (New York: W. W. Norton & Company, 1974, 1994), 408. The Bugliosi/Gentry book is an encyclopedic version of the state's perspective.

3. Charles Manson as told to Nuel Emmons, *In His Own Words, The Shocking Confessions of "The Most Dangerous Man Alive"—Rolling Stone* (New York: Grove Press, 1986), 222.

4. Charles Watson as told to Chaplain Ray Hoekstra, *Will You Die For Me?* (Old Tappan, N.J.: Fleming H. Revell Company, 1978), 69–74.

5. Ibid., 71–72.

6. Bugliosi, *Helter Skelter, The True Story of the Manson Murders*, 237.

7. Manson, *In His Own Words, The Shocking Confessions of "The Most Dangerous Man Alive"—Rolling Stone*, 91.

8. Ibid., 108.

9. Ibid., 108–119.

10. Ibid., 119.

11. Ibid., 111.

12. Sanders, *The Family: The Story of Charles Manson's Dune Buggy Attack Battalion*, 42.

13. Susan Atkins with Bob Slosser, *Child of Satan, Child of God* (Plainfield, N.J.: Logos International, 1977), 80–81.

14. Sanders, *The Family: The Story of Charles Manson's Dune Buggy Attack Battalion*, 38.

15. Bugliosi, *Helter Skelter, The True Story of the Manson Murders*, 225.

16. Sanders, *The Family: The Story of Charles Manson's Dune Buggy Attack Battalion*, 193–194.

17. Bugliosi, *Helter Skelter, The True Story of the Manson Murders*, 232.

18. Dave Smith, "Mother Tells Life of Manson as Boy," *Los Angeles Times*, 27 January 1971.

19. Atkins, *Child of Satan, Child of God*, 87.

20. Bugliosi, *Helter Skelter, The True Story of the Manson Murders*, 322.

21. George Bishop, *Witness to Evil* (Los Angeles: Nash Publishing, 1971), 386–387.

22. Atkins, *Child of Satan, Child of God*, 87.

23. Sanders, *The Family: The Story of Charles Manson's Dune Buggy Attack Battalion*, 47.

24. Bugliosi, *Helter Skelter, The True Story of The Charles Manson Murders*, 154.

25. Ibid., 155.

26. Ibid., 225.

27. Laurence Merrick/Robert Hendrickson documentary film, *Manson*, 1972. Paul Watkins and other Family members speak openly about life with Manson.

28. Sanders, *The Family: The Story of Charles Manson's Dune Buggy Attack Battalion*, 47.

29. Ibid., 151.

30. Bishop, *Witness to Evil*, 355, and Laurence Merrick/Robert Hendrickson, *Manson*.

31. Watson, *Will You Kill For Me?*, 127–128. Manson also blames Watson in *In His Own Words*.

32. Sanders, *The Family: The Story of Charles Manson's Dune Buggy Attack Battalion*, 200.

33. Atkins, *Child of Satan, Child of God*, 127.

34. Ibid., 129.

35. Manson, *In His Own Words, The Shocking Confessions of "The Most Dangerous Man Alive"—Rolling Stone*, 194.

36. See Bugliosi, *Helter Skelter, The True Story of the Manson Murders*, 236–238 and elsewhere throughout the book.

37. Watson, *Will You Die For Me?*, 135.

38. Ibid., 140, and Sanders, *The Family: The Story of Charles Manson's Dune Buggy Attack Battalion*, 276.

39. Sanders, *The Family: The Story of Charles Manson's Dune Buggy Attack Battalion*, 284.

40. Ibid., 271–288.

41. Atkins, *Child of Satan, Child of God*, 159–161.

42. Watson, *Will You Die For Me?* 139.

43. Sanders, *The Family: The Story of Charles Manson's Dune Buggy Attack Battalion*, 285.

44. Charles Manson, *In His Own Words, The Shocking Confessions of "The Most Dangerous Man Alive"—Rolling Stone*, talks about the Tate murders beginning on page 201.

45. Atkins, *Child of Satan, Child of God*, 145.

46. Watson, *Will You Die For Me?*, 147.

47. Ibid., 148.

48. Bugliosi, *Helter Skelter, The True Story of the Manson Murders*, 407.

49. Sanders, *The Family: The Story of Charles Manson's Dune Buggy Attack Battalion*, 353.

50. "Police Raid Ranch, Arrest 26 Suspects in Auto Theft Ring," *Los Angeles Times*, 17 August 1969.

51. Charles Champlin, "The Pyramiding Truth on Image of Hollywood," *Los Angeles Times, Calendar Magazine*, 17 August 1969.

52. Dial Torgeson, "Anatomy of a Mass Murder in Hollywood," *Los Angeles Times*, 17 August 1969.

53. United Press International coverage of Woodstock appeared in the 17 August 1969 *Los Angeles Times*. Subsequent stories were similar, but not all as disparaging.

54. George Bishop, *Witness to Evil*, 1–29 and elsewhere.

55. Bugliosi, *Helter Skelter, The True Story of the Manson Murders*, 84.

56. Ibid., 95.

57. Ibid., 409.

58. Atkins, *Child of Satan, Child of God*, 159–161.

59. Susan Atkins, "Susan Atkins' Story of 2 Nights of Murder," *Los Angeles Times*, 14 December 1969.

60. Susan Atkins, "Story Behind Two Nights of Violence," *Miami Herald*, 14 December 1969.

61. Bugliosi, *Helter Skelter, The True Story of the Manson Murders*, 408.

62. "Waiting for Charlie," *Life*, 21 August 1970, 40–43.

63. "A Special Report, Charles Manson, The Incredible Story of the Most Dangerous Man Alive," *Rolling Stone*, 25 June 1970, cover.

64. Stuart Loory, "Nixon Explains," and "Manson Guilty, Nixon Declares," *Los Angeles Times*, 4 August 1970.

65. Bishop, *Witness to Evil*, 341.

66. Ibid., 386–388; Bugliosi, *Helter Skelter, The True Story of the Manson Murders*, 388–392. Manson discusses his testimony in *In His Own Words*, and various Internet sites have extensive Manson materials, including *Access Manson* (http://atwa.com/), which has materials copyrighted by Sandra Good, who has been with Manson nearly from the beginning of his notoriety.

67. Dial Torgeson, "Tearful Polanski Tells of His 'Truly Happy' Life with Wife," *Los Angeles Times*, 20 August 1969.

68. Bugliosi, *Helter Skelter, The True Story of the Manson Murders*, 474–483.

69. Ibid., 322.

70. Manson, *In His Own Words, The Shocking Confessions of "The Most Dangerous Man Alive,"—Rolling Stone*, 225.

71. Ibid., 226.

14

The Case of Lieutenant William Calley
(1970)

"We were all kind of crazed."

Heartbeats rivaled the speed of blades keeping helicopter troop transports aloft. The throbbing concussion of those blades, the roar of engines, and the wind blasting through open doorways smothered other sound. There was little of interest to see through those doors as the copters approached the landing zone.

But the soldiers of C Company, Task Force Barker, did not need their senses to tell them what waited ahead. They had been to Vietnam's Son My village before. They had been told what they would find on this trip—elements of the 48th Viet Cong Local Force Battalion.

It was the worst and the best of news.

Briefers had told Task Force Barker that the 48th had heavy weapons, including rockets and mortars. Company C, whose job was to assault the subhamlet of My Lai within Son My, might be outnumbered as much as two to one.

But at least it would be a stand-up fight against a known enemy. On previous operations in the area Task Force Barker had been mauled by a largely unseen foe whose primary weapons were booby traps, mines, and wraith-like snipers. Services held just before the briefings for Staff Sgt. George J. Cox, killed by a mine, were a reminder of unsettled scores.

Everyone Task Force Barker would meet on this operation would be VC or VC sympathizers. Intelligence had said the villagers would be gone to Saturday market by the time the assault forces landed. Troopship door gunners had free-fire clearance.

The unit was told to sweep through the area, close with and destroy the opposition. Everything—success, safety, survival—depended upon aggressiveness.

Company C's soldiers knew exactly which bastards to kill, and payback was going to be a bitch.

But the information was wrong. The direct confrontation with a potentially superior force never materialized that March day in 1968. And, tragically, the civilian population of Son My had not gone to market.

Like a tidal wave rushing upon an unprotected shore, the assault's momentum carried it, out of control, through Son My. As one member of C Company remembered: "We were all kind of crazed. We were so psyched up we didn't know what we were doing. We went into the village expecting to receive fire. We knew there would be VC troops, and we had to hit first."[1]

According to army estimates, more than 400 Vietnamese may have been killed that day at My Lai. Members of B Company killed as many as ninety more at the nearby subhamlet of My Khe. Almost all Vietnamese killed that day were unarmed civilians. Most were elderly, women, children, infants.[2]

The suffering didn't end there.

The Peers Commission, an army investigative team, concluded that "the crimes visited on the inhabitants of Son My Village included individual and group acts of murder, rape, sodomy, maiming, and assault on noncombatants and the mistreatment and killing of detainees."[3]

Not everyone participated in the atrocities committed that day. Some Americans at Son My tried to end the rampage. One soldier reportedly shot himself in the foot to avoid participating in the slaughter.[4] However, the Peers Commission concluded that responsibility for the slaughter was shared widely throughout the membership of TF Barker. Six men eventually faced court-martial for their actions at Son My or the subsequent cover-up.

Only one, William Laws "Rusty" Calley Jr., was convicted of criminal charges for his actions. Calley, who at the time of the attack was a twenty-five-year-old second lieutenant commanding C Company's First Platoon, was convicted of the premeditated murder of not fewer than twenty-two Vietnamese civilians.

Calley's story is among the best metaphors for the war that was like a vague, macabre nightmare. It happened. The almost 58,000 Americans killed or listed as missing at its end more than twenty years ago are testament to that.[5] But many details remain fuzzy, unclear.

Similarly, the details of Calley's story seem to emerge from a Lewis Carroll fantasy. Unlike most murder trials, the identity or even the number of victims was never established by the government. Fixing the scene of the crime was confusing even for army investigators familiar with the area. According to their maps, Calley's platoon was at My Lai, one of five subhamlets located within Son My village.[6] Vietnamese government maps labeled the subhamlet Thuan Yen. Local residents called it Xom Lang.[7]

But names were irrelevant. Regardless of what it was called, on March 16, 1968, the hamlet was a slaughterhouse.

Calley's description of events, delivered during nine hours of testimony over two and half days near the conclusion of his trial, was chilling. The story seemed even more horrific because Calley, with his unimposing frame (5 feet 3 inches, 160 pounds), receding auburn hair and youthful, oval face, looked more like an altar boy than a mass murderer. It was grueling testimony with Calley tense throughout. He continually raised his eyes to the ceiling, rubbed his chin, and massaged his hands, and he often seemed to be searching for the right words to answers for many of the questions. Throughout, Calley punctuated each answer with the word "sir."[8]

Latimer [George Latimer, Calley's civilian attorney]: Now, did you see some live Vietnamese while you were going through the village?

Calley: I saw two, sir.

Latimer: All right. Now, tell us, was there an incident concerning those two?

Calley: Yes, sir. I shot and killed both of them.

Latimer: Under what circumstance?

Calley: There was a large concrete house and I kind of stepped up on the porch and looked in the window. There was about six to eight individuals laying on the floor, apparently dead and one man was going for the window. I shot him. There was another man standing in a fireplace. He looked like he had just come out of the fireplace, or out of the chimney. And I shot him, sir. He was in a bright green uniform.

Calley [later in the questioning as he described the actions of one of men]: . . . molesting a female. . . . I told him to get his pants back up and get over to where he was supposed to be.

Latimer [later in the questioning about My Lai residents who were allegedly taken into a ditch and executed]: What did you do after you saw them shooting in the ditch?

Calley: Well, I fired into the ditch also, sir. . . .

Latimer: Now, did you have a chance to look and observe what was in the ditch?

Calley: Yes, sir.

Latimer: And what did you see?

Calley: Dead people, sir.

Latimer [later in the questioning]: Did you at any time direct anybody to push people in the ditch?

Calley: Like I said, I have the order to take those people through the ditch and had also told Meadlo if he couldn't move them, to waste them . . . I never stood up there for any period of time. The main mission was to get my men on the other side of the ditch and get in that defensive position, and that is what I did, sir.

Latimer [later in the questioning]: I am going to ask you this: during this operation, My Lai Four, did you intend specifically to kill Vietnamese—man, woman, or child?

Calley: No, sir, I did not.

Latimer [soon after]: Did you form any impression as to whether or not there were children, women, or men, or what did you see in front of you as you were going on?

Calley: I never sat down to analyze it, men, women and children. They were enemy and just people.[9]

Son My, which sits in a basin, was part of a farming region on the South China Sea. Concrete and straw houses and thatched huts dotted the rolling hills. Many residents had simple pens for their goats, pigs, and water buffalo. To the west of the village lay acres of green rice paddies. About 400 people lived in the five hamlets that comprised Son My, the most notable being Pinkville[10] which was separated from the other hamlets by a wide, shallow body of water.[11]

According to the Peers Commission, Company C's First Platoon, under Calley's command, began its sweep through the southern portion of My Lai just before 8 a.m. Troops entered the subhamlet firing on the Vietnamese indiscriminately, killing livestock and destroying property. Two large groups of surviving villagers were herded together. Between seventy and eighty Vietnamese were placed in a drainage ditch east of My Lai. The other group of between twenty and fifty villagers was taken to a trail south of the subhamlet. Everyone in both groups was, in the terminology of those serving in Vietnam, "wasted."

Calley admitted to ordering and participating in the killing of unarmed civilians, yet he maintained that he was innocent of murder. Despite the court-martial verdict, many agreed. He was even a hero to some. Public opinion eventually would force President Richard Nixon, who had earlier called for the swift punishment of those guilty of criminal acts at Son My, to intercede on Calley's behalf.

The incident followed on the heels of what was perhaps the most costly victory in American military history—Tet.

As 1967 drew to a close, military and political leaders told the American people that communist forces would soon be so weakened that South Vietnam would be able to conduct the fight alone, and the United States could begin withdrawals. This was welcome news to a country that had seen its commitment grow from 100 U.S. Army Special Forces advisers in 1961 to more than 500,000 troops. Increasingly, responsibility for the war had shifted until the entire conflict had been turned upside down. The war had become Americanized, with U.S. troops increasingly shouldering responsibility for fighting North Vietnamese regulars and Viet Cong guerrilla units.[12]

But optimism met with reality when communist forces used the cover of Tet cease-fire agreements to launch assaults against locations across South Vietnam on the night of January 30–31, 1968. They attacked the U.S. Embassy in Saigon and captured the ancient imperial capital city of Hué.

The Tet Offensive was a clear tactical defeat for the communists. According to U.S. military estimates, more than 30,000 communists were killed during the first two weeks. The communists were unable to accomplish any of the campaign's goals. They failed to capture the embassy.

Nor were they able to kill or capture Ambassador Ellsworth Bunker, who had escaped. Though there was great loss of civilian life and much destruction in Hué, U.S. troops retook the historic city in twenty-five days of bitter fighting.[13]

More important, the assault failed to inspire a popular uprising in the South, a major objective of the plan.

But while Tet may have been a military defeat for the communists, it was a political victory. Tet shattered American confidence. How could an enemy supposedly rocking on its heels mount such a major attack at the same time that its forces had the U.S. Marine base at Khe Sanh surrounded and under siege? How could it kill 973 Americans in the first two weeks of Tet, when U.S. losses had been averaging only 140 per week? The United States would eventually "lose" in Vietnam, the only time it would lose a war. Some observers believe Tet caused that loss.[14]

In the immediate aftermath of Tet, the American military had a public relations problem. The solution would be victories. At that time victory meant impressive statistics—large body counts of enemy dead and similar symbolic indexes of success.

Those statistics were hard to come by during Task Force Barker's two February operations in the Son My area.

Insurgents there operated under the guidelines of the first phase of the three-step communist strategy for conducting the war. The plan, used so effectively against the French, dictated "starting with hit-and-run guerrilla strikes, then mounting larger actions and, finally, as the balance of force tilted in their direction, staging conventional battles."[15]

During the first phase, small units applied constant pressure, continually harrying American units with ambushes, booby traps, sapper attacks, and sniper fire. The objective was to break down morale by hurting the enemy and avoiding opportunities for retaliation. The plan's success required support of the local population.

The entire Quang Ngai Province, where Son My is located, was ideally suited for the needs of communist strategy. Quang Ngai had long been a breeding ground for rebellion. Its people began resisting French colonialism in the 1800s and continued to do so until France relinquished its control of the country under the 1954 Geneva Accords. Pro–Viet Cong sentiments ran strong there. "[A] whole generation of young people had grown up under the control" of Viet Cong influence, according to assessments by the South Vietnamese government.[16] Most people living in the village were escapees from the South Vietnamese Protected Hamlet Program, a plan designed to deny insurgents access to popular support by relocating villagers in fortified settlements. In the opinion of the South Vietnamese government, everyone living in Son My was "either VC or VC sympathizers."[17]

Six Americans had been killed and forty-three wounded during the two Son My area operations in February. Snipers and mines had caused most of these casualties. And there was little to show for the cost.

Although the unit reported body counts totaling 155 Viet Cong, it captured only six weapons and one prisoner. The numbers didn't satisfy brigade command.

During briefings before the March 16 assault, Task Force Barker was told it had not been aggressive enough on previous operations. It had allowed the VC to mingle with the local population and escape. It had let civilians carry away munitions that should have been captured. This time the 48th VC Local Force Battalion, which had fought during Tet, would be dealt with "once and for all."[18]

The plan was simple. The attack would begin with an artillery barrage and an assault by helicopter gunships to soften up the landing zones. C Company—Calley's—would hit My Lai. Orders called for Company B to then land near another subhamlet referred to as "Pinkville."[19] The companies would link up for night defensive positions northeast of My Lai(4). Company A would remain north of Son My throughout the operation. Its job was to prevent enemy troops from escaping.

The raid was a basic search-and-destroy mission. The military defined these missions "as those operations conducted for the purpose of seeking out and destroying enemy forces, installations, resources, and base areas."[20]

Very few "resources" escaped Company C's attention that day. After the soldiers of C Company had completed their sweep through the Vietnamese subhamlet, "not a house was standing, not a well was unpolluted, not an animal was still alive, and almost all of the people . . . were dead."[21]

While the First Platoon was conducting its sweep, the Second and Third platoons were also contributing to the carnage.[22] The Second killed about seventy villagers as it moved through the northern portion of My Lai and Binh Tay, a nearby subhamlet. Trailing in the wake of the First and Second, the Third Platoon "burned and destroyed what remained of the houses in My Lai(4) and killed most of the remaining livestock. Its members also rounded up and killed a group of 7-12 women and children."[23]

The Peers Commission found that only about ten members of B Company had taken part in the slaughter at My Khe (Pinkville), but that they had killed as many as ninety civilians.

Killing civilians during combat operations wasn't unique to the Son My assault or even to the Vietnam War. Collateral deaths, as the American military now refers to them, are expected whenever civilians are in close proximity to fighting. Given the nature of the warfare waged in Vietnam, civilians were often nearby.

But My Lai was different. Too many had died. And, as Richard Hammer wrote, the killing took place "not in the heat of combat but during the course of what was almost an unhampered stroll in the warm Vietnamese sun."[24] There was only one American casualty in Company C that day, a soldier wounded by the discharge of his own pistol. Mines and booby traps caused all of B Company's casualties—one killed and seven wounded. A helicopter pilot had radioed that he was under fire, but his report was never confirmed.

The story remained buried with the dead for almost two years. An initial investigation within the Americal Division was a whitewash. The Peers Commission reported that officers "[a]t every command level within the Americal Division" participated in the cover-up.[25] Despite rumblings and protests by survivors, the official version of the incident was that Son My had been a hard-fought battle and an important victory. General William C. Westmoreland, commander of U.S. forces in Vietnam, even commended Company C for its performance.

The carefully woven tapestry began to unravel when a returning soldier, Ronald Ridenhour, wrote a letter to the Secretary of Defense, among others, describing rumors he had heard after his transfer from the 11th Light Infantry Brigade's headquarters company to Company E. Ridenhour wrote about accounts of three privates, Butch Gruver, Michael Terry, and William Doherty, all veterans of Charlie Company. The letter, written in March 1969, contained inaccuracies, but the basic story was true. He wrote:

Any villagers [from Pinkville] who ran from Charlie Company were stopped by the encircling companies. I asked "Butch" several times if all the people were killed. He said he thought they were, men, women, and children. He recalled seeing a small boy, about three or four years old, standing by the trail with a gunshot wound in one arm. The boy was clutching his wounded arm with his other hand, while blood trickled between his fingers. He was staring around himself in shock and disbelief at what he saw.[26]

The letter prompted the Department of the Army to conduct its own investigation. Westmoreland, now Army Chief of Staff, ordered an inquiry by the Army Inspector General's office in late April. By July sufficient evidence had been amassed to bring in the Provost Marshal's Criminal Investigation Division. In November Westmoreland and Secretary of the Army Stanley R. Resor directed Lt. Gen. William R. Peers to form a commission to examine the cover-up.

As a result of these inquiries, the army would eventually charge twenty-five men either with war crimes for their part in the massacre or with violating military policy for their part in the cover-up. But court-martial convictions would prove difficult because of the delay. Soldiers who were no longer in the army were beyond the reach of military justice, and enlistments were running out.

Calley actually came within a few days of avoiding his court-martial. In June the army told Calley, who had earlier extended his enlistment by six months, that he was facing possible murder charges. But formal charges were not filed until the day before his enlistment expired.

The army may have intentionally drawn things out to avoid the public attention trials generate. As Richard Hammer wrote, "[T]he political repercussions of revelations about a slaughter of unarmed Vietnamese civilians by American soldiers might be so intense and so vast and the public repugnance over the war be so great as a result of such disclosures as to lead to renewed and greater protests in the streets and on the campuses than had taken place in recent years."[27]

Despite the investigations and charges, the army managed to keep the incident out of the headlines. Formal charges against Calley, once filed, got only a one-paragraph story on a back page in the *New York Times*.

The days of obscurity for the massacre ended in November 1969. The story first broke in the November 12 issue of the *Alabama Journal* under Wayne Greenhaw's byline. Greenhaw, tipped off by Pentagon sources, had begun investigating the details of Calley's arrest in September.[28]

But a Dispatch News Service report by Seymour M. Hersh, which appeared in about thirty papers the following day, drew national and international attention. His article "triggered an avalanche of publicity concerning the incident and . . . [Calley's] role therein. Within a period of a few days virtually every form of news service in the country, and indeed in the world, had deluged its hearers, viewers and readers with extensive and intensive coverage of . . . [Calley's] plight."[29] Hersh would go on to win the Pulitzer Prize for ferreting out and publishing the rest of the My Lai story.

During the interim between Hersh's first article and the start of Calley's trial on November 17, 1970, the news media had worked mightily to make up for their nineteen months of virtual silence on My Lai. When the trial began, about half of the fifty-nine spectators who filled the available seating in the Ft. Benning, Georgia, courtroom were members of the media.[30]

"Never in the history of the military justice system, and perhaps in the history of American courts, has any accused ever encountered such intense and continuous prejudicial publicity as did the Petitioner herein," U.S. District Judge J. Robert Elliott later wrote in reviewing Calley's appeal following conviction.[31] Press coverage was so intense during the twelve days following Hersh's original story that the first day the court-martial impaneled, November 25, 1969, the defense and prosecution filed a joint motion for a gag order. Both sides wanted the court to prohibit the media from publishing any additional comments by potential witnesses.

Had the motion been granted, it might have been too late to prevent whatever impact press coverage would have on the court-martial panel. The media had already carried a detailed interview with a Company C soldier who would later appear as a key prosecution witness. Vietnamese identified as survivors of the My Lai massacre had told their stories for television news cameras. Former army photographer Ronald Haeberle, one of two army correspondents on the Son My operation, had made $54,500 selling his photos to *Life* and *Time* magazines and to other publications during the mid-November rush. The color photos became the focal point for media discussion of the case. The prosecution later used some as evidence.[32]

Not only was the coverage pervasive, a significant portion was inflammatory. Headlines read "Massacre Compared to Nazi Murders," "Pinkville Symbolizes Brutalism," and "Just Speed That Trial." Calley was called a "ghoul."[33] The media carried interviews with people, like Ridenhour, who had not witnessed the event, but could only repeat second-hand stories.

Little could have been done to prevent this early onslaught of coverage. As Elliott noted, the defendant in a court-martial has less potential for court protection from pretrial publicity than do defendants called before a civilian court. "Unlike the civilian system, in the military system there is no judge with the judicial powers to protect the individual until the case is *referred to trial* by court-martial."[34]

Although the presiding officer, Colonel Reid W. Kennedy, refused the November 25 motion aimed at the media, he did try other approaches to protect the defendant's Sixth Amendment rights. He enjoined potential witnesses from granting additional interviews. He told potential members of the court-martial panel present to avoid press coverage.

But these efforts had little real effect. The order did not apply to five members of the six-member jury who were later selected before the trial's start one year later. The order regarding interviews by witnesses was routinely ignored. When Kennedy examined his options for enforcing the decree, he concluded that as a military judge he lacked pretrial contempt-of-court authority to enforce his instructions. Kennedy suggested that attorneys turn to other courts for help. The Court of Military Appeals, responding to a joint petition, refused to intercede.

On paper Calley's defense team overmatched the opposition. The sixty-nine-year-old Latimer headed a four-member group. During World War II he had risen to the rank of colonel and had served as chief-of-staff with the 40th Infantry Division. His legal career was equally distinguished. A practicing attorney since 1924 and viewed as one of Utah's top trial lawyers, he had served on both the Utah Supreme Court and the U.S. Court of Military Appeals.

Calley's top military representative, Major Kenneth A. Raby, was a career attorney with the Judge Advocate General's Office. The thirty-five-year-old major was considered a brilliant scholar with an impressive knowledge of precedent. However, some observers initially felt his rigid style of delivery would limit his effectiveness before a jury.[35]

Calley's other civilian counsel lacked Latimer's reputation. A fifty-two-year-old personal injury lawyer from Ohio, Richard B. Kay's chief distinction was a failed bid for the U.S. Senate on the George C. Wallace ticket. Kay agreed to work for free, however, hoping that the publicity would earn him a vice-presidential nomination when Wallace made his next bid.[36] Captain Brooks S. Doyle Jr., a second military lawyer, rounded out the defense unit. He was a twenty-seven-year-old graduate of Wake Forest University Law School.

Facing Latimer and Raby were two JAG attorneys in their twenties. Captain Aubrey Marshall Daniel III, a twenty-eight-year-old draftee with less than three years of legal experience, headed the prosecution team. Captain John Patrick Partin, the twenty-five-year-old trial assistant, had only recently joined the army.

The prosecution, however, had a strong case. Though the defense would concede nothing, thereby forcing Daniel to call witnesses to establish each point in his case, there was really little dispute over the basic story. Calley gave the orders to "waste" Vietnamese civilians. He had also personally killed Vietnamese civilians with his M-16 rifle.

Calley never denied issuing the orders or killing Vietnamese civilians that day. He did not see why he should. Calley argued that he merely followed the direct orders of Captain Ernest L. Medina, commander of C Company.

The prosecution, maintaining that Medina never ordered the death of civilians, called witnesses, including Medina, to support its position. As a legal matter, the existence or absence of such orders should have been irrelevant. The Nuremberg trials at the end of World War II established the legal precedent that blind adherence to orders was no defense for criminal acts. Even under U.S. military regulations, a soldier is not required to obey all orders, but to follow all "lawful orders." What took place at My Lai violated both international law and military regulations.

It was important for Daniel to keep the trial focused on Calley's actions. His witnesses did that.

Robert Maples, a nineteen-year-old machinegunner in Calley's platoon. He testified that Calley ordered a group of Vietnamese into a ditch, then asked Maples to use the machinegun. "What did you do?" Daniels asked. "I refused." Daniel then asked if the people were armed. Maples response: "No."[37]

Pvt. 1st Class Paul Meadlo. "We just gathered up people and started leading them to a designated area." Meadlo said about thirty-five or forty unarmed people, including women with babies in their arms, were taken to a clearing. Meadlo testified that Calley said, "You know what to do with them, Meadlo." "I assumed he meant guard them, and I said 'yes.'" Meadlo added that when Calley returned, he asked, "How come they're not dead? . . . I want them dead." Meadlo said, "He told me to shoot them," adding that both he and Calley then shot the villagers and that Calley used about four or five magazines.

Meadlo also testified that later he went to a drainage ditch where Calley waited with about 100 villagers. "We got another job to do, Meadlo," he said Calley told him. "Lt. Calley started shoving them off and shooting them in the ravine."[38]

Rennard Doines of Fort Worth, Texas. Doines described killing livestock and dogs as they entered the hamlet. Then he told how fifteen people were taken from thatched hooches. "Most of them were women, children and old men, trying to hide." Doines said the prisoners were taken to Calley. When Doines returned later, "I went over there and looked and there was a bunch of dead people; about ten or fifteen dead people. Most of them were little kids, babies like, and old women. They were lying there, bleeding."[39]

Charles Sledge, the radio operator. Sledge described a man in monk's robes being brought to Calley for questioning. "The Priest would say, 'No Viet,' and he held his hands in this shape (as though in prayer). Calley asked him a few more questions and he bowed his head and he still said, 'No Viet.' [probably 'nobiet,' 'I do not know'] Then he hit him with the butt of his rifle in the mouth." When answering a question about what the priest did next, Sledge answered, "He didn't do nothing but fall back, doing this with his hands again, sort of like pleading. Lt. Calley took his rifle at point-blank and pulled the trigger in the priest's face. Half his head was blown off."[40]

Sledge also described another incident later that morning involving a child about two years old. Sledge explained that the "little baby" was running from the drainage ditch mentioned in earlier testimony. "Lt. Calley grabbed it by the arm and threw it into the ditch and fired." When asked how many shots Calley had fired, Sledge responded: "One."[41]

Daniel's witnesses provided powerful testimony. But the case might be crippled if the defense were allowed to roam too far afield. Close examination of the legality of orders generally would have been counterproductive. After all, in Vietnam habitual disregard of the rules governing warfare was tolerated if not encouraged by the leadership. Some even argued, as Calley's attorneys would try to do during the trial, that the standard weapon of the American soldier was illegal. The 5.56mm bullet of the M-16 rifle, traveling at more than 1,000 meters per second, began to tumble when it hit the human body, turning it into a buzzsaw chewing an unpredictable path through its victim. Surely this broke international conventions prohibiting weapons "calculated to cause unnecessary suffering."[42]

Intense press coverage continued throughout the trial. Elliott found that coverage actually increased after the trial judge's attempt to restrict it. Statements from witnesses and trial participants were still published. Public officials, including those speaking for the president—commander-in- chief of everyone involved with the trial, including the judge and jury—issued comments on the incident. Elliott wrote that "segments of the press not only recognized that Calley was being isolated and prosecuted by the press to the extent that it might be impossible for Calley to have a fair trial, but they actually indulged in self-praise of their prosecution of the man."[43]

The press had relatively free access to most participants. Even Judge Kennedy would visit with reporters over drinks. Calley and Daniel were perhaps the most reclusive. Whenever possible, Daniel limited his contact with reporters to "no comment" statements.

Calley, acting on advice of counsel, was also circumspect in his dealings with the media throughout most of the trial. However, *Esquire* paid Calley $20,000 for the rights to his story.[44] John Sack, who became an editor/writer for the magazine in 1968, worked with Calley on the three-article series, which was written in Calley's own words. The series, later republished in book form,[45] provoked bitter criticism even within the magazine's staff.

The first article, published in the November 1970 issue and illustrated by a cover photo of a smiling Calley in uniform surrounded by four small Asian children, cost the magazine $200,000 when advertisers pulled ads from the next issue. Both Porsche and Volkswagen threatened never to advertise in the magazine again.

Newsweek published an article attacking not only the cover's propriety, but also questioning the morality of paying Calley so much for his story. (*Newsweek* incorrectly reported that he had received $50,000.) There were accusations that the magazine was withholding discussion of the My Lai assault for publicity reasons and criticism of Sack's refusal to surrender 60 hours worth of notes to the court.[46]

But once again, acting on the advice of counsel, Calley had not told Sack what had happened at My Lai until after the trial.

During Calley's three days of testimony near the trial's end, he maintained that he was responsible for far fewer deaths than the army was alleging. Even then he said he was following orders.

Calley said his group had been told to kill the communists in My Lai and destroy everything that might be of use to them. In his testimony, Medina denied directly ordering that any prisoners be shot.

The verdict did not come easy for the jury. Deliberations, at times heated, took almost ninety hours over thirteen days. Sequestered for the first time during the trial, the six jury members, all decorated combat veterans and all but one with tours in Vietnam, sifted through the testimony of 104 witnesses delivered during the four-and-one-half months of proceedings.

On March 29, participants and observers gathered to hear the jury's finding. Calley, originally charged with the murder of at least 109 people on six separate specifications, still faced four charges in the death of at least 102 people. Conviction on each of the charges required a two-thirds vote.

The jury found Calley guilty on each of the charges. However, because conflicting testimony made it difficult to firmly establish the actual number of people killed, the jury reduced the total, convicting Calley for the murder of at least twenty-two people.

Two days later, after hearing statements by the defense and prosecution, the jury sentenced Calley to life in prison. Its only other option would have been a death sentence. Daniel did not ask the jury for a death sentence in his statement prior to sentencing.

Calley's saga did not end with the jury's decree. He became a specter haunting the American social and political landscape for years to come.

Both hawks and doves rallied to Calley's defense. Calley received as many as 5,000 pieces of mail in a single day immediately after the decision. Overall, correspondence ran at least 100 to 1 in his favor,[47] and a poll just after the trial showed that almost 80 percent of Americans strongly opposed the verdict and that 20 percent believed Calley's actions were not even criminal.[48] Even those who deplored his actions felt it unfair to send him to prison when so many others connected with the affair or its concealment had escaped punishment. *Time* and *Newsweek* had cover stories on Calley after the trial, and both deflected blame from Calley, pointing out that he was the only one going to jail while others just as guilty would not. Alabama Senator John Sparkman said Calley was a "scapegoat" for the sins of everyone connected with the incident.[49]

Washington Post reporter William Greider, who covered the court-martial and reported on events for more then four months, wrote: "Americans have chosen some strange popular heroes in the last decade, but none of them was a convicted mass murderer."[50]

As a result of public outcry, President Nixon one day after the sentencing preempted the military appeals process by ordering that Calley be kept under house arrest pending the outcome of the review required by the military's criminal justice system. Daniel, two weeks away from his own separation date, strongly condemned the action in a letter addressed to the president.

Calley's sentence would later be reduced twice. In August 1971, Third Army commander Lieutenant General Albert O. Conner decreased Calley's sentence to twenty years. In April 1974, Nixon's Secretary of the Army, Howard H. Callaway, cut the sentence to ten years.

Calley would be a legacy to Jimmy Carter. During the 1976 presidential campaign, Democratic candidate Carter was forced to explain his position on Calley's conviction.[51]

Calley's case also challenged the independence of the military's criminal justice system. Not satisfied with the results of the army's appeal process, Calley had filed for review by civilian federal courts. Both parties continued to press the issue in the federal courts even after Calley's effective parole date in November 1974. The army wanted to avoid precedent wherein civilian courts reversed a court-martial decision. Although no longer under confinement, Calley wanted the conviction overturned.

U.S. District Judge J. Robert Elliott (who would be a guest at Calley's 1976 wedding) overturned the conviction, citing the intense press coverage of the trial. Much of the sixty-three-page opinion was in fact devoted to chastising the media.

The U.S. 5th Circuit Court of Appeals in New Orleans reversed Elliott's ruling. In its reading of the law, the court found that in order to justify overturning a conviction, an appellant must not only establish the existence of potentially prejudicial press coverage, but must also show how this information actually had an impact on the trial process. In an 8 to 5 decision, the court determined that Calley had failed to meet this burden.

In April 1976, the Supreme Court of the United States announced, without comment, its refusal to hear the case.

Calley actually spent very little time in prison. He was paroled November 19, 1974, after serving about one-third of his ten-year sentence,[52] the minimum amount required for early release. Most of that time was spent under house arrest, at Ft. Benning rather than in the military prison at Ft.

Leavenworth, Kansas, as would normally have been the case. Under house arrest he had his own apartment and was allowed visitors. He was also twice freed on $1,000 bonds while the federal courts were examining the case.

Calley's only stay at Ft. Leavenworth was from late June to early November 1974. Even there he got special accommodations. He was placed alone in a room normally holding ten men and given his own television.

After the U.S. Supreme Court announcement, Calley tried to regain the anonymity of his former life.[53] He refused all interviews and has continued to do so. In 1976 Calley married Penny Vick, daughter of a Columbus, Georgia, jeweler. After the wedding, Calley became a jeweler also, and the couple settled in Columbus.

Although Calley himself has tried to reclaim obscurity, My Lai and his actions there will forever remain significant historical icons.

But then Calley the man was never really the issue anyway. As Hammer wrote: "Practically no one was willing to look at Calley himself and at what he had done; almost everyone wanted to make him more than he was, wanted in a large sense to turn him into a symbol and as a symbol to reject or accept what they saw him standing for."[54]

NOTES

1. Wayne Greenhaw, *The Making of a Hero: The Story of Lieut. William Calley Jr.* (Louisville, Ky.: Touchstone Publishing, 1971), 139.

2. See, generally, Williams R. Peers, *The My Lai Inquiry* (New York: Norton, 1979). See also the United States Dept. of the Army, *The My Lai Massacre and its Cover-Up: Beyond the Reach of Law?* (New York: Free Press, 1976).

3. U.S. Dept. of the Army, *My Lai Massacre*, 315.

4. Richard Hammer, *The Court-Martial of Lt. Calley* (New York: Coward, McCann & Geoghegan, 1971), 25.

5. Stanley Karnow, *Vietnam: A History* (New York: Viking Press, 1983), 9.

6. There were a number of subhamlets within Son My. Six were labeled My Lai on U.S. Army maps and were distinguished from one another by numbers. Company C assaulted My Lai(4).

7. William R. Peers, *The My Lai Inquiry.* (New York: Norton, 1979). See also *The My Lai Massacre and its Cover-Up: Beyond the Reach of Law?*

8. Hammer, *The Court-Martial of Lt. Calley*, 240.

9. Ibid., 249–253, 256–257.

10. My Lai (1).

11. Greenhaw, *The Making of a Hero: The Story of Lieut. William Calley Jr.*, 84.

12. Karnow, *Vietnam: A History.*

13. Ibid., 523–545; Philip B. Davidson, *Vietnam at War/ The History: 1946–1975.* (Novato, Calif.: Presidio, 1988), 473–528; William Weir, *Fatal Victories* (Hamden, Conn.: Archon Books, 1993), 220–237.

14. Weir, *Fatal Victories*, 236.

15. Karnow, *Vietnam: A History,* 182.

16. U.S. Dept. of the Army, *My Lai Massacre,* 59.

17. Ibid. 60.

18. Ibid. 89.

19. Although known as Pinkville, its name was My Lai(1).

20. The United States Dept. of the Army, *My Lai Massacre,* 87–88. The army would later stop using the phrase search-and-destroy.

21. Hammer, *The Court-Martial of Lt. Calley,* 18.

22. The United States Dept. of the Army, *My Lai Massacre,* 45.

23. Ibid.

24. Hammer, *The Court-Martial of Lt. Calley,* 5.

25. The U.S. Dept. of the Army, *My Lai Massacre,* 316.

26. The complete text of the letter can be found in the U. S. Dept. of the Army, *My Lai Massacre.*

27. Hammer, *The Court-Martial of Lt. Calley,* 30.

28. See generally, Greenhaw, *The Making of a Hero: The Story of Lieut. William Calley Jr.*

29. *Calley v. Callaway,* 382 F.Supp. 650 (M.D. Ct. Ga., 1974), 657.

30. Hammer, *The Court-Martial of Lt. Calley,* 73.

31. *Calley v. Callaway,* 382 F.Supp. 650 (M.D. Ct. Ga., 1974), 657.

32. Ibid., 660.

33. Ibid., 658–661.

34. Ibid., 657.

35. According to Hammer's account in *The Court-Martial of Lt. Calley,* Raby performed beyond expectations, while Latimer's work fell far short of what was anticipated.

36. Hammer, *The Court-Martial of Lt. Calley,* 63–64.

37. Greenhaw, *The Making of a Hero: The Story of Lieut. William Calley Jr.,* 129.

38. Ibid., 128.

39. Ibid., 130–131.

40. Ibid., 132–133.

41. Ibid., 134.

42. Hammer, *The Court-Martial of Lt. Calley,* 12.

43. *Calley v. Callaway,* 382 F.Supp. 650 (M.D. Ct. Ga., 1974), 669.

44. For a more complete discussion of the *Esquire* coverage of Calley, see Carol Polsgrove, *It Wasn't Pretty, Folks, But Didn't We Have Fun?: Esquire In the Sixties* (New York: W. W. Norton & Co., 1995), 219–236.

45. Calley and Sack split a $100,000 contract from Viking for the book rights.

46. Sack avoided a contempt of court sentence on a procedural technicality.

47. "Second Thoughts About Calley," *Newsweek,* 19 April 1971, 29.

48. Hammer, *The Court-Martial of Lt. Calley,* 374.

49. Greenhaw, *The Making of a Hero,* 190.

50. Ibid., 210.

51. See Charles Mohr's article in the 21 May 1976 issue of the *New York Times.*

52. Calley was released on bail ten days before the parole took effect and never returned to confinement. November 19 was the official parole date.

53. In July 1972, concern over media coverage caused Calley to forego attending his father's funeral. See the 16 July 1972 issue of the *New York Times*.

54. Hammer, *The Court-Martial of Lt. Calley*, 375.

15

The Case of O. J. Simpson
(1995)

"No closer to Greek tragedy than Oedipus Hertz"

Paul Thaler

The stillness of the balmy, late evening in Brentwood was pierced by the Akita, frantically barking. Something about the desperate sound alerted neighbors that something had gone terribly wrong.

When the police finally arrived, the dog's paw prints formed a speckled pattern in the wash of blood puddled along the entryway of a condominium at 875 Bundy in West Los Angeles. There they found the bodies: a thirty-five-year-old woman, curled in a fetal position, both her carotid arteries and jugular vein severed, knife wounds cutting so deeply as to nearly decapitate her. She had lost seven-eighths of the blood in her body. The other victim was a twenty-five-year-old man, his body slashed sixty-four times by the killer's knife, with slices across his neck and throat: One wound penetrated so deeply it cut into the abdominal aorta. In no sense were these ordinary homicides: According to an investigating detective, this was an attack of rage.

If so, it was an act of calculated, cold-blooded rage. A trail of bloody size-12 footprints belonging to the killer first led away from the bodies then back again. Murderers generally flee a killing scene quickly. But, as one law enforcement official speculated, in this case, the killer's stride was short, indicating that he was unhurried, seemingly amazed at his own butchery.[1]

That the murders took place in fashionable Santa Monica was news enough. But the realization that one of the victims, Nicole Brown Simpson, was the former wife of football legend O. J. Simpson, made this story something else. Despite the aura of wealth and celebrity already attached to the murders, no one could have imagined that by the time the case was resolved, the entire world would be galvanized—and stunned—by the murderous events surrounding the night of June 12, 1994.

Leo Wolinsky, the metro editor at the *Los Angles Times* first received word of the murders as the story flashed across the City News Service, which sends advisories to local news outlets. The first advisory failed to identify the victims. Wolinsky's instincts told him that the bodies were likely dumped in the exclusive neighborhood better known for its upscale cafes than serious crime. He sent a single reporter. "We still were thinking of it as a curiosity," he said.[2]

Soon afterward, another advisory identified the victims. Nicole Simpson was the estranged wife of the former football hero. Ronald Goldman was a waiter at a nearby restaurant called Mezzaluna. He had been on a good-will mission to Nicole Simpson's condominium to return a pair of eyeglasses left earlier at the restaurant—a good deed that cost him his life.

The murders were big news in Los Angeles, and the local press pounced with stories from unidentified police sources that Simpson was a prime suspect in the case. The national news media were initially more restrained. Network news featured twenty-second sight bites of the murder scene, of O. J. Simpson leaving police headquarters, another of Simpson in handcuffs being questioned by investigators. Although O. J. Simpson had yet to be officially implicated in the crimes, the media pictures foreshadowed his arrest. Five days after Brentwood neighbors were awakened by Nicole Simpson's Akita and the gruesome discovery of the two victims, Simpson was formally charged with the murders.

For much of the nation, the Simpson murder story began June 17, 1994, after a surreal set of circumstances that led to his arrest—an event that would be known simply as "the chase." As many Americans settled around their TV sets that Friday evening, the commerce of television abruptly came to a halt. Network after network dropped all regular programming to take viewers live to Los Angeles. Viewers first saw the videos before they heard the announcement—overhead shots of a white Bronco van moving slowly across the California interstate. Only when the shot widened did viewers realize that the van was being followed by a phalanx of police cars. Anchors then disclosed that O. J. Simpson was reportedly in the back of the van driven by his friend Al Cowlings.

These images were juxtaposed against footage taken earlier at the Los Angeles Police Department in Parker Center. A visibly angry police spokesperson told reporters that Simpson had fled an arrest warrant and that the LAPD was "actively searching" for him. TV viewers could hear reporters' collective gasp at the announcement—a reaction that seemed to reflect the sense of stunned disbelief that reverberated across the nation. Was Simpson, this charismatic media personality wanted for two brutal slayings, now on the run? The news would only get worse. Soon after the police announcement, the Bronco had been spotted. A reportedly despondent Simpson had told a police dispatcher on his cellular phone that he was holding a gun to his head and was prepared to pull the trigger. Then Simpson's friend, Robert Kardashian, read a purported suicide note from Simpson who asked the public to "think of the real O. J. and not this lost person."

TV news helicopters followed as the scene unfolded. The scene was described as a chase or a slow-speed pursuit but resonated more like a funeral procession. Television news anchors, visibly grim, questioned aloud how Simpson, the former gridiron star and a celebrity on the American media landscape for the past twenty-five years, could be tied to the gruesome murders. Could his shining public personality have disguised the murderous passions that lurked under his telegenic veneer?

NBC's Tom Brokaw told viewers: "For people who have known the public O. J. Simpson or even the private, it is inconceivable that it could come to this . . . a man who has spent most of his adult life in the public eye, almost always in adulation. Now, the dark side of his role in public life."[3]

The two-hour chase was elevated into a new symbolic realm as media commentators searched for a deeper meaning. The chase evoked the Greek myths and stories about the fall of the "great man." Simpson's life story was in fact an inspirational saga of a young bowlegged boy rising from the slums of San Francisco to emerge as one of the preeminent athletes in professional sports. For most Americans, though, he was perhaps better known for hawking Hertz rental cars, or for his minor screen roles in mostly slapstick movies. Ironically, Simpson attained a cultural stature in his televised flight that surpassed anything he had achieved in real life. He would find the apex of his fame as the most celebrated accused murderer in twentieth-century American history.

For some critics, to imbue Simpson with heroic qualities spoke more to the disintegration of popular culture in America than anything else. Richard Corliss, of *Time* magazine, said Simpson was no more than "a minor pop star . . . in big trouble." Simpson perfectly fit the new-age media-molded celebrity, someone celebrated for his "well-knownness" through his appearances on sports shows and commercials. "Perhaps in an age long depleted by kings," said Corliss, "we can come no closer to Greek tragedy than Oedipus Hertz."[4]

Television also gave pictures of Simpson's "fans" who lined freeways and overpasses, waiting for the Bronco to pass. They held signs urging Simpson to "Go, Juice, Go," cries of adulation he once heard on the football field. TV commentators condemned the scene, perplexed at the hero-worshipping and breakdown in moral sensibility. There was little commentary if any about media's role in this strange cultural celebration of celebrity.

For the next fifteen months, the Simpson story dominated the media agenda in a way no story had in the history of American journalism. Simpson's peaceful surrender to police at his Rockingham estate in Santa Monica did not signal the end but the beginning of a media frenzy that in itself would become historic. Not even the media armies that surrounded the trials of Harry K. Thaw, Bruno Hauptmann, Charles Manson, and other "trials of the century," would compare to the spectacle surrounding the Simpson trial.

While there was no escaping the fact that the Simpson trial was a tremendous story, even journalists were stunned by the sheer breadth of coverage and frenetic competition that ensued in the aftermath of the chase. Even before Simpson appeared for his preliminary hearing, the case was caught in a media maelstrom spinning out of control. The press furiously pursued the story and often did it badly. Mistakes were endemic in the plethora of news reports based on unidentified sources and unverified information. The media world became an echo chamber in which erroneous information was first reported and then repeated by other news outlets. Soon it was difficult to discern what was real or fiction—a damning credibility gap for an institution that rises or falls on perceptions of truth that Americans hold it to. With each day appeared another bad story. A *Los Angeles Daily News* exclusive reported a bloodstained entrenching tool had been found near the murder scene. That a murder weapon was uncovered was big news—but soon that story was shelved without comment. Leaks from the coroner's office led some media to surmise the victims were "decapitated"—a vivid picture, but not accurate. Then there were reports that a bloody ski mask had been found at the murder scene—a piece of evidence that did not exist.

Key participants found themselves victimized by sloppy reporting. KCBS reported that they had time-coded videotape showing Deputy District Attorney Marcia Clark at Simpson's estate before a search warrant had been issued. Such information, if true, could have seriously hampered the prosecution's case. Only days later, after angry denials by the district attorney's office, did the station finally back off its erroneous story.

Beyond the obvious concerns about factual errors lay a broader critique regarding the press and the Simpson case. Indeed, the Simpson trial hit the American landscape at a time of significant technological and psychological changes in journalism and in the popular culture at large. The confluence of these forces came together, seeming to implode the delicate relationship between the press and the courts.

Throughout the next months, the Simpson case would be linked, and magnified, by a vast modern technological machine. Television's satellite links enabled Americans to see immediate live pictures, first of the chase, and then of the hearings, trial, and verdict. Viewers were effectively positioned into various roles as spectators, commentators, and witnesses. Americans now were a collective, a tribe of viewers, huddled around an electronic storyteller where terrible tales about murder were being unraveled. These stories were all the more unsettling because they reflected in some ways who *they* were as a people, a race—and where they had arrived in the waning moments of the twentieth century.

Other instruments also extended the boundaries of the Simpson case. A vast home computer network enabled millions to speak to each other and to on-line media outlets: Throughout the year, the Simpson case was the preeminent "hot topic," with special links to the wealth of legal documents, daily trial transcripts, press articles, television transcripts, and video clips.

There were other interactive links apart from cyberspace: Both television and radio talk shows were a way in which listeners not only contributed their ideas to this "Great Conversation," but, in essence, became a part of the Simpson story itself.

When media weren't talking about the case, they were usually talking about what Americans were saying about the case. Using polls as a favorite weapon in their arsenal, the media came to conclusions—however ephemeral—about what Americans believed about Simpson's guilt or innocence. These broad-based surveys tended to create a racial world of "us" versus "them"—with black and white Americans divided over Simpson's culpability in the murders. As they became a mainstay in media reports, the polls ultimately became a racial litmus test, a reflection that revealed less about the Simpson case and more about race politics in America.

Without question, however, the most significant connection and influence in this symbiotic relationship between the media and the courts was a small and seemingly innocuous looking machine—a TV camera situated on the wall of Department 103 in the Los Angeles Criminal Courthouse, the site of the Simpson trial. While television has been present in criminal cases since the mid-1950s, the days of noisy motor drives and harsh klieg lights were long gone. The modern, light-sensitive camera works in silence, indeed, without even a technician visible to man its controls. Although the camera no longer called attention to itself—an old criticism articulated by the U.S. Supreme Court in the 1965 Estes decision—it did something far more insidious: it fundamentally altered the very nature of the Simpson trial itself, including, it can be argued, the final verdict in the case.

Up until the Simpson case, the debate about whether television cameras belonged in American courtrooms was typically relegated to state legislative halls, legal seminars, or scholarly discourses on media and justice. After forty years of controversy concerning the "effects" of television on trials, the camera and the court seemingly settled into a cozy relationship. By the time the Simpson case came to trial, forty-seven states permitted some form of televised trials. From time to time, a few complaints could be heard but, for the most part, Americans seemed to love their court TV.

There were, of course, some outspoken critics raising serious concerns about the upcoming televised Simpson trial. Even a wary Federal Judicial Conference voted days before the start of the Simpson trial to stop a national experiment allowing televised civil trials in federal courts. But in the beginning of the Simpson case, the euphoria was too high to allow such thinking to be taken seriously. Like a nation going to war, virtually all media organizations rallied around the courtroom camera, heralding the camera as a major weapon for democracy. Whether or not democracy and justice would flourish at the televised Simpson trial, the one certainty was that the camera would make careers, bringing fame and fortune to more than a few trial players standing before it.

Television itself seemed to suddenly discover a new genre—something I call the "Television Trial"—intense and extended coverage of sensational cases with popular appeal.[5] In the 1980s a few trials were broadcast extensively, including the trials of Claus von Bulow in 1982 and the defendants in the "Big Dan's tavern" gang rape case in New Bedford, Massachusetts, in 1984. But as commercial TV fare, trials were too long and tedious and never seriously considered a part of television's future. The expansion of cable television and, specifically, the rise of Court TV changed that thinking. With its gavel-to gavel-coverage of selected trials, Court TV revolutionized court reporting and, indeed, the very notion of the public trial. The Television Trial transcended local boundaries to become a national trial; and courtroom doors now opened to a vast American public tuned to the case.

There were other ramifications resulting from this new television age. For one, defendants became the latest American celebrities: William Kennedy Smith, Erik and Lyle Menendez, Lorena and John Bobbitt, Amy Fisher, Joey Buttafuoco. While advocates of courtroom cameras applauded Court TV for opening the courts to more public scrutiny, critics warned that American trials soon may become something else—entertainment. Then the Simpson case arrived.

No defendant in modern American jurisprudence could compare to the likes of O. J. Simpson, who wore the mantle of celebrity even before he sat down at the defense table in Department 103 at the Los Angeles Criminal Courts Building. The media never had a defendant with the star-like qualities of Simpson and, for fifteen months, he would be the object of their obsession.

A huge media contingent gathered in and around the courthouse, many settling into a media shantytown erected in a nearby parking lot nicknamed "Camp O. J." Nine towering television platforms were built giving television reporters a backdrop of the Criminal Courts Building during their on-air reports. Miles of television cable were strung in and around the courthouse; satellite dishes were strategically placed; and dozens of trailers and mobile production trucks housed hundreds of reporters, producers, and technicians from scores of television stations. The courthouse area had the feeling of being under siege, which, in fact, it was.

The case began in earnest with the preliminary hearing, a six-day event beginning in late June 1994 that immediately spiraled into a media extravaganza.

The legal purpose of the preliminary hearing was to determine if enough evidence existed to hold Simpson over for trial. Such hearings are normally perfunctory and draw little, if any, media interest. But with the chase as the opening act to the ensuing frenzy, the Simpson preliminary hearing was already positioned as a media spectacular.

The decision by ABC, NBC, CBS, CNN, Court TV, and a myriad of local stations to cover the hearing in its entirety was unprecedented. When the proceedings weren't being aired live, network news magazines and talk shows placed Simpson center stage. The respected "Nightline" became a devotee of the hearings and the Simpson case dominated its weekly agenda. CNN, the once all-news network, was transformed into the all-O. J. network. Ratings soared fivefold during the hearings, audience numbers the network hadn't seen since its groundbreaking coverage of the 1991 Persian Gulf War.

The six-day preliminary hearing became the single most important event in the United States if judged by the nation's media coverage. Indeed, virtually all other news was pushed to the back burner, including Yasir Arafat's arrival in Jericho, a historic moment in Middle East politics, and the death of North Korean leader Kim Il Sung during a time of critical tension between the United States and North Korea. These stories were mere blips on the electronic landscape.

Television coverage compelled the print media to compete, and most of the major papers carved out large sections of their news hold for coverage of the case. Once, print coverage of trials largely consisted of reciting the day's testimony. With television already giving viewers that story, newspapers were free to expand coverage outside the courtroom—and they eagerly did so.

The *Los Angeles Times*, in particular, became the paper of record for the Simpson case. From the time of the murder to the trial's end, the newspaper would run 398 front-page articles about the case—more than 1,500 stories in all. (By comparison, the *New York Times* ran 52 front pagers.) The sheer scope of coverage was like nothing seen before in the history of the paper. Five reporters were assigned the Simpson case full time; other reporters worked part time on the story. The newspaper also created special columns such as "The Spin" and "The Legal Pad."[6]

Henry Weinstein, the paper's veteran legal analyst, found his job recast once the case came to trial. Of the 154 stories he wrote for 1995, 126 were about the Simpson case—82 percent of his entire workload for the year. No other topic had so dominated his work. A veteran reporter of twenty-six years who covered important legal issues involving farm workers and asbestos litigation, he was astounded at the intensity of his own coverage. "I'll bet I haven't written 126 stories on asbestos litigation in all of the twenty or so years that I've been covering it," he said.[7]

By the time Simpson was brought to trial, his story had transcended the earthly boundaries of the "news." As one critic commented, the case had "hijacked" the culture. It was virtually impossible to turn anywhere on the media landscape and not come into contact with the Simpson case. Tabloid circulation skyrocketed, as did virtually any radio or TV talk show where Simpson was the topic. With the exception of sex-related topics, the Simpson case dominated cyberspace's chat lines. Thousand of articles were already written and soon a spate of books would be published. Hundreds of American lawyers found new careers as TV commentators on Simpson-related shows across the nation. Before the trial was over, one research group estimated that American companies had lost $40 billion in productivity costs from workers chatting about the case during extended coffee breaks or at copy machines.

The Simpson case had also become a leading American export. The case bannered across the front pages of Israeli newspapers, was broadcast live in Britain, and debated at dinner tables in Iman and Beirut. Eugene Roberts, managing editor of the *New York Times*, said that during his trip to Asia he found "people who don't even understand the [English] language were watching it on TV and having it explained to them." When Russian President Boris Yeltsin visited the country, his first statement coming off his plane was reportedly, "Do you think O. J. did it?"[8]

Perhaps no other story in recent memory did more to exacerbate the tenuous relationship between the media and their constituencies. Although Americans continued avidly to watch and read about the case, there was a growing sense of anger that the media was exploiting the story and exploiting them. Reaction to complaints was mixed. Leading journalists argued that Americans could simply turn off the TV set or turn the pages of their newspaper to bypass the Simpson story. But others were more introspective. Tom Brokaw, the NBC "Nightly News" anchor, said he could not recall another story that created "so much angst" at the network. Brokaw conceded that NBC staffers were constantly questioning their own roles in producing and showcasing the story, asking themselves: "How much is too much? Are we all prostituting ourselves to the O. J. thing? Have we been driven by the lowest common denominator?"[9]

Even before the trial opened on January 24, 1995, the case had taken on various incarnations. After the release of two 911 emergency tapes earlier in the case, in which Simpson is heard breaking into Nicole Simpson's home shouting profanities, the case became a touchstone for a national seminar on wife battering. The prosecution and police's early media campaign painting Simpson as a wife abuser, paid dividends. For many Americans, Simpson was no longer seen as a celebrity but a wife abuser, and, possibly, a murderer.

But the powerful messages of wife beating were overwhelmed by an even more hot-buttoned topic: race. While mainstream media at first tried to downplay or outrightly ignore the significance of Simpson's color, they soon become entangled in a case loaded with racial implications. Their early reticence to cast the case in racial terms, soon gave way to a political climate that was also exploited by a defense strategy to move attention away from the murder and to the LAPD and its handling of the case.

It was impossible to look at the "message" without its context. The trial of O. J. Simpson took center stage with the painful memory of the police beating of Rodney King, the trials of the police officers involved, and the subsequent riots, still fresh in the minds of many Angelenos. Though the Simpson case began as a murder mystery, within the black community, it soon became the latest symbol of black oppression.

In the days leading up to trial, the race issue tumbled into American living rooms through the camera lens as trial attorneys angrily debated whether the use of the word "nigger" would be allowed when a prosecution witness, Detective Mark Fuhrman, took the stand. An earlier *New Yorker* magazine article helped to float a defense theory that Fuhrman was possibly a rogue cop, and also a racist, who planted a bloody glove on Simpson's estate the night of the murders to implicate Simpson. Although no evidence was produced to prove that Fuhrman set up Simpson then—or at any time during the coming year—the theory would remain at the heart of the defense strategy.

Before a national audience, prosecutor Christopher Darden pleaded with Judge Lance Ito to prohibit defense lawyers, planning to vigorously challenge Fuhrman's attitudes about black Americans, from using "the n-word" before the jury.

"It is the dirtiest, filthiest word in the English language," Darden told the court. "It will upset the black jurors. It will issue a test, and the test will be: Whose side are you on, the side of the white prosecutors and the white policemen, or are you on the side of the black defendant and his very prominent black lawyer?"

Johnnie Cochran, the lead attorney for the "dream team," called Darden's objections insulting to the mostly black jury panel and then issued an apology to the black community for Darden's slight. Taking advantage of the full reach of the camera, Cochran not only addressed the courtroom, but the nation. It would not be the last time that he would use the court podium as a pulpit for political messages about race in America.

The Simpson case soon settled into the muck of an extended race argument even as prosecutors introduced what they called a "mountain of evidence" against Simpson. First, evidence pointing to motive: Simpson's stormy, violent treatment of his ex-wife. And second, evidence pointing to his role in the murders: hair found in a cap at the murder scene that was compatible with Simpson's hair; a trail of blood that was Simpson's type leading from the murder scene, to Simpson's Bronco, to the pathway leading to Simpson's house, on socks found in Simpson's bedroom, and on a brown glove found next to his home. Other blood samples—those from the victims—were also found in and around Simpson's possessions.

The defense team tried to downplay the physical evidence by pointing to sloppy police work. Police had improperly collected blood evidence, and then failed to refrigerate it, a fact that could degrade such samples. Barry Scheck, one of the defense lawyers, launched the DNA war, arguing at great length over the discrepancies in the prosecution's blood evidence. He pointed to inconsistencies in the composition of the DNA—a drop of blood contains about 1,500 nanograms of DNA, he maintained, yet some of the blood gathered contained 2 to 35 nanograms.

The technical and long-winded scientific debate over blood was central to the case, but it may very well have been overwhelmed by the race issue—personified in the being of Mark Fuhrman. The media hype surrounding the confrontation between Fuhrman and F. Lee Bailey, another member of the defense team, was astounding. Bailey promoted his cross-examination, promising to break the detective on the stand and reveal the detective as the racist cop he had been characterized as from the start of the trial.

Throughout the three-day questioning, Bailey grilled Fuhrman about his racial views. Repeatedly, he would ask whether he had used the racial slur "nigger" any time in the past ten years. Fuhrman said he had not. The race banter between the lawyer and the detective continued and, having failed to shake the detective, Bailey promised to deliver a witness named Max Cordoba, to discredit Fuhrman's testimony. In dramatic overstatement, Bailey intoned: "I have spoken with (Cordoba) on the phone personally, Marine to Marine, and I don't have the slightest doubt that he will march up to the witness stand and tell the world what Fuhrman called him."

In a plot development so audacious as to make even a veteran Hollywood screenwriter blush, Cordoba could be seen that very evening on NBC-TV's "Dateline," declaring that he had in fact never even spoken to Bailey. (Later modifying his viewpoint, he said his memory of such a conversation was jogged in a dream.) The following day, the prosecution's reaction was swift and furious. With open disdain, prosecutor Marcia Clark accused Bailey of being an outright liar, and, when the famed defense lawyer tried to protest, she told him, in essence, to sit down and shut up. The moment for millions of TV viewers was pure theatrical drama.

Even reporters found the legal antics hard to believe. A dismayed Greg Jarrett, NBC's co-anchor, asked rhetorically: "It makes you wonder what's going on here."

Having raised public expectations to a Perry Mason–like cross-examination, the media was not in a forgiving mood when the reality of this performance failed to live up to the hype. The media was openly contemptuous. Commentary was more akin to theater "reviews" and, clearly, the famed attorney had flopped. The *New York Time's* David Margolick, in his 1,600-word essay on Bailey's performance, concluded: "Mr. Bailey's theatricality and bombast seemed silly at times, the kind of shtick that may have worked well when lawyers still wore flowers in their boutonnieres but no longer."[10]

But the issues revolving around race and Mark Fuhrman would not disappear. And, in a development more akin to TV court dramas than real life courtrooms, the defense revealed the existence of audio tapes in which Fuhrman is heard speaking to a screenwriter by the name of Laura Hart McKinny. The tapes were first played in the courtroom in the absence of the jury, but in the presence of millions of TV viewers. For two hours, Fuhrman could be heard spewing out invectives against minorities. He had used the word "nigger" more than forty times, but the tapes went further. The detective spoke about beating people and pounding their faces into "mush," and also about how he would plant or manufacture evidence to "set niggers up."

Although jury members heard only small portions of the tape, the rest of America listened repeatedly as the tapes made the media rounds. On every television station, mainstream newspaper, and radio news and talk show across the country, the Simpson trial had dramatically turned into the trial of Mark Fuhrman. And he was guilty, at the very least, of perjury.

When the verdict came down, it was a stunning moment. It had taken jury members less than three hours to reach a decision in a trial that had lasted nine months. America appeared to stand still as the verdict was announced in Department 103. When Simpson was acquitted, the media impressions were vivid—with pictures of black Americans jumping in jubilation at the news; white Americans staring in disbelief. For some observers, the reality of the deep divisions between black and white America were as startling and disillusioning as the pronouncement from Los Angeles.

As part of media's iconic world, O. J. Simpson also evolved. No longer the desperate, former football star taking flight down the freeway and cheered by his fans for his celebrity, he had been relegated to another status: that of the black man, conspired against by a racist police system, now cheered for his blackness. The case which began as a TV megaevent, would end in a bizarre and surreal coda. Following his acquittal, yet another white van would take him home to Brentwood along the same California freeway he traveled a year before. At his estate he would be embraced by A. C. Cowlings, his friend and accomplice during the chase. As these scenes unfolded, the ubiquitous helicopters' TV cameras captured these moments for a vast American audience and for posterity.

Even before the trial had begun, Judge Lance Ito had held the promise that the Simpson case could be a golden civics lesson by which Americans could learn about the process of justice. In the end, perhaps Ito felt the same bitter irony experienced by Americans who believed that the trial had exacerbated deep-seated racial tensions in this country and that justice itself had less to do with truth than wealth, status, and, in the end, a play to racial fears.

Although the jury had reached a verdict, much to the relief of those who believed the case would end in a mistrial, the nagging question remained whether they reached the *right* verdict. Undoubtedly, their judgment will long be debated as to whether reasonable doubt existed to exonerate Simpson. But what will continue to embitter many Americans is *how* the verdict was reached. Jurors had effectively nullified all evidence and testimony to reach a decision seemingly based on a snap judgment.

Some critics tied the verdict to racial motives among the nearly all black panel, but other explanations could also account for the nearly instantaneous verdict. The case had been distended beyond recognition, finally ending with a frustrated jury anxious to end their nine-month ordeal, sequestered from their family and day-to-day life. Here a finger was pointed at television and its power within the courtroom.

After the trial, Christopher Darden acknowledged that the camera had hurt the process of justice. He accused the judge of being so "infatuated with the idea of being the judge in the 'trial of the century,'" that ultimately he lost control of the trial. Darden also accused lawyers of arguing endlessly and questioning witnesses beyond the scope of reason. Television, he said, "had caused each lawyer to change their natural courtroom style."

"With millions watching, and pundits watching every move and scoring 'points' as to who is ahead and who is behind," he said, "lawyers became more abrasive, combative and long-winded." He added: "That style of justice never helps achieve justice. It only tarnishes it."[11]

By the time the Simpson trial had ended, the once overwhelming support for cameras in the court plummeted. Judges in several high-profile cases banned televised court coverage. Among them were Superior Court Judge Stanley Weisberg, who refused to allow cameras into the court for the second trial of Erik and Lyle Menendez, accused of killing their parents, after the first high-profile, televised proceeding ended in mistrials.

While the verdict ended the O. J. Simpson trial, it did not end the O. J. Simpson story. The television trial, especially this one, has a peculiar afterlife. Now free of the constraints of the courtroom, trial participants could now cash in on the celebrity status they have achieved. Following the trial, most of the key players soon discovered, if they hadn't already known, that they had become the next hot property. The goods and services already produced from the Simpson case were estimated at $2 billion, more than the GNP of many small countries. Now in the posttrial marketplace, Marcia Clark, Christopher Darden, Robert Shapiro, Johnnie Cochran, and O. J. Simpson himself, were prepared to take their cut from the pie. Each walked away from the trial with a million-dollar-plus book deal, a TV series, or other lucrative deals. With the winners and losers replaying the evidence and testimony again and again, the Simpson case continues to find life well after the trial is over. In an age of devalued heroes and instantaneous story-making, the Simpson case had become legendary.

As for the media, they have moved onto the next story. O. J. Simpson's forays to Europe to sell his own version of the case, or his involvement in a civil trial, which has become less enthralling. After all the clamor, the case has a remarkable deflating effect, the fatigue finally settling in after a wearisome and depressing trial.

But the media, as well as the American justice system, will be challenged to critically examine their own roles in this so-called "trial of the century." Was the Simpson trial merely an aberration, as some observers conclude—a once-in-a-lifetime mystery featuring a famous defendant and a gruesome double murder, played against the backdrop of Hollywood and the celebrity culture it helped to spawn? Or was the Simpson trial inevitable—a collision between the courts and the media, both coming to grips with a powerful technological age that has defined their very existence? Out of the smoke and noise we may find a deeper understanding about what happened here—what turned law and justice into entertainment and spectacle. If so, this may be the Simpson trial's most lasting and meaningful legacy.

Editor's Note: Simpson's civil trial represented, figuratively and literally, a reversal of fortune for the former football star. In early February of 1997, Simpson was found liable for the deaths of his ex-wife and Ronald Goldman. Jurors awarded $25 million in punitive damages, $12.5 million each to the estates of Nicole Brown Simpson and Ronald Goldman. In addition, $8.5 million in compensatory damages was awarded.

NOTES

1. Christopher Darden, *In Contempt* (New York: ReganBooks, 1996).

2. Interview with Leo Wolinsky, August 1996.

3. Tom Brokaw's statement made on a live news special on NBC-TV, 17 June 1994.

4. Richard Corliss, "It's Already a TV Movie," *Time*, 18 July 1994.

5. Paul Thaler, *The Watchful Eye: American Justice in the Age of the Television Trial* (Westport, Conn.: Praeger, 1994).

6. David Shaw, "The Story That Hijacked America," *Los Angeles Times,* 9 October 1995, special report.

7. Interview with Henry Weinstein, May 1996.

8. Shaw, "The Story That Hijacked America," S3.

9. Ibid, S10.

10. David Margolick, "A Cross-Examination Ends, and Judging Begins for Simpson Lawyer," *New York Times*, 30 March 1995.

11. Darden, *In Contempt*, 260.

16

The Verdict

Michael Maher and Lloyd Chiasson Jr.

Why does the press love spectacular trials? In the wake of the O. J. Simpson trial, the answer that comes first to mind is that trial coverage is little more than collective rubber-necking. Trials are real-life soap operas that allow the public to gawk at others' malfeasance and tragedy.

In this perspective, media attention to "trials of the century" diverts the public from considering more substantive matters. Such a view is offered by television journalist Christiane Amanpour, who has covered many of the wars of the 1990s: "It is not OK for the press to focus inordinate amounts of attention on the O. J. Simpson case and virtually ignore the massacre of between 500,000 and 1 million Rwandans!"[1]

If we look through the lens of Social Responsibility theory,[2] we find little support for the kind of press coverage the preceding chapters have analyzed. The trial of Charles Manson or of Lizzie Borden, the tragedy of Charles Lindbergh or of Nicole Brown Simpson, has little material bearing on the lives of the millions who read those stories. In matters that really affect them, Americans would be better informed by reading about tax legislation or the federal deficit. The media tell us what to think about, as agenda-setting studies have shown, but they tell us to think about the wrong things when they devote so much space to, say, O. J. Simpson prosecutor Marcia Clark's hair.

From a social responsibility perspective, press coverage of trials is little more than a pernicious distraction from weightier matters of civic responsibility. But it has been well established that, in market-driven journalism, the media must give the public what it wants rather than what it needs.[3] A more interesting question about trial coverage focuses not so much on the press, but on the public: Why do people read and watch trial coverage with such avidity?

A considerable body of press criticism now looks at media coverage not in terms of its accuracy or its biases, but as a compendium of stories, much like literature. And these stories can be interpreted like any other anthropological artifacts, as cultural indicators.[4]

Trials are also cultural events, which is probably why they interest the public so much. They have all the elements of good fiction: conflict, suspense, rising and falling action, deception and surprise, heroes and villains. Like a sports event, a trial ends with a clear-cut winner and loser. Trials provide a continuing source of news pegs, as each new witness and each new bit of evidence creates a new premise for a story.

But thousands of trials happen every day. Why do only certain trials achieve "trial of the century" status? What is it about the trials discussed in the previous chapters that so captures the public interest? Many top trials involve celebrities: O. J. Simpson, Sharon Tate, Charles Lindbergh, the Chicago White Sox. But John Scopes was a high school football coach prior to the Great Monkey Trial; the Scottsboro boys were hoboes; and Lizzie Borden was an innocuous single woman living in her father and step-mother's home. So celebrity status is not a common factor.

Many of the preceding chapters describe violent crime: Charles Manson, Lizzie Borden, O. J. Simpson, John Brown, William Calley, Bruno Hauptmann—all were accused of murder. But what about John Scopes, the Black Sox, John Peter Zenger, the Chicago Seven? Violence is not a common factor.

Viewed collectively within a broad historical frame, the preceding chapters show us that the common factor is not some aspect of the trial. Rather, the common factor is that all these trials broached deep-seated public anxieties.

Consider:

The unusual trial of John Peter Zenger. It would be easy to say that the arrest of an eighteenth-century printer generated interest throughout the colonies because he was treated unfairly, because his adversary was hugely disliked, because free speech was at stake. But that is a short-sighted view. The Zenger trial was important because it marked an early—perhaps the earliest—sign of colonial discontent with England. It marked a moment in time when the colonies displayed more different than shared values with the homeland. The colonists' interest in the Zenger trial had more to do with a forced dependence on England and a corresponding desire by the colonists for more independence, than it ever had to do with Zenger. The Zenger case became widely known throughout the colonies because it suggested that a greater freedom of expression—both in print and in governance—might be possible. It created interest because it pitted the English against the colonists. The trial was no magical moment; it foretold no coming revolution. But it clearly demonstrated early signs of the "us" versus "them" mentality that prevailed throughout the Revolutionary Period and that dominated the Boston Massacre trials.

Honor and duty: These were the intangibles that embodied the trials of

John Brown and William Calley. In part, each trial was reduced to, and decided upon, these concepts. But the key question in each trial both horrified and galvanized the public: Were they devils or soldiers? Yet the verdicts in both cases had less to do with the crimes than they did in defining *how* Americans fight war and *why*. Slavery, not John Brown, stood trial in 1859. More than 100 years later, the Calley trial forced many Americans to reconsider their support for another war and probably hastened our withdrawal from Southeast Asia.

The bomb in Haymarket Square fanned fears of socialism, communism, and anarchy. The result: Five men died, capital gained ground that labor lost, and justice was roundly defeated. But it was fear that made this trial special—fear of change, fear of the unknown. For what could be more frightening than anarchy? A communist state, perhaps? Little wonder the anarchists were found guilty. But there is more to the story—public anxiety over communism may have been soothed, but it was only temporary. The shouts of the anarchists would reverberate into the next century and surface in the Scottsboro, Hiss, and Rosenberg trials.

Two trials seem to have little to recommend them as pressure gauges measuring public anxiety. At first glance, the Lizzie Borden trial appears to have been no more, and no less, than a murder trial. A sensational one, no doubt, but a murder trial nonetheless. Charles Manson's trial was chiseled from the same granite. But pick up the rock, and lying underneath is the public's fascination with the bizarre. The crimes for which Borden and Manson were charged were not murders as much as acts of slaughter. Bestial, macabre mutilations recounted in newspapers, in kitchens, over back fences. The key question in the Borden trial: Could a woman commit such a brutal murder? The key question in the Manson trial: How could anyone commit such inhuman acts? An underlying question in both trials: How could our society produce anyone capable of that? And in seeking the answer, we are drawn to the trials. But there is more. The public's fascination with the Borden trial rested upon the emerging women's movement and women's demand for more equality in American society. Women wanted off the pedestal upon which men had sequestered them. Could a woman have done such a heinous thing? The ironic answer is that the jury essentially said no, women were not equal to men. Lizzie was not capable of an ax murder. In many ways the verdict was consistent with the times—it was chauvinistic and against full equality for women.

Many observers of the Harry K. Thaw trial believed the wrong person was tried. No question Harry committed the deed, but Evelyn Nesbit, they pointed out, planted the seed. As the trial played out, the central figures stood for the changing times and a new set of standards unlike those of the nineteenth century. Stanford White, Harry Thaw, and Evelyn Nesbit became as famous for their libertine escapades as for their roles in the murder. The real defendant at this trial, the carnival barker nudging the public into the cloaked tent, was sexual mores.

In retrospect, the public's attitude about the Black Sox scandal was clear: Indict the players, not The Game. That players cheated, that gamblers wormed their way into the soul of baseball, and that owners were a part rather than a solution to the problem, somehow, miraculously, never touched The Game. The media didn't report it that way. If it had, the national pastime would have been sullied. The players might be dirty, but never The Game. The public's immediate interest was focused on the players and the World Series, but its hopes, and fears, were with The Game.

For the most part, the famous Monkey Trial of John Scopes was reported like the World Series six years before. Science versus religion; Darrow versus Bryan; Tennessee versus the world; evolution versus God. In many ways it was not unlike the O. J. Simpson trial. It was a media circus; it offered up a gaggle of celebrities; it galvanized the public. But its real significance could be found in the larger issue that cemented all the elements together: Life in the twentieth century had inexorably changed the human condition and that was frightening and captivating at the same time. As science seemed to erode Biblical accounts of who we are and where we come from, every American became a stranger in a strange land. Write jokes about monkeys. Write about Darrow. Write about Bryan. Just don't write about a world we no longer understand or feel comfortable in.

Charles Lindbergh was the Neil Armstrong of his day, and his fame was as great following his New York to Paris solo flight in 1927. The arrest, conviction, and electrocution of a Bronx carpenter more than six years later made the name Bruno Richard Hauptmann almost as well known. But the men were a study in contrasts. Lindbergh was wealthy, celebrated, admired. Hauptmann was an unknown immigrant laborer of modest means. Their social, intellectual, and economic worlds were far apart. The names Lindbergh and Hauptmann, when linked, have come to connote good versus evil, justice versus injustice. Hauptmann's was a contentious trial for many reasons, but it was framed by the status of the participants and the hard times of the Depression. In the end, the public perceived the trial in the most American of storylines—rich man versus poor man.

The Scottsboro boys' cases crystallized two of the twentieth century's great "isms": racism and communism. These nine black hoboes were tried for raping two white women at a time when lynching was still common for such a crime, when blacks were still excluded from juries, and indeed when blacks were simply not accepted as having equal human rights in the South. Their trials allowed world public opinion to focus on this system of apartheid, and helped change it—even though the defendants were convicted in every trial.

In 1931 the American Communist Party inserted itself as champions of the Scottsboro boys, through its legal arm, the International Labor Defense. At the time capitalism seemed to be failing; millions were out of work. Hundreds of thousands of Americans attended rallies or signed petitions on behalf of the Scottsboro boys in an era that was this country's most serious flirtation with communism. But the communists failed to convince Americans that theirs was the best solution, even during this dark decade.

The fear of communism was by no means over by the next decade, for no two trials encapsulated the fear and anxiety of the cold war more than the Hiss and Rosenberg trials. The threat of spies, the claims of guilt, the cries of innocence, the intrigue, the suspense—all were elements of a classic Eric Ambler "whodunit." But the dominant theme emanating from these trials was the fragility of the status quo. Each crime—and it follows, each trial—was based upon the erosion—or fear of erosion—of democracy. Little wonder they translated into such huge media events.

Chicago was a scary place to be in 1968, primarily because America was a scary place to be. Remember: Americans were fighting among themselves about a war they couldn't explain and an enemy they didn't understand, all for a cause they couldn't clearly define. This was the decade of civil rights marches, of assassinations, of Watts, of Neil Armstrong's moon walk, of Woodstock, of free love, of long hair, and bell bottoms. It was a decade of change, and change fosters interest and anxiety. Like the Manson trial, the trial of the Chicago Seven was about a lot of things, but mostly it was about the culture of the baby boomers. The rebellion, the alternative solutions to mainstream society norms—these were on trial.

If the fascination with the Manson trial was, on the one hand, about the inhuman acts committed, the other hand was about the whole counterculture movement of the 1960s. The peace/love flower children optimism of the midsixties seemed to be degenerating into something evil. The Manson murders resonated with a public that was suspicious of youth culture. In fact, Joan Didion wrote that the Manson murders essentially ended the optimism of the sixties: "Many people I know in Los Angeles believe that the Sixties ended abruptly on August 9, 1969, ended at the exact moment when the word of the murders on Cielo Drive traveled like brushfire through the community."[5]

Perhaps no trial created as much public debate—in part because of the astounding amount of media coverage, in part because the accused was a celebrity—than the last trial included in this book. Of all the trials, not one left the public as unsettled as did O. J. Simpson's. The question is, why? Was it because the vast majority of white people thought a guilty man was unfairly acquitted, or was it that the majority of blacks believed an innocent man escaped white man's justice? The answers are yes. O. J. was important only insofar as he was a black man. The trial, not the murders, was about race. The defense wallowed in it; the prosecution ran from it. And from the beginning, the public, consciously or not, was fascinated with and frightened by it.

Elements of the trial intrigued us—O. J.'s celebrity status, the now-famous police "escort" of the white Bronco, the incidents of spousal abuse—but race was the trump card. The defendant's blackness and his wife's whiteness. The selection of a minority jury. The death of two whites at the hands, possibly, of a black. The possibility of manipulation of condemning evidence by a white against a black. More than anything else, that the reactions of blacks and whites to the verdict were poles apart was a verdict of its own: America has never adequately resolved its racial differences. The problems between the races have not been solved, they have metamorphosed. Ask the Scottsboro boys.

In conclusion, this text tilled fertile soil. No hyperbole was needed. The coverage of these cases proved that the press is "on trial" every time it reports on a crime. But the real story here is not the crime, nor the trial, nor the media coverage. The real story is found in what the significance of the trial was, or is, or will be.

Is it possible to find a distinguishable pattern woven from the threads of trials spanning three centuries? Are they nothing more than separate events whispering just bits and pieces of history? Has this collection presented no more than sixteen trials, sixteen verdicts? If there is social significance to these trials, what, exactly, is it?

And the answers. Yes, there is a pattern to be found. No, these sixteen trials do not whisper, they shout. And their message is simple: Our preoccupation with these trials reflects not so much an interest in the individual event but in the American landscape at that point in time. Each trial reflects what is happening in America and what Americans think about it. Trials are social barometers of the times.

Our final verdict is this: Spectacular trials achieve such notoriety because they touch a tender nerve in the public psyche. The label "trial of the century" tells us a lot more about the century than it does about the trial.

NOTES

1. Christiane Amanpour, *Quill*, April 1996, 16.

2. See F. Sieber, T. Peterson, and W. Schramm, *Four Theories of the Press*. (Urbana: University of Illinois Press, 1963).

3. See J. McManus, *Market-driven Journalism: Let the Citizen Beware?* (Thousand Oaks, Calif.: Sage, 1994).

4. See, for example, T. Koch, *The News as Myth: Fact and Context in Journalism* (Westport, Conn.: Greenwood Press, 1900); R. Hart, *The Sound of Leadership: Presidential Communication in the Modern Age* (Chicago: University of Chicago Press, 1987); R. Darnton, *Writing News and Telling Stories*. (Daedalus 104(2), 175–194; H. McCartney, "Applying Fiction Conflict Situations to Analysis of News Stories," *Journalism Quarterly* (1987): 163–170; S. Bird and R. Dardenne, "Myth, Chronicle, and Story: Exploring the Narrative Qualities of News," in *Media, Myths, and Narratives: Television and the Press* , ed. J. W. Carey (Newbury Park, Calif.: Sage), 67–86.

5. Joan Didion, *The White Album* (New York: Pocket Books, 1979).

Selected Bibliography

BOOKS AND JOURNALS

Abramson, Phyllis Leslie. *Sob Sister Journalism*. New York: Greenwood Press, 1990.

Diary and Autobiography of John Adams. Edited by Lyman H. Butterfield et al., 4 vols, Cambridge, Mass.: Harvard University Press, 1963.

Adams, John. *The Works of John Adams*. Edited by Charles Francis Adams. Boston: Little, Brown, 1856.

Alexander, Charles C. *Our Game: An American Baseball History*. New York: Henry Holt and Company, 1991.

Anzieu, Didier. *Freud's Self-Analysis*. Madison, Conn.: International Universities Press, Inc., 1986.

Aronson, James. *Deadline for the Media: Today's Challenges to Press, TV and Radio*. Indianapolis and New York: Bobbs-Merrill, 1972.

Asinof, Eliot. *Eight Men Out*. New York: Holt, Rinehart and Winston, 1963.

Atkins, Susan, with Bob Slosser. *Child of Satan, Child of God*. Plainfield, N.J.: Logos International, 1977.

Baer, Rosemary. *Reflections on The Manson Trial, Journal of a Pseudo-Juror*. Waco, Texas: Word Books, 1972.

Bailyn, Bernard. *The Ideological Origins of the American Revolution*. Cambridge, Mass.: Belknap Press of Harvard University Press, 1967.

Baughman, James. *Henry R. Luce and the Rise of the American Century*. Boston: Twayne, 1987.

Belfrage, Cedric. *The American Inquisition, 1945–60*. New York: Columbia University Press, 1973.

Belknap, Michael R., ed. *American Political Trials*. Westport, Conn.: Greenwood Press, 1981.

Berg, William J., and Laurey K. Martin. *Emile Zola Revisited*. New York: Twayne Publishers, 1992.

Bishop, George. *Witness to Evil*. Los Angeles: Nash Publishing, 1971.

Botein, Stephen, ed. "Mr. Zenger's Malice and Falsehood." In *Six Issues of the New-*

York Weekly Journal. Worcester, Mass.: American Antiquarian Society, 1985.

Boyer, Richard O. *The Legend of John Brown.* New York: Alfred A. Knopf, 1973.

Brill, A. A., ed. *The Basic Writings of Sigmund Freud.* New York: Random House, 1938.

Brown, Arnold. *Lizzie Borden: The Legend, The Truth, The Final Chapter.* Nashville, Tenn.: Rutledge Hill Press, 1991.

Bryan, William Jennings. *In His Image.* London: Fleming H. Revell, 1922.

Bugliosi, Vincent, with Curt Gentry. *Helter Skelter, The True Story of the Manson Murders.* New York: W. W. Norton & Company, 1974, 1994.

Buranelli, Vincent, ed. *The Trial of John Peter Zenger.* New York: New York University Press, 1957.

Burk, Robert F. *Never Just a Game: Players, Owners, and American Baseball to 1920.* Chapel Hill: University of North Carolina Press, 1994.

Busch, Francis X. *Guilty or Not Guilty?* Indianapolis and New York: Bobbs-Merrill, 1952.

Calley v. Callaway, 382 F. Supp. 650 (M.D. Ct. Ga., 1974).

Calley v. Callaway, 519 F.2d 184 (5th Cir, 1975).

Calley, William L., with John Sack. *Lieutenant Calley/His Own Story.* New York: Viking Press, 1971.

Campbell, K. K., ed. *The Autobiography of Albert R. Parsons.* Labor Day 1995. Toronto: eye WEEKLY (http://www.interlog.com/eye/Misc/ Labor/Haymarket), 1995.

Carter, D. *Scottsboro: A Tragedy of the American South.* Baton Rouge: Louisiana State University Press, 1969.

Caudill, Edward. "The Roots of Bias: An Empiricist Press and Coverage of the Scopes Trial." *Journalism Monographs,* No. 114 (July 1989).

Caute, David. *The Great Fear: The Anti-Communist Purge Under Truman and Eisenhower.* New York: Simon and Schuster, 1978.

Chambers, Whittaker. *Witness.* Chicago: Regency Gateway Inc., 1952.

Chenery, William L. *Freedom of the Press.* Westport, Conn.: Greenwood Press, 1977.

Chiasson, Lloyd, Jr., ed. *The Press in Times of Crisis.* Westport, Conn.: Praeger, 1995.

Cobb, Irwin S. *Exit Laughing.* New York: Bobbs-Merrill Co., 1941.

Condon, John F. *Jafsie Tells All!: Revealing the Inside Story of the Lindbergh-Hauptmann Case.* New York: Jonathan Lee Publishing, 1936.

Cooke, Alistair. *A Generation on Trial: U.S.A. v. Alger Hiss.* London: Rupert Hart-Davis, 1951.

Cooper, David E. *The Manson Murders: A Philosophical Inquiry.* Cambridge, Mass.: Schenkman, 1974.

Daniels, Jonathan. *They Will Be Heard.* New York: McGraw-Hill Book Company, 1965.

Darden, Christopher. *In Contempt.* New York: ReganBooks, 1996.

Darrow, Clarence. *The Story of My Life.* New York: Scribner's, 1932.

Darwin, Charles Robert. *On the Origin of Species by Means of Natural Selection; or, The Preservation of Favoured Races in the Struggle for Life.* London: John Murray, 1859.

David, Henry. *The History of the Haymarket Affair: A Study in the American Social-Revolutionary and Labor Movements.* New York: Russell and Russell, 1958.

Davidson, Philip B. *Vietnam at War/ The History: 1946–1975.* Novato, Calif.:

Presidio, 1988.

de Camp, L. Sprague. *The Great Monkey Trial.* Garden City, N.Y.: Doubleday & Company, 1968.

DeWitte, Benjamin Parke. *The Progressive Movement.* Seattle: University of Washington Press, 1915.

Didion, Joan. *The White Album.* New York: Pocket Books, 1979.

Drew, Thomas. *The John Brown Invasion: An Authentic History of the Harper's Ferry Tragedy.* Boston: James Campbell, 1859.

Dupuy, R. Ernest, and Trevor N. Dupuy. *The Harper Encyclopedia of Military History: From 3500 B.C. to the Present.* New York: Harper Collins, 1933.

Ebner, Michael H., and Eugene M. Tobin, eds. *The Age of Urban Reform: New Perspectives on the Progressive Era.* Port Washington, N.Y.: Kennikat Press, 1977.

Edelstein, Tilden G. *Strange Enthusiasm: A Life of Thomas Wentworth Higginson.* New Haven, Conn.: Yale University Press, 1968.

Ely, James W., Jr. "The Chicago Conspiracy Case." In *American Political Trials,* edited by Michael R. Belknap, Westport, Conn.: Greenwood Press, 1981.

Endleman, Robert. *Johnstown and the Manson Family: Race, Sexuality, and Collective Madness.* New York: Psyche Press, 1993.

Epstein, Jason. *The Great Conspiracy Trial: An Essay on Law, Liberty and the Constitution.* New York: Random House, 1970.

Everett, George. "The Age of New Journalism, 1883–1900," 275–302. In *The Media in America.: A History,* 3rd ed., edited by William David Sloan and James D. Startt. Northport, Ala.: Vision Press, 1996.

Fisher, Jim. *The Lindbergh Case.* New Brunswick, N.J.: Rutgers University Press, 1987.

Gabler, Neal. *Winchell: Gossip, Power, and the Culture of Celebrity.* New York: Alfred A. Knopf, 1994.

George, Waller. *Kidnap: The Story of the Lindbergh Case.* New York: The Dial Press, 1961.

Ginger, Ray. *Six Days or Forever.* Boston: Beacon Press, 1958.

Gitlin, Todd. *The Whole World Is Watching: Mass Media in the Making and Unmaking of the New Left.* Berkeley: University of California Press, 1980.

Glock, Charles Y., and Rodney Stark. *Religion and Society in Tension.* Chicago: Rand McNally and Company, 1965.

Goodwin, Maud Wilder. *Dutch and English on the Hudson.* New Haven, Conn.: Yale University Press, 1919.

Grebstein, Sheldon Norman, ed. *Monkey Trial.* Boston: Houghton Mifflin, 1960.

Greenhaw, Wayne. *The Making of a Hero: The Story of Lieut. William Calley Jr.* Louisville, Ky.: Touchstone Publishing, 1971.

Grodzins, Morton. *Americans Betrayed.* Chicago: The University of Chicago Press, 1949.

Halberstam, David. *The Powers That Be.* New York: Alfred A. Knopf, 1979.

Hammer, Richard. *One Morning in the War: The Tragedy at Son My.* New York: Coward-McCann, 1970.

_____. *The Court-Martial of Lt. Calley.* New York: Coward, McCann & Geoghegan, 1971.

Hosokawa, Bill. *Thirty-five Years in the Frying Pan.* San Francisco, Calif.: McGraw-Hill, 1978.

Hudson, Frederic. *Journalism in the United States.* New York: Harper & Brothers,

Publishers, 1873.

Infeld, Leopold. *Albert Einstein: His Work and Its Influence on Our World.* New York: Scribner's, 1958.

Isaacs, Alexander J. *The Haymarket Riot.* 1st ed., Chicago: Alexander J. Isaacs, 1956.

Jensen, Richard J. *Clarence Darrow: The Creation of an American Myth.* New York: Greenwood Press, 1992.

Jones, Robert W. *Journalism in the United States.* New York: E. P. Dutton & Company, 1947.

Karnow, Stanley. *Vietnam: A History.* New York: Viking Press, 1983.

Kaul, Arthur J. "The Unraveling of America." In *The Press in Times of Crisis,* edited by Lloyd Chiasson Jr. Westport, Conn.: Praeger, 1995.

Kennedy, Ludovic. *The Airman and the Carpenter: The Lindbergh Kidnapping and the Framing of Richard Hauptmann.* New York: Viking, 1985.

Kessner, Thomas. The *Golden Door: Italian and Jewish Immigrant Mobility in New York City 1880–1915.* New York: Oxford University Press, 1977.

Knowlton, Steven R. "The Media and Popular Sovereignty." In *The Significance of the Media,* edited by James D. Startt and William David Sloan. Northport, Ala.: Vision Press, 1994.

Lee, James Melvin. *History of American Journalism.* Garden City, N.Y.: The Garden City Publishing Co., 1923.

Levine, Lawrence W. *Defender of the Faith, William Jennings Bryan: The Last Decade, 1915–1925.* New York: Oxford University Press, 1965.

Levitt, Morton, and Michael Levitt. *A Tissue of Lies: Nixon v. Hiss.* New York: McGraw-Hill, 1979.

Lincoln, Victoria. *A Private Disgrace: Lizzie Borden By Daylight.* New York: G. P. Putnam's Sons, 1967.

Livsey, Clara G. *The Manson Women: A "Family" Portrait.* New York: Richard Marek Publishers, 1980.

Lizzie Borden: (http://web2.xerox.com/digitrad/song=FALLRIVR)

Lowenfish, Lee, and Tony Lupien. *The Imperfect Diamond: The Story of Baseball's Reserve System and the Men Who Fought to Change It.* New York: Stein and Day, 1980.

Luhrs, Victor. *The Great Baseball Mystery, the 1919 World Series.* New York: A. S. Barnes and Co., 1966.

Manson, Charles, as told to Nuel Emmons. *In His Own Words, The Shocking Confessions of "The Most Dangerous Man Alive"—Rolling Stone.* New York: Grove Press, 1986.

Maury, Terry. *The Ultimate Evil: An Investigation into America's Most Dangerous Satanic Cult.* Garden City, N.Y.: Doubleday, 1987.

Meany, Tom. *Baseball's Greatest Teams.* New York: A. S. Barnes and Company, 1949.

Merrick, Laurence/Henrickson, Robert. *Manson.* Documentary film, 1972.

Michener, James A. *Kent State: What Happened and Why.* New York: Fawcett Crest, 1971.

Mooney, Michael. *Evelyn Nesbit and Stanford White: Love and Death in the Gilded Age.* New York: William Morrow and Company, 1976.

Morris, Richard B. *Fair Trial: Fourteen Who Stood Accused from Anne Hutchinson to Alger Hiss.* Norwood, Mass.: Plimpton Press, 1952.

Mott, Frank Luther. *American Journalism.* New York: The Macmillan Company,

1942.

"Murder of the Century." *The American Experience.* WGBH Educational Foundation, Boston, 1995.

Navasky, Victor S. *Naming Names.* New York: Viking Press, 1980.

Nelson, Bruce C. *Beyond the Martyrs: A Social History of Chicago's Anarchists, 1870-1900.* New Brunswick, N.J.: Rutgers University Press, 1988.

Nelson, Truman. *The Old Man: John Brown at Harper's Ferry.* New York: Holt, Rinehart & Winston, 1973.

Neville, John F. *The Press, the Rosenbergs, and the Cold War.* Westport, Conn.: Praeger, 1995.

Niebuhr, H. Richard, and Daniel D. Williams. *The Ministry in Historical Perspectives.* New York: Harper & Brothers, 1956.

Norris, C., and S. Washington. *The Last of the Scottsboro Boys.* New York: G. P. Putnam's Sons, 1979.

Oates, Stephen B. *To Purge This Land with Blood: A Biography of John Brown.* New York: Harper & Row, 1970.

Parks, Stephen, ed. *Three Trials: John Peter Zenger, H. S. Woodfall and John Lambert.* New York: Garland Publishing Co., 1974.

Parsons, Lucy. "Famous Speeches of the Eight Chicago Anarchists." In *Mass Violence in America,* edited by Robert M. Fogelson and Richard E. Rubenstein. New York: Arno Press and the *New York Times,* 1969.

Patterson, H., and Conrad Patterson. *Scottsboro boy.* Garden City, N.Y.: Doubleday, 1950.

Payne, George Henry. *History of Journalism in the United States.* New York: D. Appleton and Company, 1920.

Peers, William R. *The My Lai Inquiry.* New York: Norton, 1979.

Phillips, Arthur S. *The Phillips History of Fall River.* Fall River, Mass.: Dover Press, 1944, 1946.

Porter, Edwin H. *The Fall River Tragedy.* Fall River, Mass.: J. D. Monroe, 1893.

Quarles, Benjamin, ed. *Blacks on John Brown.* Urbana: University of Illinois Press, 1972.

Redpath, James. *The Public Life of Capt. John Brown, with an Auto-Biography of his Childhood and Youth.* Boston: Thayer and Eldridge, 1860.

Rights in Conflict: The Violent Confrontation of Demonstrators and Police in the Parks and Streets of Chicago During the Week of the Democratic National Convention of 1968, A Report Submitted by Daniel Walker, Director of the Chicago Study Team, to the National Commission on the Causes and Prevention of Violence. "Walker Report." New York: Bantam Books, 1968.

Riordon, William L. *Plunkitt of Tammany Hall.* New York: E. P. Dutton, 1963.

Royko, Mike. *Boss: Richard J. Daley of Chicago.* New York: E. P. Dutton, 1971.

Rutherfurd, Livingston. *John Peter Zenger.* New York: Arno Press, 1970.

Sanborn, F. B. *The Life and Letters of John Brown, Liberator of Kansas, and Martyr of Virginia.* Boston: Roberts Brothers, 1891.

Sanders, Ed. *The Family: The Story of Charles Manson's Dune Buggy Attack Battalion.* New York: Avon Books, 1971.

Sayer, James Edward. *Clarence Darrow: Public Advocate.* Dayton, Ohio: Monography Series No. 2, Wright State University, 1978.

Scaduto, Anthony. *Scapegoat: The Lonesome Death of Bruno Richard Hauptmann.* New York: G. P. Putnam's Sons, 1976.

Scholfield, Ann. "Lizzie Borden Took an Axe: History, Feminism, and American

Culture." *American Studies*, April 1993.

Schultz, John. *Motion Will Be Denied: A New Report on the Chicago Conspiracy Trial*. New York: William Morrow and Company, 1972.

Seymour, Harold. *Baseball: The Golden Age*. New York: Oxford University Press, 1971.

Smith, John Chabot. *Alger Hiss: The True Story*. New York: Holt, Rinehart and Winston, 1976.

Snyder, Louis L., and Richard B. Morris, eds. *A Treasury of Great Reporting*, as reported by Irwin S. Cobb for the *New York Evening World*, 7 February 1907. New York: Simon and Schuster, 1962.

Spiering, Frank. *Lizzie*. New York: Random House, 1984.

St. Johns, Adela Rogers. *The Honeycomb*. Garden City, N.Y.: Doubleday & Company, 1969.

Swanberg, W. A. *Luce and His Empire*. New York: Charles Scribner's Sons, 1972.

Tebbel, John. *The Compact History of the American Newspaper*. New York: Hawthorn Books, 1969.

Thaler, Paul. *The Watchful Eye: American Justice in the Age of the Television Trial*. Westport, Conn.: Praeger, 1994.

The Conflict of Naturalism and Humanism. New York: Teachers College, Columbia University, 1910.

The World's Most Famous Court Trial: State of Tennessee v. John Thomas Scopes [Complete Stenographic Report of the Court Test of the Tennessee Anti-Evolution Act at Dayton, July 19, 1925, Including Speeches and Arguments by Attorneys.] New York: DaCapo Press, 1971.

Tompkins, Jerry R., ed. *D-Days at Dayton, Reflections on the Scopes Trial*. Baton Rouge: Louisiana State University Press, 1965.

Tripp, Bernell. *Origins of the Black Press in New York, 1829-1849*. Northport, Ala.: Vision Press, 1992.

Villard, Oswald Garrison. *John Brown, 1800–1859: A Biography Fifty Years After*. Boston: Houghton Mifflin Co., 1910.

Voigt, David Q. *America Through Baseball*. Chicago: Nelson-Hall, 1976.

Watkins, Paul. *My Life With Charles Manson*. New York: Bantam Books Inc., 1979.

Watson, Charles, as told to Chaplain Ray Voekstra. *Will You Die For Me?* Old Tappan, N.J.: Fleming H. Revell Company, 1978.

Weinstein, Allen. *Perjury: The Hiss-Chambers Case*. New York: Alfred A. Knopf, 1978.

Weir, William. *Fatal Victories*. Hamden, Conn.: Archon Books, 1993.

Werner, M. R. *Bryan*. New York: Harcourt, Brace and Company, 1929.

Whipple, Sidney B. *The Lindbergh Crime*. New York: Blue Ribbon Books, 1935.

Williams, T. Harry, Richard Current, and Frank Freidel. *History of the United States Since 1865*. 3rd ed. New York: Alfred A. Knopf, 1969.

Wills, Gary. *Nixon Agonistes: The Crisis of the Self-Made Man*. Boston: Houghton Mifflin, 1970.

_____. *The Press and the Cold War*. Boston: Beacon Press, 1973.

Zaehner, Robert Charles. *Our Savage God: The Perverse Use of Eastern Thought*. New York: Sheed and Ward, 1974.

Zamora, William. *Trial By Your Peers*. New York: Maurice Girodias Associates, 1973.

Zeligs, Meyer A. *Friendship and Fratricide: An Analysis of Whittaker Chambers and Alger Hiss*. New York: The Viking Press, 1967.

Zetterberg, Peter, ed. *Evolution versus Creationism: The Public Education Controversy.* Phoenix, Ariz.: Oryx Press, 1983.

Zobel, Hiller B. *The Boston Massacre.* New York: W. W. Norton, 1970.

NEWSPAPERS

Atlanta Constitution
Baltimore American
Baltimore Exchange
Baltimore Patriot
Boston Daily Advertiser
Boston Gazette
Boston Globe
Boston Sunday Post
Central Presbyterian
Chattanooga Daily Times
Chicago Journal
Chicago Tribune
Cleveland Weekly Leader
Fall River Daily Globe
Freedom's Champion (Atchison City, Kansas)
Hartford Evening Press
Liberator
Illustrated American
London Evening Echo
London Morning Post
London Sphere
Los Angles Times
Miami Herald
New Bedford Evening Standard
New Bedford Times
New Orleans Daily Picayune
New York Herald
New York Observer
New York Sun
New York Times
New York World
Philadelphia Christian Observer
Providence Journal
Richmond Enquirer
Springfield (Massachusetts) *Republican*
St. Louis Post Dispatch
Tallapoosa (Alabama) *Times*
Weekly Portage (Ohio) *Sentinel*

MAGAZINES

Calendar Magazine, Los Angeles Times
The Commonweal

Editor & Publisher
Esquire
Life
National Review
Newsweek
Quill
People Magazine
The Rolling Stone
Time

PAMPHLETS

Boston Massacre
Common Sense

Index

About the Editor and Contributors

LLOYD CHIASSON JR. is a journalism historian specializing in literary journalism and the role of the press in periods of crisis. He is a professor of mass communication at Nicholls State University. His books include *Reporter's Notebook* (1993) a journalism interactive computer textbook, *The Press in Times of Crisis* (Greenwood Press, 1995). He has also published numerous book chapters and journal articles about Frederick Douglass, George Ripley, Noah Webster, Truman Capote, the encampment of the Japanese-Americans during World War II, the John Brown raid at Harpers Ferry, and the slavery literature of the Antebellum Period.

DONALD R. AVERY has written broadly on the colonial and early republic periods, as well as the party press period. A former president, secretary, and treasurer of the American Journalism Historians Association, he has served as managing editor of *American Journalism* and is on the editorial boards of *American Journalism* and *Journalism Monographs*. He is a professor of communication at the Communication Department at Eastern Connecticut State University.

JANET S. BOYLE holds degrees in psychology and in medical technology. She is an expert regarding the Harry K. Thaw trial, and has done considerable research on the lives of Thaw, Evelyn Nesbit, and Stanford White.

ROBERT DARDENNE is an associate professor in the School of Mass Communications, University of South Florida at St. Petersburg. He wrote *The Conversation of Journalism* with Rob Anderson and George M. Killenberg, contributed chapters to *Myth, Media, and Narrative* and other books, and has published articles and essays in various journals. He has studied and written on narrative as a news form, particularly from an historical perspective, and has varied research interests, including crime and crime news.

ALFRED N. DELAHAYE is professor emeritus of journalism at Nicholls State University in Thibodaux, Louisiana. He worked as managing editor of the *Houma Courier* and the *Terrebonne Press* before becoming director of publications and public relations at Nicholls State University. In retirement Dr. Delahaye has taught reporting and technical writing classes and is writing a history of Nicholls State University.

CAROL SUE HUMPHREY is an American historian of the eighteenth century, specializing in the newspapers of the American Revolutionary era, and she is an associate professor of history at Oklahoma Baptist University in Shawnee, Oklahoma. She has written *'This Popular Engine': New England Newspapers During the American Revolution, 1775-1789* (1992), and *The Press of the Young Republic, 1783-1833*, (Greenwood Press, 1996). She has also published numerous articles and book reviews about the press of the revolutionary era in *American Journalism, Journalism History, Journalism Quarterly, Rhode Island History, Virginia Magazine of History and Biography, Pennsylvania Magazine of History and Biography, The Historian, Georgia Historical Quarterly,* and *Media History Digest.* She is currently working on a study of the role of ritual in the American Revolution as expressed in the weekly newspapers.

ARTHUR J. KAUL is a professor and chair of the Department of Journalism at the University of Southern Mississippi. His scholarly interests include media history and ethics and literary journalism. He has published in *American Journalism, Critical Studies in Mass Communication, Dictionary of Literary Biography,* and *Journal of Mass Media Ethics,* and has edited a volume on literary journalism for the *Dictionary of Literary Biography.*

MICHAEL MAHER is an assistant professor of communication at the University of Southwestern Louisiana, where he teaches writing, editing, and desktop publishing courses. Besides co-writing the concluding chapter of *The Press in Times of Crisis* (Praeger, 1995), he has also written a chapter dealing with the news coverage of world overpopulation and natural resources. His research expertise centers on the media's coverage of the environment.

JOSEPH MCKERNS is an associate professor of journalism at the Ohio State University. He is the author of the *Biographical Dictionary of American Journalism* (Greenwood Press, 1989), *News Media and Public Policy: An Annotated Bibliography* (1985), and articles on the history of the American news media published in scholarly journals. McKerns is a past president of the American Journalism Historians Association and past editor of *Journalism Monographs*.

KITTRELL RUSHING is an associate professor and the head of the Communication Department at the University of Tennessee, Chattanooga. His current research interest includes newspapers of the Antebellum and Civil War eras.

JAMES STEWART is an assistant professor and director of print journalism at Nicholls State University. His research areas are history, communication, and ethics.

PAUL THALER is Director of Journalism and Media at Mercy College, in Dobbs Ferry, New York, and is the author of *The Spectacle: Media and the Making of the O.J. Simpson Story* (Praeger, 1996), and *The Watchful Eye: American Justice in the Age of the Television Trial* (Praeger, 1994). He is a leading authority in on-going debates concerning media and the criminal justice system and frequently appears on network television, radio, and in the national press as a commentator addressing media-law issues.

BERNELL TRIPP is an associate professor in the School of Journalism at the University of Florida. She has published several book chapters on the nineteenth century black press and is the author of *Origins of the Black Press, 1827-1847* (1992).

GENE WIGGINS is a professor of journalism and director of the School of Communication at the University of Southern Mississippi. He has authored numerous articles on press law and history. His most recent publication is a media law book for the state of Mississippi.

ISBN 0-313-30022-4

90000>

EAN

9 780313 300226

HARDCOVER BAR CODE